African History Archive

Over the past forty years, Zed has established a long and proud tradition of publishing critical work on African issues, offering unique insights into the continent's politics, development, history and culture. The African History Archive draws on this rich backlist, consisting of carefully selected titles that even now have enduring relevance years after their initial publication. Lovingly repackaged, with newly commissioned forewords that reflect on the impact the books have had, these are essential works for anyone interested in the political history of the continent.

Other titles in the archive:

A History of Africa
Hosea Jaffe

No Fist Is Big Enough to Hide the Sky: Th
and Cape Verde, 1963–74
Basil Davidson

Yours for the Union: Class and Community Struggles in South Africa
Baruch Hirson

About the author

Jeff Crisp is a research associate at the Refugee Studies Centre, University of Oxford, and an associate fellow at Chatham House. He has previously held senior positions at the Office of the United Nations High Commissioner for Refugees (UNHCR) and the Global Commission on International Migration. He is also a respected historian who has written widely on African labour history and current affairs.

Gavin Hilson is a leading global authority on the environmental and social impacts of the small-scale mining sector and has published over a hundred journal articles, book chapters and reports on the subject. He is currently professor and chair of sustainability in business at the University of Surrey.

The Story of an African Working Class

Ghanaian Miners' Struggles 1870–1980

Jeff Crisp

With a new Foreword by Gavin Hilson

ZED

Zed Books

LONDON

The Story of an African Working Class: Ghanaian Miners' Struggles 1870–1980 was first published in 1984 by Zed Books Ltd, The Foundry, 17 Oval Way, London SE11 5RR, UK.

This edition was published in 2017.

www.zedbooks.net

Cover design by Kika Sroka-Miller.

A catalogue record for this book is available from the British Library.

ISBN 978-1-78699-067-9 hb
ISBN 978-1-78360-976-5 pb
ISBN 978-1-78360-975-8 pdf
ISBN 978-1-78360-973-4 epub
ISBN 978-1-78360-974-1 mobi

CONTENTS

FOREWORD BY GAVIN HILSON

Jeff Crisp's book, *The Story of an African Working Class*, offers invaluable analysis of the labour dynamics and organizational structures in Ghana's mining sector over 110 years spanning the country's colonial period and independence from Great Britain. The text focuses heavily on labour control, capturing the essence of the day-to-day struggles faced by indigenous mine workers during this time. It explains how, through strikes, unions and informal forms of resistance, indigenous workers challenged authority in a bid to improve their quality of life. The book has attracted some criticism over the years, but for the most part it has been acclaimed for its accurate and detailed description of Ghana's mining sector during this period, its strong historical narrative and its Marxist lens. It, along with Peter Greenhalgh's *West African Diamonds, 1919-1983: An Economic History*, are today regarded as the two landmark texts on Ghana's mining history.

Over the years, the book has catalysed scholarly interest in, and research on, the mining sector in Ghana. At the time of its publication, there was already an impressive body of work in circulation on mining in Southern Africa, headlined by contributions from scholars such as Robert Kubicek, Frederick Johnstone, Ian Phimister and Charles Van Onselen. Most of this work was also Marxist in tone, chronicling the rise of mining and the organization of its operations and labour in the Witwatersrand, and Northern and Southern Rhodesia. *The Story of an African Working Class* was instrumental in bringing into the spotlight Ghana's equally rich and turbulent mining history. At approximately the same time the first rough diamonds were being harvested in Kimberley, South Africa, the foundations for present-day Ghana's first industrial-scale gold mines were being laid. Jeff Crisp captures these details through extensive research, including a detailed analysis of well-preserved documents contained in the country's National Archives. These documents would provide the bedrock for more recent seminal publications on mining in Ghana, which Jeff Crisp's work no doubt helped to inspire. Notable among these is Don Robotham's *Mining or Proletarians? The Economic Culture of Underground Miners in Southern Ghana, 1906-1976* and Raymond Dumett's *El Dorado in West Africa: The Gold-Mining Frontier, African Labor and Colonial Capitalism in the Gold Coast, 1875-1900*.

In recent years, however, *The Story of an African Working Class* has taken on additional significance: offering a glimpse of how mines *should* perform in

Ghana and sub-Saharan Africa more broadly. Jeff Crisp spoke at length about unionization and resistance in the country's mining sector, the general implication being that by taking action, whether moderate or radical, workers genuinely believed they could facilitate change capable of improving their lives. Perhaps fittingly, the rather arbitrary year of '1980' marked the end of the particular 'period' in Ghana's mining industry on which the book focuses.

Of course, the author had no idea that this would happen. In 1981, Flight Lieutenant Jerry Rawlings seized control of the Ghanaian state, removing Dr Hilla Limann, whom he had installed as president, following a successful coup d'état, in 1979. Rawlings brought political stability to Ghana, which has since had six elections and is today championed as a beacon of democracy in Africa. But during Rawlings' twelve years as Ghana's president, the country's mining sector experienced unprecedented change. Coincidentally, in 1983, the year in which *The Story of an African Working Class* was published, Ghana implemented its ambitious IMF-endorsed Economic Recovery Program, a move aimed at stabilizing the country's economy, and which would provide the bedrock for a series of World Bank-funded structural adjustment programs. Mining sector reforms aimed at attracting foreign investment in the sector were implemented alongside these programs, culminating in the passing of a new piece of legislation, The Minerals and Mining Law (PNCL 153), in 1986. As with all industries in Africa, globalization would forever change the face of the continent's mining sector.

In their book, *Africa Undermined* (1979), Greg Lanning and Marti Mueller, drawing on experiences from Zambia, Zimbabwe and the Democratic Republic of Congo, would cast light on the 'brand' of development a liberalized mining sector, populated and controlled by foreign multinationals, would bring to Africa. In Ghana, this manifested as a rapid, and at times hostile, acquisition of rights in localities such as Prestea and Tarwka, as well as the closing down of the State Gold Mining Corporation's operations in the towns of Bibiani and Konongo. Today, Ghana boasts the tenth-largest gold mining economy in the world, and the second largest in Africa. It is, however, a very different industry to that which Jeff Crisp studied so meticulously and reported on extensively. Alongside a series of large-scale mining 'enclaves' and innumerable mineral exploration activities, there is a burgeoning artisanal and small-scale segment populated by hundreds of thousands of men and women, many of whom once worked at the sites - now closed or under private ownership - which the author details in his book.

In an era of globalization, the 'labour question' which Crisp so eloquently broached is very different. For a sector that was struggling to establish itself in a landscape devoid of infrastructure, the challenge - or the 'labour question' - was determining how to establish a reliable and efficient workforce comprised of 'natives' who were willing to work for low salaries. This, in large part, provided the impetus for the unionization, resistance and protests which Crisp describes. But whilst scholars have frequently commented on the appalling work conditions endured by African mine labourers during the colonial period and beyond, many fail to explain how a demand for indigenes in the industry put them in a strategic position to negotiate and improve their livelihoods by bringing about change through deliberate action.

As mentioned, the mining landscapes in Africa are very different today in a 'rolled back' state. Machines have replaced manual labour; there is a demand for workers but for more specific skills – in particular, geologists and engineers – which the host country can only partly satisfy; and scores of people once found working in large-scale projects are now seen labouring at artisanal and small-scale sites. In Ghana, the government must rely on multinationals, such as Gold Fields and Newmont, to 'create' jobs and facilitate local economic development as part of their corporate social responsibility (CSR) programmes. In recognition of these very different policy concerns, the academic debates on mining in Africa have shifted pronouncedly. They have moved from a discussion on labour structures and Marxist critique towards a general debate on political economy which reflects on why mineral-rich sub-Saharan Africa is so poor, a phenomenon popularly referred to as the 'resource curse'. Whilst large-scale mine production is, indeed, booming across the continent, the 'returns' from this activity have been underwhelming. To 'correct' this, policymakers and donors are now asking mining companies to think more creatively about their CSR programmes, as well as implement Local Content policies which mandate the industry to engage with indigenous businesses and hire – in this particular case – Ghanaians.

This is why Jeff Crisp's book is so valuable: it offers a glimpse of a mining sector in which there is some accountability and 'space' to engineer change from within. It was written at a time when protest had an impact and large-scale mines were truly 'growth poles', capable of spawning downstream and upstream linkages. For Ghana, where leaders continue to struggle to find ways to transform mining into a catalyst for development, perhaps revisiting the past through texts such as *The Story of an African Working Class* could provide valuable insight moving forward.

Professor Gavin Hilson
University of Surrey
December 2016

PREFACE TO THE FIRST EDITION
BY ROBIN COHEN

Jeff Crisp's book on the mine workers of Ghana is one of the best-written and most carefully-researched studies of African labour history I have read. It will be placed on my shelf next to that classic account of mine workers in Southern Rhodesia, Chibaro, by Charles van Onselen (1976). The comparison is apt not only in terms of the quality of Crisp's account, but also the subjects of both books. As Crisp shows, the distinctive character of mine workers' struggles often hinges on their occupational (and not necessarily class) consciousness. Men brought together to break, blast and hoist massive tonnages of low-grade ore in dirty, confined and dangerous conditions, rapidly learn the practical benefits of solidarity.

This occupational solidarity arises even though workers are often assembled from scattered geographical areas and are employed on annual contracts. The pattern of using short-term contract labour from distant labour reservoirs was successfully pioneered in Southern Africa and has only recently been subject to some modifications there. Consolidated Gold Fields, a South African company which bought into the Ghana diggings, attempted to impose the whole package of pass laws, compounds and a monopsonistic labour-recruiting agency on their co-employers in Ghana. As Crisp demonstrates, this strategy could not be superimposed on Ghana, partly because there were at first conflicts of interest between the colonial state and the companies, partly because there was competition for relatively scarce labour by the cocoa industry and the armed services, but largely because the level of underdevelopment of rural Ghana was insufficient to force large numbers of rural cultivators to abandon their own means of production. It was only in the late 1920's that the Northern Territories and the neighbouring country of Volta were sufficiently impoverished to provide an assured labour supply.

By this time too, and in marked contrast to the Southern African mines, where whites occupied these layers, African workers in more skilled occupations (on machines or hammering and blasting) had begun to stabilise themselves and their families in settlements around the mining areas. Again, although the mining companies were by no means enthusiasts for unions, unlike in Southern Africa, the colonial state showed a sufficient sophistication to permit unionisation, if only as a more advanced means of labour control. The mine workers' union soon, however, found itself having to respond to rank-and-file protest or face disappearance as an effective intermediary between the workers and the companies. In the 1930's and then in 1947 and 1955/6, in the general strikes of those years, the workers made the running and the union officials became the reluctant articulators of their grievances.

In the Convention People's Party period (1945-1966), the union became a prime target of the nationalist party's regulatory apparatus. Through legislative restrictions, buying off the leadership and integrating the mine workers' union into the officially-sponsored TUC, Nkrumah hoped to bring the anomolous independence of the mine workers into line. The apparent ease of this process misled many contemporary observers into overrating the 'modernising' or 'centralising' capacity of independence parties like the CPP and grossly underestimating the workers' strength. Crisp makes no such error. He shows how rank-and-file militancy bypassed official cooptation, not only under the Nkrumah government, but also during the successive military and civilian regimes in the 1966-1980 period. What was striking about the post-Nkrumah period, was that the frequent changes of personnel and ideological direction in the state apparatus, exposed the police, army and judiciary to the wrath of the mine workers who once attacked Tarkwa, at the centre of the gold-mining area, 'like an invading army' armed with bows and arrows, sticks, cudgels and iron rods. Crisp concludes his account of the post-war era like this:

> The neat formulae of labour control devised by capital and the state were fatally flawed by their failure to recognise the strength of mine workers' militancy and solidarity. More than 100 years of struggle in the gold mines have demonstrated that it is a militancy and solidarity which cannot be legislated out of existence, eliminated by the incorporation of the Mine Workers' Union and its leaders into the machinery of state, or suppressed by the use of crude coercive tactics.

Though Crisp tells a story of resistance - even heroism - against extreme odds, he also seeks a realistic appreciation of the limits to the mine workers' consciousness and action. As I've mentioned, the strength of the bonds which unite mine workers are occupationally distinctive, and Crisp argues that this has limited their capacity to act as flag bearers for other sections of the working class. In addition, their incapacity to create an alternative political bloc to the circulation of elite figures drawn from the military, professional politicians, business stratum and intelligentsia, has meant that mine workers have been unable to assume the role of what Marx called the 'general representatives' of their society.

In short, Crisp successfully paints a picture of worker resistance somewhere between what he calls 'radical pessimism' and 'proletarian messianism'. The general implications of his view for the study of African labour history are well set out in his first chapter. He is kind enough to say that his views were informed by an article of mine on African workers' resistance and hidden forms of consciousness (the most accessible version of this was published in The Review of African Political Economy, No. 19,

September–December 1980). In fact, his own exposition extends, clarifies and supplements the scheme I proposed. Both at the level of an elegant exposition of his case study and in his taut reordering of theoretical priorities, this study is to be greatly welcomed. I hope it will gain the wide readership it deserves.

Professor Robin Cohen
University of Warwick
March 1984

ACKNOWLEDGEMENTS

I would like to offer my sincere thanks to everyone who has assisted me in the preparation of this book, especially those who gave me access to archives in England and Ghana and those who allowed me to interview them about their experiences in Ghana's gold mining industry. Parts of chapter 6 were previously published as 'Union Atrophy and Worker Revolt: Labour Protest at Tarkwa Goldfields, Ghana, 1968-1969', in Canadian Journal of African Studies, vol. 13 no. 1-2, 1979. Parts of Chapters 6 and 7 were previously published as 'Rank-and-File Protest at the Ashanti Goldfields Corporation, Ghana, 1970-1972', in LABOUR, Capital and Society, vol. 14 no. 2, 1981. Parts of Chapter 5 appear as 'Productivity and Protest: Scientific Management in the Ghanaian Gold Mines, 1947-1956', in Struggle for the City: Migrant Labor, Capital and the State in Urban Africa, by Fred Cooper (Ed.), Sage Publications, 1983.

ABBREVIATIONS *

ABA	Amalgamated Banket Areas
AGC	Ashanti Goldfields Corporation
AGM	Annual General Meeting
APS	Aborigines' Protection Society
ARA	Annual Report on Ashanti
ARCM	Annual Report of the Gold Coast/Ghana Chamber of Mines
ARGC	Annual Report on the Gold Coast
ARLD	Annual Report on the Labour Department
ARMD	Annual Report on the Mines Department
ARMedD	Annual Report on the Medical Department
ARWP	Annual Report on the Western Province
CCA	Chief Commissioner, Ashanti
CCNT	Chief Commissioner, Northern Territories
CCWP	Chief Commissioner, Western Province
CGF	Consolidated Gold Fields of South Africa
CIL	Chief Inspector of Labour
CL	Chief Labour Officer
CO	Colonial Office
COL	Commissioner of Labour
COM	Gold Coast/Ghana Chamber of Mines
CPP	Convention Peoples' Party
CS	Colonial Secretary
DC	District Commissioner
EGM	Emergency General Meeting
JNC	Joint Negotiating Committee
LAC	London Advisory Committee of the Chamber of Mines
LOT	Labour Officer, Tarkwa
m.d.l.	Man-days lost
MEU	Mines Employees' Union
MIF	Miners International Federation
MJNC	Mines Joint Negotiating Committee
MSNC	Mines Standing Negotiating Committee
MWU	Mine Workers' Union

* Archival abbreviations are listed in the Bibliography

NEC	National Executive Council
NLC	National Liberation Council
NRC	National Redemption Council
NT's	Northern Territories
PP	Progress Party
RLO	Regional Labour Officer
SGMC	State Gold Mining Corporation
SM	Secretary for Mines
SMC	Supreme Military Council
SS	Secretary of State
T and A	Tarquah and Abosso Mine
TO	Transport Officer
TUC	Trades Union Congress
UAC	United Africa Company
WACM	West African Chamber of Mines
WAYL	West African Youth League

THE GOLD COAST MINES' EMPLOYEES' UNION

GENERAL STRIKE No. 2

23RD. DECEMBER. 12 O'CLOCK, MIDNIGHT

LOCAL CONDITION FOR A. B. A. BRANCH.

STRIKE ACTION BEGINS.

(1) Night Shift - 7 a. m. - Morning of 23rd.

(2) Day Shift - 4.30 p. m.

(3) Afternoon Shift - 12 O'clock Midnight

UNION Officers will check up the Afternoon Shift workers to prevent any unfair play.

SOLIDARITY MINE WORKERS.

Solidarity in this industrial POSITIVE ACTION for economic freedom.

DOWN WITH CHAMBER'S STUPID

deplomacy. Salaries or not, forward ever. Down with stupid ideology of mass dismissal and re-employment of Who? Yorkshire Miners? Never to Compromise. Months or Years The Struggle Continues. One For Each in The Struggle For

Food Peace & Freedom.

The West African Raw Press. Tko.

J. K. Mensah.
Acting President.
A. O. A. Okudolo
Acting Secretary.

MEU General Strike Poster, 1954

This leaflet may win you a valuable cash prize !!

STUDY IT CAREFULLY

Do Not Lose It

WATCH THE ASHANTI TIMES FOR FURTHER ANNOUNCEMENTS

This may be your lucky number → **D** № 001398

The Truth Of The Matter

1. Whatever else you may be told **your employer is always interested in your welfare**.

It is in his interest as well as yours that you should live a healthy, happy, contented life.

2. Since 1952 the wages of mining employees have been increased by about 18%. Be fair and remember that.

Since then gratuities have been doubled.
Leave conditions have been greatly improved.
The starting rates have been increased.

3. You will find details of all these and other concessions on notice boards about the mine. **Read them carefully**. If anyone tries to destroy those notices it will mean that they do not want you to know about them.

4. Think also of the services which the mining companies give to their employees.

   (a) Free medical attention for you **and for your dependents**.
   (b) Housing at rents far below those charged by outside landlords.
   (c) Piped water and electric light.
   (d) Clubs, sports fields & recreational facilities.

5. Do other employers give all these things? Think fairly and clearly and you will know in your heart that your wages with a mining company are worth very much more to you than they would be elsewhere.

6. Be fair and think of this too: the price the companies get for the gold you help to produce is lower now than in 1952: but you receive not lower but higher wages.

7. There has been no recent rise in the cost of living.

8. All this is the **truth**. Then why strike and lose money?

TRUTH WILL PREVAIL

AGC Anti-Strike Leaflet, 1955-56

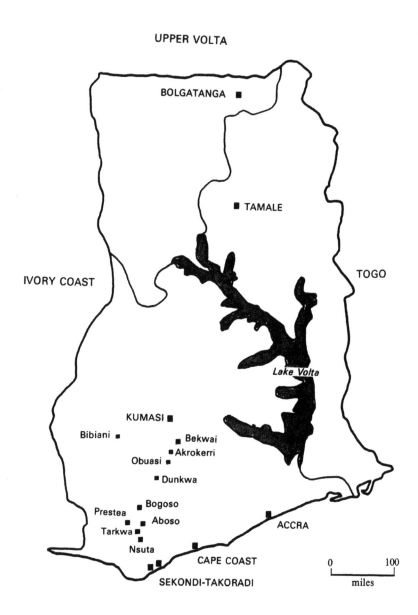

GHANA
Towns and Gold Mining Centres

Chapter 1

A CONCEPTUAL FRAMEWORK FOR AFRICAN LABOUR HISTORY

Without contraries is no progression.

William Blake, The Marriage of Heaven and Hell.

This book tells the story of Ghana's mine workers, one of the oldest and most militant groups of wage labourers in Africa. For more than 100 years the mine workers have been struggling to improve their conditions of life and employment, encountering in the process enormous and frequently violent opposition from mining capital, the colonial and post-colonial state. This chapter provides a brief examination of the conceptual framework which has been used to describe and analyze the changing pattern of that struggle in Ghana's gold mining industry.

Labour Control and Labour Resistance

The conceptual framework employed in this book is based on the two central themes of labour control and labour resistance. The first, labour control, is used to denote those activities of the representatives, allies and collaborators of capital which are designed to assert authority over wage labour and thereby incorporate it into the capitalist mode of production. The second, labour resistance, is used to denote those activities of wage labour, its representatives and allies, which defy the authority of capital, assert the autonomy of the worker, and thereby obstruct the incorporation of labour into the capitalist mode of production. Labour control and labour resistance are integral and inseparable features of the capitalist mode of production. To rephrase Marx, they presuppose the existence of each other, condition the existence of each other, and reciprocally bring forth each other:

> The directing motive, the end and aim of capitalist production, is to extract the greatest possible amount of surplus value, and consequently to exploit labour power to the greatest possible extent. As the number of cooperating labourers increases, so too does their resistance to the domination of capital, and with it, the necessity to overcome this resistance by counterpressure. The control exercised by the capitalist is...consequently rooted in the unavoidable

antagonism between the exploiter and the living and labouring raw material he exploits.[1]

Labour resistance and labour control are, therefore, a necessary manifestation of capital's principal objective, the accumulation of the surplus value created by labour power. More specifically, resistance and control are a function of four characteristics of the process through which capital seeks to achieve that objective.

Firstly, capital cannot accumulate surplus value unless it is able to purchase as much (or as little) labour power as it requires at any time, and bring it into connection with the means of production. It must, therefore, control the supply of labour to, and its occupational and geographical distribution within, the wage labour market. In advanced capitalist societies this form of control is the source of few problems for capital, as the vast majority of the population has been divorced from the means of production and can only subsist by the sale of its labour power. In contrast, in societies where the capitalist mode of production has not fully developed, and coexists with pre-capitalist modes of production, much of the population can subsist, and enter the cash nexus, without entering the labour market. In the absence of sufficiently strong ecological pressures or financial incentives to induce them into the labour market voluntarily, rural producers, traders and craftsmen must be forced to abandon their existing economic activities, to become dependent on wages as a means of subsistence, and to endure the rigours and uncertainties of capitalist employment.

Secondly, to maximize the surplus value which it appropriates from labour, capital must control, and thereby minimize, the wages paid to the worker, and habituate the worker to the unequal distribution of the product of their labour. Workers however, like capitalists, seek to sell the commodity at their disposal, labour power, for the highest price the market will pay. Indeed, they are encouraged to do so by capital, which makes new goods and services available to them. Consequently, workers must resist the efforts of capital to force down wages, and use whatever means are at their disposal to force them up.

Thirdly, capital can also maximize the surplus value appropriated from labour by controlling, and thereby maximizing, the productivity of the worker, and by habituating the worker to the unequal distribution of effort and authority in the workplace. Resistance to this aspect of the capitalist mode of production is again a particular problem for capital in societies where the wage labour force is rooted in pre-capitalist modes of production and has not internalized the norms and values ('ideology') of capitalism. Rural producers, traders and craftsmen who enter the labour market are accustomed to working at a self or communally determined rate. In their previous activities they have individually or jointly controlled the labour process, and have been free, within physiological limits, to sacrifice income for leisure. Consequently they have a marked tendency to resist the efforts of capital to realize their full potential as the creators of surplus value.

Capital's principal objective of accumulating surplus value is, therefore, threatened by the resistance of workers and potential workers to these three features of the capitalist mode of production. One function of the state, an administrative and juridical structure relatively autonomous of capital, is to minimize the impact of such resistance on the rate at which surplus value is created and appropriated. Inevitably, in the course of their resistance, workers come into conflict with the state, and participate in various forms of organization and action in an attempt to make it more susceptible to their interests. To protect capital, and to safeguard their own privileged status, the ruling elites of the state must control this <u>political activity</u>, and induce the wage labour force to recognize the legitimacy of their governing role.

Strategies of Control and Modes of Resistance

Having identified the features of the capitalist mode of production which give rise to the 'unavoidable antagonism' of labour and capital, it is now possible to examine the concrete manifestations of this antagonism. The methods used by capital to assert its authority over labour, and the means whereby labour asserts its autonomy of capital, are described in this book as <u>strategies of control</u> and <u>modes of resistance</u>.

In order to control the supply, wages, productivity and political activity of labour, capital and the state employ a variety of labour control strategies. Some examples of these strategies are listed in the matrix on the following page. As the matrix indicates, these strategies can be subdivided and classified in three ways.

Firstly, they can be grouped according to which of the four forms of capitalist control they are designed to reinforce. Taxation, for example, has commonly been used as a means of forcing rural populations off the land and into the labour market, and is therefore designed to control the supply of labour. The purpose of supervision, a universal feature of capitalist production, is to control the work-rate or productivity of labour. The majority of labour control strategies are more complex in motivation and are designed to assert more than one form of control over labour. To provide just one example, capital and/or the state might employ the strategy of importing labour in order to counteract local resistance to wage employment (supply), because foreign workers are cheaper to hire than local workers (wages), because they work harder (productivity), and because they are less likely to participate in movements which challenge the legitimacy of the ruling elites (political activity).

Strategies of labour control can also be classified according to the nature of their target. One set of strategies, including promotion, bonus schemes and deductions from wages, are designed primarily to influence the behaviour of the individual worker, whereas another set of strategies, including supervision, paternalism and the lock-out, are designed to control groups of

STRATEGIES OF LABOUR CONTROL

Labour Control Strategy	OBJECTIVE SUPPLY	WAGES	PRODUCTIVITY	POLITICAL ACTIVITY	TARGET INDIVIDUAL	GROUP	INSTITUTION	METHOD COERCION	INCENTIVE	IDEOLOGY
Imported Labour	X	X				X			X	
Indentured Labour	X	X			X				X	
Forced Labour	X	X			X			X		
Rural Taxation and Underdevelopment	X	X			X	X		X	X	
Monopsonistic Recruitment	X	X			X	X		X	X	
Supervision			X		X	X		X		
Mechanization	X		X		X	X		X		
Reorganization of Labour Process	X	X	X		X	X		X		
Bonus Schemes		X	X		X	X			X	X
Pensions, Gratuities, Long Service Awards	X	X			X	X			X	X
Promotion				X	X				X	X
Paternalism	X		X	X	X	X				X
Fines and Wage Deductions	X	X	X		X	X		X		
Dismissal		X	X		X	X		X		
Corporal Punishment and Imprisonment			X	X	X			X		
Institutionalization of Bargaining		X	X	X		X			X	X
Intimidation of Union and Party Members		X	X	X	X	X	X	X		X
Coopting of Union and Party Leaders		X	X	X		X	X		X	X
Restrictions on Union Autonomy		X	X	X			X	X		X

workers. A final type of strategy is represented by those designed to influence the institutional behaviour of labour. For example, the state is able to use a wide range of legislative measures to obstruct the unionization of workers, to restrict the financial and administrative autonomy of established unions, and to prevent workers from leaving weak trade unions to join or create a more militant organization.

The matrix also indicates that strategies of labour control vary in their method. Coercion forms the basis of strategies such as forced labour and corporal punishment, whereas bonus schemes, gratuities and promotion work on the principle of incentive. Another group of strategies seeks to control the behaviour of the wage labour force through the use of ideology. Paternalism, for example, is intended to encourage workers to adopt a loyal and deferential attitude towards their employer. Similarly, the state uses the ideology of 'national interest' to divert workers' attention away from the inequalities of capitalist society, and to persuade trade union members and officials to increase output, forgo wage increases and avoid disruptive political activities. Several strategies on the matrix combine more than one method of control. For example, a government which is trying to gain the cooperation of trade union leaders might do so by simultaneously offering them rewards of money or social status (incentive), by intimidating and threatening them (coercion), and by appealing to their sense of patriotism (ideology).

The means whereby workers express their antagonism and resistance to the objectives and strategies of capital are equally varied. As the matrix on the following page demonstrates, the concept 'mode of resistance' encompasses this wide range of activities and includes familiar forms of working class action such as strikes and go-slows, and less obvious forms of resistance to the capitalist mode of production, such as absenteeism, malingering and theft. For analytical purposes, this conceptual framework classifies the many modes of resistance according to their visibility, inclusiveness and duration.

Visibility refers to the extent to which a mode of resistance is visible to and perceived as a threat by capital and the state. Communal revolts against labour recruitment, strikes, demonstrations and rallies demand the overt participation of workers and potential workers, whereas they can participate in modes of resistance such as malingering and absenteeism in a covert manner. Overt modes of resistance require the conscious participation of workers, and therefore tend to be regarded most seriously by capital and the state. In contrast, covert modes of resistance might not even be perceived as forms of resistance by workers themselves, and therefore tend to be tolerated unless they become a serious threat to the economic and political objectives of capital and state.

As the matrix indicates, visibility is frequently (but not invariably) related to the inclusiveness or scale of resistance.

MODES OF LABOUR RESISTANCE

	Mode of Resistance	VISIBILITY Overt	VISIBILITY Covert	INCLUSIVENESS Collective	INCLUSIVENESS Individual	DURATION Limited	DURATION Intermittent	DURATION Continuous
'INFORMAL RESISTANCE'	Absenteeism		x		x		x	
	Malingering		x		x		x	
	Sabotage	x	x	x	x	x		
	Theft		x	x	x	x	x	
	Bonus Cheating		x	x	x	x	x	
	Restricted Output	x	x	x	x		x	
	Desertion/Breaking Contract	x	x	x	x		x	
	Temporary Withdrawal of Labour		x		x	x	x	
	Permanent Withdrawal of Labour		x		x	x		
'COLLECTIVE RESISTANCE'	Strike	x		x		x		
	Riot	x		x		x		
	Rally	x		x		x		
	Demonstration	x		x		x		
	Go-Slow/Work to Rule	x		x		x		
	Communal Withdrawal and Revolt	x		x		x		
	in Rural Labour Reservoir						x	
'INSTITUTIONAL RESISTANCE'	Party Formation/Membership	x		x	x			x
	Pressure Group Formation/Membership	x		x	x			x
	Trade Union Formation/Membership	x		x				x

Overt modes of resistance normally involve collective action, whereas covert modes of resistance are more often pursued on an individual basis. Some forms of resistance, such as theft, sabotage, bonus cheating and restricted output, are commonly undertaken by both groups of workers and individuals.

Finally, modes of resistance vary in their duration. Some manifestations of conflict between labour and capital, such as strikes and riots, are by definition of limited duration, whereas others, such as absenteeism, malingering or restricted output, represent intermittent activity. Other forms of resistance, such as membership of a trade union, political party or pressure group, require continuous commitment or participation.[2]

Using the three criteria of visibility, inclusiveness and duration, it is possible to identify three broad types of resistance. Informal modes of resistance are usually pursued on an individual or small-scale basis, intermittently and in a covert manner. In Hyman's words, informal or 'unorganised' activity 'is not normally part of a deliberate strategy to remedy the source of grievance; indeed it may well derive from a generalized sense of dissatisfaction rather than consciousness of a specific grievance, and so may not be conceived as industrial conflict at all'.[3] In contrast, collective modes of resistance are more inclusive, overt, and of specific duration. Such action 'normally involves a deliberate attempt to change the situation which gives rise to conflict; it is purposeful activity designed to achieve some concrete improvement'.[4] Thirdly, institutional forms of resistance are collective, normally overt, and require continuous commitment. Workers participating actively in such modes of resistance recognize their exploitation and subordinate status, and seek, often in an incremental manner, to ameliorate their situation.[5]

Those modes of resistance defined as 'collective' in this taxonomy vary so widely that it is necessary to refine the concept by introducing three secondary classifications. Firstly, collective modes of resistance can be classified according to the number of workers or potential workers participating. A general strike involving thousands or even millions of workers clearly represents a different order of resistance to a demonstration involving only 40 or 50 workers. Secondly, they can be classified according to the defining characteristics of the participants - whether the participants reflect or supercede cleavages of occupation, age, sex, ethnic origin, skill and status in the labour force. Thirdly, collective modes of resistance vary in the way they are mobilized. A strike, for example, might be mobilized by the representatives of a political party, by national or local trade union officials, or by certain groups or individuals within a labour force. The methods whereby workers are mobilized also vary, and include intimidation, persuasion, the offer of financial or other incentives, and appeals to class, party, occupational, ethnic or religious allegiances.

The Structure of Conflict in Ghana's Gold Mines

Hitherto, this discussion of labour resistance and labour control has focused on the conflicting interests of three abstract entities, 'labour', 'capital', and 'the state'. While they are analytically useful, reality is more complex than these concepts suggest. Strategies of control and modes of resistance are the product not of such clearly defined entities, but of specific individuals, groups and institutions, which vary from country to country, industry to industry, and enterprise to enterprise. At this stage of the analysis, therefore, it is necessary to move away from a purely theoretical disicussion of the conflict between labour and capital, and to examine the peculiar structure of conflict in the analytical unit of this study, the Ghanaian gold mining industry.

As the diagram on the following page indicates, the political economy of Ghana's gold mining industry can be conceptualized as a pyramidical, hierarchically structured network of authority relationships. At the top of this hierarchy (Level 1) are the representatives of international and metropolitan capital and the core states of the world capitalist system. This group includes the directors, senior management and large shareholders of expatriate mining companies, financiers and bankers, senior government decision-makers and the ruling elites of the colonial and post-colonial state. They are, in Cardan's words, the 'order-givers', those 'who really manage, in whose interests everything finally functions, who take the important decisions, who reactivate and stimulate the working of the system.[6]   At the bottom of the hierarchy are the mine workers, the 'order-takers' whose surplus value is appropriated by the superior components of the hierarchy, and whose exploitation and subordination is the principal objective of the order-givers who control it.

These top and bottom levels of the hierarchy are analagous to the two 'pure' classes of marxian political economy, the bourgeoisie and proletariat. The order-givers own and control the means of production, while the order-takers are divorced from it and sell their labour power as a means of subsistence. Interposed between these groups are two intermediate strata whose class location is more ambiguous. Level 2 of the hierarchy, the 'subordinate order-givers', includes junior mine management and supervisory staff, central and local state bureaucrats, and members of coercive state agencies such as the army, police force and judiciary. They are subject to the dictates of the order-givers, and their function is to devise, coordinate and implement the strategies of control needed to extract surplus value from the labour force. They also have their own, distinct interests which reinforce their need to perpetuate the subordination and exploitation of those beneath them.

The final stratum in the hierarchy, the 'brokers' (Level 3) occupy the most ambiguous position. Groups such as mine headmen (foremen), trade union officials, tribal heads and chiefs all have close socio-economic links with the bottom stratum of

The Structure of Authority
in Ghana's Gold Mining Industry

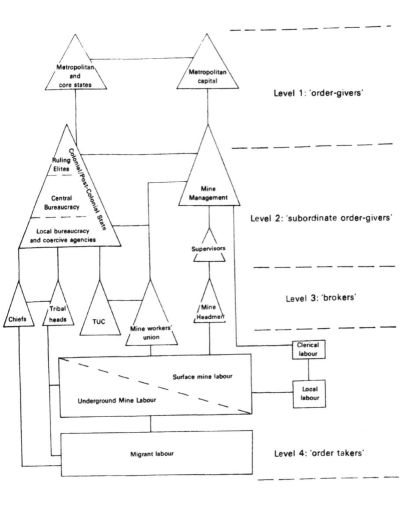

workers, but they also enjoy a privileged status and share some of the order-giving functions of the higher strata. As brokers they are expected to articulate the demands of the labour force to the higher levels of the hierarchy, but they are also expected to communicate the orders of those higher levels to the labour force. Moreover, all the brokers have their own disciplinary powers which can be used against members of the labour force who pose a threat to their intermediary role. Thus the problem for the brokers is to avoid a total identification with the objectives and actions of those above or below them in the hierarchy, for to do so would be to destroy their ability to maintain the communication which holds the system together.

Neither those components of the hierarchy which participate in modes of resistance (Levels 3 and 4), nor those components which impose strategies of control (Levels 1, 2, and 3) form monolithic units of conflict. As suggested already, there is a clear potential for disagreement between the labour force and the brokers given their different functions and status within the hierarchy. Moreover, the labour force itself is divided by vertical cleavages into local and migrant workers, manual and clerical workers, surface and underground workers, and by horizontal cleavages of age, skill, experience, status and political orientation. So although all members of the labour force have a common interest in resisting their exploitation and subordination, the precise objectives of different workers, and the modes of resistance they use to achieve those objectives, may well differ and even conflict.

The potential conflicts which exist between the order-giving components of the hierarchy are equally apparent. In fact, three such conflicts can be identified. Firstly, the order-giving components of the hierarchy can be divided into separate substructures, each of which seeks to reinforce a different form of capitalist control. For example, the productivity of the mine workers is controlled by five components: the directors of a mine, who control its broad production strategy; the mine's senior management, which sets specific productivity targets; supervisors and headmen, who impose discipline in the workplace to ensure that those targets are attained; and officials of the mine workers' trade union, who are empowered to negotiate 'productivity deals' on the workers' behalf. Other configurations of order-giving components form substructures which control the supply, wages and political activity of the labour force. Although these substructures share the broad objective of controlling labour, their specific aims and the strategies they employ to achieve those aims can prove mutually destructive. For example, the productivity substructure might successfully boost output by intensifying workplace discipline, but only at the expense of making employment in the industry less attractive, thereby contradicting the efforts of the labour supply substructure to recruit and retain an adequate number of workers.

Contradictions also arise from divisions within each of the four order-giving substructures, particularly between those components ultimately controlled by capital (whose immediate aim is the maximization of the surplus value accumulated) and those components ultimately controlled by the state (whose immediate aim is the maintenance of a stable political status quo). For example, the ruling elites and bureaucracy of the state might aim to control working class political activity through the encouragement of moderate trade unionism, while the directors and managers of a mine simultaneously attempt to control the political activity of its labour force by using coercive strategies of control designed to prevent the formation of trade unions. The two strategies are, of course, incompatible.

A third set of contradictions in the functioning of the order-giving substructures arises from the ambiguous position of the brokers. To serve the interests of capital and state, the brokers must be controlled tightly enough to ensure their obedience, but sufficiently independent to retain the confidence of the labour force. In practice, this delicate balance is almost impossible to maintain. On one hand, brokers who have few restrictions placed upon their financial or administrative autonomy are likely to prove responsive to pressure from below, and to become the mobilizers and organizers of labour resistance. On the other hand, brokers who are unambiguously controlled by capital and state will be unresponsive to the demands of rank-and-file workers. In this situation, the workers are likely to reject the brokers' intermediary role and to defend their interests through independent modes of resistance. Thus however much or little freedom is given to the brokers, the hierarchy cannot guarantee the passive, order-taking labour force which it demands.

Towards a History of the African Working Class

In 1976 Cohen wrote that 'worker protest against, and resistance to the labour process has thus far only been inadequately described in the African context. This deficiency has less to do with the quality of the relevant literature produced than with the limited questions that have been posed'.[7] The purpose of the conceptual framework outlined in this chapter is to overcome some of the deficiencies in the existing literature, and to stimulate research into questions that have hitherto been ignored or neglected by African labour historians.

To quote Cohen again, the first generation of African labour histories tended to concentrate on 'the more evident forms of protest (predominantly strikes, unionization, and overt political activity).'[8] While such modes of resistance are evidently of great importance, a preoccupation with these more obvious forms of working class dissent has a number of undesirable effects. It encourages an excessively institutional approach to the subject, a narrowly intra-elitist perspective which focuses on the pronouncements of union and party leaders, but neglects the activities, attitudes and aspirations of the rank-and-file worker. This institutional approach also limits the chronological scope of enquiry, encouraging researchers to ignore the vitality of working class resistance in periods when trade unions and radical political parties do not exist, are banned, or have been transformed into instruments of labour control.

Conventionally, historians and social scientists have tended to draw sharp distinctions between the different arenas of conflict between labour and capital identified in the first part of this chapter. Workers are said to act 'politically' when they participate in organizations that have a recognized role in the national political process, or when they challenge directly the legitimacy of the state's ruling elite. When they attempt to maintain or increase the level of their wages they are liable to be described (and even dismissed) as acting in an 'economistic' manner, and when they take action over workplace issues they are said to be acting 'industrially'. The conceptual framework employed in this study rejects such a mystifying categorization of labour resistance, and encourages the researcher to show how the struggle between labour and capital proceeds simultaneously in the workplace, the community, the national political arena and in the rural labour reservoir. While it recognizes that overtly political resistance often has a more profound and more immediate impact on the relationship between labour, capital and state than other forms of action, by redefining 'politics' in terms of the efforts of individuals, groups and institutions to assert and resist authority, this framework rejects the suggestion that 'economistic' and 'industrial' struggles are apolitical in either motivation or effect. Industrial struggles question the organization and control of a labour process which is dependent on and a reflection of a particular configuration of authority relationships, while economistic struggles question the differential distribution of benefits inherent to that configuration. The order-giving substructures described earlier form an integrated (if contradictory) whole, and working class struggle against all four sub-structures is needed to promote progressive political change. There is no need to elaborate on the fate of workers in states where a 'revolution' in the national political arena has not been accompanied or followed by a corresponding revolution in the distribution of benefits or the organization of production.

Finally, the conceptual framework used here to describe and analyze the story of Ghana's mine workers has been devised to illuminate the dialectical nature of the struggle between labour, capital and state. This framework enables the researcher to show not only how workers respond to the strategies of control imposed upon them, but also how workers constantly take the initiative against capital and state, shifting between informal, collective and institutional modes of resistance according to the perceived economic and political environment, forcing capital and state to respond with new strategies of control. Such an approach might prove a useful antidote to both proletarian messianism and to radical pessimism, demonstrating that African workers can promote progressive change even within a coercive political context, while identifying the many ways in which capital and state can prevent such change from attaining 'revolutionary' proportions.

Notes

1. Marx (1901) p.321.

2. This assumes that the workers in question are voluntarily members of such organizations. As later chapters will show, compulsory membership of trade unions and parties is a strategy of control commonly employed by the state.

3. Hyman (1975) p.198.

4. ibid.

5. As Cohen has stated, 'some of the forms of resistance, indeed if one has a Coserian view of the functionality of conflict, all the forms of resistance, may be re-rendered as "forms of adaptation"'. Like Cohen, this study assumes that 'the resistance of workers is more salient...than is their adaptation, though they have, perforce, to adapt to the capitalist mode'. Cohen (1976) pp.7 and 20. Much of this chapter has been informed by Cohen's observations.

6. Cardan (n.d.) p.11.

7. Cohen (1976) p.3.

8. ibid.

Chapter 2

THE LABOUR QUESTION AND THE
CONTRADICTIONS OF CONTROL, 1870-1906

The native himself seems to be the only person who
can stand the climate and who should do the work,
but the question is, how is he to be induced to do
it in order that it shall be profitable to those who
invest their capital?

George MacDonald, The Gold Coast Past and Present, 1898.

In 1471 Portuguese explorers first reached the West Coast of
Africa in search of gold. For the next 400 years they and other
Europeans made repeated attempts to gain control of gold production in the area, but they enjoyed little success. Although
indigenous rulers in the Gold Coast were happy to trade in gold,
they refused to reveal the location of their mines and continued
to control production either directly, through the use of slave
labour, or indirectly, through the tribute system. It was not until the last quarter of the 19th Century, when Britain 'pacified'
and annexed the Gold Coast hinterland, that European entrepreneurs finally gained direct access to the colony's mineral
deposits. This chapter describes the early development of
capitalist mining in the Gold Coast, and examines the problems
which the first mining companies encountered in their efforts to
control local labour.

The Origins of the Labour Question, 1870-1900

The establishment of a capitalist mining industry in the Gold
Coast proved to be a very risky enterprise, and many investors
saw their capital wasted on mines which failed to produce a single
ounce of gold. A number of obstacles confronted the first mining
companies. The lack of infrastructural development in the colony
at this time meant that the establishment of a new mine was a
long and expensive process. Political instability and the absence
of concession legislation prolonged this process further, and
wasted the scarce capital resources of the many speculative
mining companies which appeared on the London Stock Exchange
during the 'jungle boom' of the 1880's. Such enterprises were
further weakened by climatic and health conditions on the West

Coast, which took a severe toll of expatriate mining personnel and discouraged experienced engineers from working in the colony.

The most important obstacle to the development of modern mining was what became known amongst British entrepreneurs and investors as the 'labour question'. Thomas Haughton, for example, writing to the <u>Mining Journal</u> from the coast in 1883, complained that 'the labour question is undoubtedly one of the greatest troubles'. Twelve years later the shareholders of the Côte d'Or mine were informed that 'labour is the most difficult of the local questions'.[1] What exactly was the labour question? The answer is provided in another statement by Haughton. 'The great consideration', he wrote, 'is that the mines...have a constant supply of first class labour, and that at a cheap rate'. Thus mining capital wanted three things: a regular and adequate supply of native workers; a labour force that was efficient and reliable, and one that was willing to work for low wages. These demands, and the failure of the mining industry to satisfy them, constituted the labour question of the late 19th Century.

Expatriates in the Gold Coast had no doubt that the labour question had its origins in the inherent laziness of the local population. In Burton and Cameron's words, 'their <u>beau idéal</u> is to do nothing for six days in the week and to rest on the seventh'. Edwin Cade was even more scathing. The Ashanti people, he said, were:

> ...useless so far as any work is concerned...They have no ambition, no pastimes or zeal, art or desire beyond an animal existence. (I think I could say something in opposition to the modern general views on slavery).[2]

While this explanation had the virtue of simplicity, it had the defect of being totally false. The real origins of the labour question were to be found in the socio-economic structure of the societies inhabiting the gold-producing areas of south-western Ghana, and in the conditions of work offered to them by the new mining companies.

In the Gold Coast, as in many other areas of pre-colonial West Africa, there was more land available for cultivation than there was labour to cultivate it. Skertchley, for example, noted in 1878 that the mining area of Wassaw 'is but sparsely peopled... one vast forest with meagre villages of a dozen huts or so scattered at long intervals along the roads'. Further north in Obuasi, where the Ashanti Goldfields Corporation (AGC) was to create a large mining town, the first Mine Superintendent had found merely 'a village...of half a dozen native huts, clustered round a small patch of ground in the forest'.[3] There was, therefore, no demographic pressure forcing the local population off the land and into paid employment. This situation was not altered by the emancipation of the colony's large population of slaves after 1874. The Government's fears of unrest amongst the Ashanti ensured that the Anti-Slavery Ordinance was not rigorously enforced, and as a member of the Basel Mission predicted:

No breadless proletariat will develop, because the ex-slaves can either farm land belonging to someone else for a small proportion of their yearly product, or can go and farm the uninhabited tracts. The majority...have remained with their masters either because they are well handled, and are part of the family, or because they fear to be independent.[4]

In a society where even the poorest group of people could subsist without selling their labour power, some financial incentive was obviously needed to mobilize a labour force. The incentive which the mines offered, a daily wage of between 1/0 and 1/6 for unskilled workers, was not sufficiently attractive to achieve that objective. Inspired by the notion that local labourers would only work long enough to save a fixed cash target, the mining companies refused to increase wages and petitioned the colonial administration with indignant complaints about the supply and price of labour. The Government, however, had little sympathy for the mines, since it could rely on the use of compulsory and imported labour to satisfy its own growing demand for manpower. Indeed, the Government's use of forced labour not only depleted the reservoir of potential workers available to the mines, but also made the inhabitants of the mining areas extremely wary of volunteering for work with other expatriate employers. Not surprisingly, when troops raided local market places in search of carriers, there was a 'tremendous stampede' of men out of the area.[5]

Low wages were not the only unattractive feature of the work offered by the mines. The tasks assigned to workers during this period of mine construction were arduous, dirty and dangerous, and quite unlike the agricultural labour in which most local men and women were engaged. Moreover, in the areas where mining was traditionally the work of slaves, free men were understandably reluctant to offer their services. Finally, the methods of supervision employed by the mines acted as a further disincentive to prospective wage labourers. Expatriate entrepreneurs constantly bemoaned the indigenous attitude towards work, complaining that the local labourer 'requires that you should be continually watching him, otherwise he is sitting down, praying for night and the whistle to blow'.[6] The solution to this problem was to be found in effective supervision. As John Daw of AGC explained, 'provided efficient white foremen of sterling character be available...then the greater number of men from any of the districts will do a fair day's work'. Inevitably, though, the workers' perception of what constituted a 'fair day's work' was very different to that of the white supervisor. In Skertchley's words, for example, 'when carrying for themselves a hundredweight is not overweight, but when working for a white man anything over 30 pounds is "too much"'.[7] It was the function of white supervisors to overcome such objections and to teach the workers the virtues of the Victorian capitalist:

We freely admit that we do impose conditions which an uncivilized nation may deem to be harsh and exacting. We insist on punctuality, on rigid temperance, on morality, and on diligence.[8]

In practice, the imposition of such norms was not merely 'hard and exacting', but depended on the systematic use of physical coercion. One supervisor, who stressed the need for 'patience and common sense' when dealing with native workers, nevertheless thought it necessary to inflict 'a good hiding' on a man in order to teach him a new task. 'Lagos boys', he complained, were unsuitable workers 'because they object to being hit without reason and hit back'. The Fante worker was better, as he 'can be hit with or without cause and does not worry'.[9] Such attitudes aroused the concern of other expatriates on the coast. The Basel Mission informed the Governor that without its intervention, some mining companies would quite happily have seized the land from the local population and forced men to work for them without pay. In London, the Aborigines' Protection Society informed the Colonial Office of 'seething discontent' amongst the workers:

> The causes of such discontent are not far to find. The native employees have been brutally treated, kicked about, and often had revolvers pointed at their heads when they demanded their wages.[10]

Surveying the history of the labour question in 1909, the Colonial Office remarked:

> We get periodically statements that there is a 'general scarcity of labour', but on the Gold Coast it generally turns out that there are plenty of labourers to be had by employers who pay adequate wages and treat their men well.[11]

It was a pointed and concise indictment of the mining industry's failure to resolve the labour question.

Resistance and the Labour Question 1870-1900

Even in this first phase of capitalist gold mining, when the Gold Coast lacked a true wage labouring class, the actions of workers and prospective workers clearly contradicted the interests of mining capital. Although the evidence on this subject is fragmentary, several different modes of resistance in the mining industry can be identified. Firstly, the local inhabitants of the mining areas refused to work for the low wages offered to them, or used their bargaining power to push wages up to more acceptable levels. Skertchley describes an encounter with a group of carriers:

> Yes, all were willing to go to Wassaw, but as to pay, they would not accept anything like our terms, although they were higher than the government scale. A shilling a day wages and threepence subsistence was offered and declined a half dozen times a day.[12]

Secondly, they refused to perform most tasks except for the more familiar ones such as carrying and bush clearing, and worked at their own rate rather than that desired by their employers:

When compelled by hunger to work, he applies to the white man with the firm determination to do the least possible amount of work, and to be as dense as his nature will permit; a log of wood is not more dense, and he succeeds in playing his part like a professional.13

Thirdly, local workers refused to sign the six and nine-month contracts introduced by management, and in this way retained their mobility within the colony's embryonic labour market. As a result, mining companies which paid particularly low wages or who treated their workers exceptionally badly soon lost their employees to other mines or to other sectors of the economy.14

Although the withholding and withdrawal of labour was the dominant mode of resistance in the mines prior to 1900 it was by no means the only one. From the very beginning of modern mining workers supplemented their wages by stealing gold and other items such as candles, nails and explosives. As one Mine Manager acutely observed:

You must remember that they do not think they are taking that which does not belong to them. They look upon us as robbing them, hence in this direction their conscience is unlimited in its flexibility.15

Workers also expressed their discontent in the way they behaved towards European managers and supervisors. This mode of resistance usually took the form of 'refractory behaviour', abusive language, and the deliberate misunderstanding of instructions, but it could assume much more serious proportions. In one incident a worker stabbed an accountant to death in protest against his dismissal, and in another two workers were arrested for attempting to poison European staff. At Ashanti Goldfields a white supervisor disappeared in mysterious circumstances and was publicly said to have fallen down an abandoned shaft. Privately though, both AGC and the Government suspected that he had been murdered by the friends of a worker who had been tortured by European supervisors.16

Finally, collective modes of resistance were not unknown in the mines at this time. The reaction of workers to a delay in wage payments at one mine was described in this way:

An unsteadiness and indifference as to whether or not they continued to improve in learning how to work as miners & c. commenced to appear among them. When railed for their faults the reply would invariably be 'we get no pay'. I countered this with the only means at my disposal i.e. persuasion and starvation, but this could not prevent many pieces of work being done in a slovenly, indifferent fashion.17

For mining capital, a more serious development was the rapidity with which the mine workers learnt the power of strike action. In December 1898, Edwin Cade told AGC shareholders that 'among the hundreds - nay even thousands we have employed, we have not met with a single one who has brought against us or our method of government a single word of complaint'. Evidently Cade had a very short memory, for just five months earlier he had told the same group of people that 'we have already gone through one or two costly experiments and met with strikes and disobediences which we have dealt with to the best of our ability'.[18]

Unfortunately the documentary evidence of these strikes is very limited. John Daw reported that in January 1898 six West Indian carpenters employed by AGC stopped work because 'the native food, discipline, and hard work did not agree with them'. The men were dismissed and replacements brought from Kumasi.[19] Other mines were also affected by this mode of resistance. McCarthy reported that a shortage of coins at a mine in Tarkwa prevented the Kroo workers from being paid. 'One day about 3 p.m. the Kroos struck work and came up all armed with machetes...and demanded to be paid off'.[20] Kroo workers were also involved in a strike at Pierre Bonnat's alluvial mine. Bonnat trained the men to dive for gold, but before they would start work they went on strike to demand more pay.[21] It would appear from these examples that the first mine workers' strikes were confined to small, ethnically homogenous groups of workers who had some degree of skill and therefore greater bargaining power than their unskilled colleagues. Nevertheless, ordinary workers quickly appreciated the potential of this kind of action. In 1892 between 300 and 500 workers at the Gie Appantoo mine organized a demonstration during working time to express their 'great dissatisfaction' over poor food and delays in wage payments. The Mining Journal reported that 'the feeling against [the Mine Manager] was so strong that it was evident a radical alteration was necessary'. The manager was subsequently dismissed and replaced by a man who was instructed to be more understanding in his treatment of the workers.[22]

The Origins of the Labour Force, 1870-1900

Despite the mining industry's failure to attract the regular supply of cheap and efficient workers it required, it did manage to survive a 30-year period of erratic development between 1870 and 1900. Where then, did the early labour force of mine workers come from? To a large extent it came from outside the gold-producing areas. In 1903 (the first year for which statistics are available) under 68 per cent of the industry's labour force came from the Gold Coast, and of that contingent, 16 per cent came from outside the auriferous areas of the south-west. Local workers therefore constituted only 57 per cent of the total labour force of 17,000 men. Significantly, the majority of local workers were hired not to perform the most important task of underground mining, but the ancillary tasks of carrying, clearing, woodcutting and farming.[23]

The Kroos of the Liberian coast were numerically the most important group of non-local workers, providing 14 per cent of the labour force in 1903. They had a number of advantages for the mines, which made the 18/0 cost of recruitment per man a worthwhile investment. Kroos had a long history of employment with expatriate masters along Africa's West Coast, and they were 'docile, tractable and not fastidious as to their surroundings', 'the men to handle machines, to stoke, and to show the other natives both to work and to exercise care'. They had no objection to working underground, and were 'in a position to give continuous labour', usually contracting to work for a period of 12 months.[24]

It seems likely that many of the locally-recruited workers were members of the large population of independent gold winners in south-western Ghana. While it was the habit of these men and women to 'gravitate at various intervals towards the richest and most recently discovered gold deposit', they were not particularly keen to join foreign mining companies as paid labourers.[25] By winning gold independently they could regularly earn between 1/0 and 2/0 a day, a figure that could be increased dramatically if explosives were used to blast gold-bearing rock. Moreover, the freedom which such work offered allowed a gold strike to be celebrated by 'a general debauch among the lucky finders and their friends'.[26] Some entrepreneurs, both Europeans and coastal Africans, tried to deal with the problem of labour shortages by allowing gold winners to remain on their concessions and to work on a tribute basis. The more ambitious mining pioneers were less tolerant of a labour process where 'of supervision there was none', and where 'the miners seem to have worked at their own sweet will in whatever place or direction they liked'.[27] Cade, for example, had no time for 'this absurd system of sharing', and was determined to see the gold winners either expelled from AGC's 100-square-mile concession or turned into wage labourers. After hinting that he would use force to achieve this aim, he was able to report that 'all bother with native miners had passed away' and so there was 'no need to resort to those acts of gentle persuasion that we had in view'.[28] How many winners actually chose to become mine workers is impossible to estimate, but one mining engineer with many years experience on the coast observed in 1909 that they had been 'finally eliminated...by a process of gradual absorption'.[29]

The mining companies were also able to secure some labour through arrangements with the local chiefs who had leased their land for mining operations, and who were said to be 'commonly in the hands of one or more of the European managers who by costly presents keep them in their pay'.[30] Such arrangements were highly desirable, as they allowed the mines to negotiate a fixed, and usually low wage for the workers supplied. Thus Cade reported:

> For bush work I arranged with the King for 1/0 per day, thinking that 1/3 would be paid, although I insisted on 1/0 in the agreement.[31]

Finally, the employment of women as carriers, rock sorters and washers in this first phase of capitalist mining should not be overlooked. No data is available about the wages paid to these women, but it does seem that they were assigned to some of the most arduous tasks:

> As for the poor wretched carriers, I can only say 'God help them', for some of their loads must have often proved a fearful burden to them. Many women, each with little babies, some a few weeks old only strapped to their backs, have taken 70, 80, 90 and 100 lb. loads over this very hilly road of 120 miles. It strikes me as almost incredible.

As Edwin Cade admitted that he was 'not a believer in driving philanthropy and business with the same pair of reins', we can safely assume that the sight was not so incredible as to persuade him to provide lighter loads for his female carriers.[32]

The Contradictions of Labour Control, 1900-1906

By the turn of the century the modern mining industry on the Gold Coast had survived, somewhat precariously, for almost 30 years. The labour question had not been resolved, but the erratic pace of mining development and the availability of imported labour had averted any serious labour crisis. After 1900 several factors threatened to precipitate that crisis. As a result of the pacification of Ashanti, the closure of the South African mines during the Boer War and the construction of the Sekondi-Kumasi railway, the colony experienced a speculative gold rush in the period 1900-1902. A hard core of 40 mines survived the collapse of the boom and took delivery of the machinery required for deep-level mining, creating a heavy new demand for the few workers who were prepared to perform underground labour. In addition, the period after 1900 saw the appearance of new competitors in the Gold Coast labour market. The programme of road and rail construction promoted by Governor Nathan, and above all the rapid growth of the cocoa industry, created new income-earning opportunities, many of them more attractive than work in the mines. Finally, and perhaps most seriously, the 'foreign solution' hitherto adopted by the mines was becoming increasingly unsatisfactory. French expansion on the Liberian coast made Kroo labourers more scarce and more expensive, and Mine Managers expressed a growing unease about the Kroos' refusal to work for more than one 12-month contract.

The mining companies' initial response to the impending labour crisis was to look further afield for supplies of foreign labour. The mining lobby in London pressed the Colonial Office to allow a free interchange of labour between the British West African colonies, but the Governors of The Gambia, Sierra Leone, and Southern Nigeria were not prepared to see their own scarce labour resources being drained away into the Gold Coast. The mines then turned their attention to Asia. As early as 1873 Brackenbury had advocated the employment of Chinese coolies in the Gold Coast mines, hoping that they would 'breed in with the natives and infuse some energy into the Fanti races'.[33] This proposal fell on deaf ears in London and Accra. Missionaries and educated Africans were strongly opposed to such a scheme, and a disastrous experiment with the importation of 18 Chinese prospectors in 1897 had already convinced the Gold Coast Government that such a proposal should be rejected. At the Colonial Office, the political scandal which followed accusations that Chinese 'slave labour' was being used in the South African mines ensured that no further experiments with the 'coolie solution' would be allowed. Much to their regret, therefore, the mining companies began to look for a local solution to the problem of finding the 'supply of cheap and reliable labour' which was still 'the most important factor in facilitating the rapid development of the mining industry of the Gold Coast'.[34] The rest of this chapter describes the three principal strategies employed by the mines in seeking to avert the impending labour crisis, and analyzes the reasons for their failure.

Improving labour productivity

In the speculative era of mining between 1870 and 1900, the numerous and hurriedly-formed mining companies on the Gold Coast had given almost no systematic attention to the problems of labour utilization and productivity. After 1900, with the shortage of labour growing steadily more serious and investors clamouring for profit, the mines became much more aware that 'every nigger costs £50 a year, and that every one saved means £50 towards the dividend'.[35] In their attempt to save labour and improve productivity, the mines adopted a number of strategies. Using the recently completed Sekondi-Kumasi railway, they installed much heavier and more efficient machinery than they had been able to use when all equipment had to be head-loaded from the coast. The Mine Managers also experimented with new forms of work organization. For example, many ancillary tasks in the mines were subcontracted to competing African entrepreneurs from the coast, and payment by task was introduced in place of the fixed daily wage on the assumption that it would 'substitute the hope of gain for the drudgery given under a master'.[36]

These innovations were successful and reduced working costs by up to 40 per cent, but they failed to achieve the kind of improvements in productivity that the Mine Managers sought, and they offered no lasting solution to the problem of labour shortages. If those objectives were to be achieved, then the mines recognized that they would have to find a means of ensuring that their employees worked harder, more efficiently and more consistently than they were normally prepared to. There appeared to be only one means of attaining that end, and that was to intensify managerial and supervisory authority within the mining workplace. Significantly it was precisely at this time that an influx of South African mining capital and personnel into the Gold Coast took place. South African attitudes towards and expectations of native workers were much more rigorous than those of other expatriates on the coast. Consequently, the new campaign for better labour utilization and higher productivity came to depend on increasingly punitive and coercive managerial and supervisory techniques. Almost immediately, the Government Transport Officer began to complain of the South Africans' 'anti-negro prejudices' and 'inability to see things from the native point of view'. 'I regret to say', he told the Colonial Secretary, 'that from what I have up to the present seen of mining men from South Africa they are not as a rule to be trusted to deal fairly with employees'.[37]

In 1903 the Government made an attempt to put an end to the ill-treatment of native workers through the appointment of a Mines Inspectorate, but its members did little to mitigate the impact of the new, systematically authoritarian style of management in the mines. According to one of the more enlightened members of the Mines Department:

> The plain truth about an Inspector of Mines' work is that he has a duty to defend all employees in the mines, and particularly of course the predominating native employees in a colony from the greed of the financial interests in London.

This, however, was virtually impossible, given the close social links between most Mines Inspectors and Mine Managers:

> In fact, my chief was on far too friendly terms with these managers...If an Inspector's chief is in the habit of wining, dining and card playing with those he is supposed to control, then his lot - like that of the policeman - can hardly be a happy one.[38]

Ironically, the quest for improved productivity after 1900, which was intended to offset the acute shortage of local labour in the colony, actually perpetuated the problem of labour supply. By intensifying discipline and allowing the maltreatment of workers, managers simply deterred prospective workers from joining the mines and encouraged existing mine workers to leave for less onerous forms of employment. Governor Rodger had no doubt about the contradictory nature of the mining companies' strategy:

> I have been informed by native chiefs on more than one occasion that their people were ready and willing to do mining work provided they were paid their wages regularly and were treated fairly, but felt that they would not work for companies where their wages were withheld or where they were fined on every possible pretext.[39]

Stabilizing the labour force

The second response of mining capital to the impending labour crisis was to introduce a policy of labour stabilization. In pursuit of this objective the larger mines spent substantial sums of money building new and more attractive villages for their workers. Long service awards were introduced to foster a commitment to mine work, and with the help of the colonial administration, vigorous efforts were made to solve the longstanding problem of food shortages and high prices in the mining areas. These innovations had a limited success. In July 1904, for example, the Ashanti Goldfields Chairman noted:

> The Ashantis are beginning to realize that there is some value and pleasure in work, and they are beginning to get amusements on which they can spend their money. As we go on these will be still further provided in order to give them greater inducement to earn money.[40]

However, only skilled workers such as carpenters and mechanics showed any inclination to provide the regular, dependable labour demanded by the mines. The mass of unskilled labourers continued to work for short periods, to move from mine to mine, and to move in and out of wage employment.

Why then, did the mining industry fail to stabilize the unskilled labour force, and thereby solve the labour question? Several explanatory factors can be identified. As this chapter has already described, this was a period of rapid economic expansion in the Gold Coast, which allowed workers and prospective workers to choose from a range of other, more attractive means of securing a cash income. Despite the improvements initiated by the mining companies, living conditions in the mining towns continued to be extremely unattractive. Food supplies remained inadequate, and all efforts at price fixing in local markets met with stern resistance from traders. Workers agreed to a proposal that they should grow their own food on land provided by the mines, but demanded time off to do so, thereby defeating the whole object of the scheme. The newly constructed mining villages were usually sited some distance from the pit-head in low-lying, damp and malarial locations 'which no ingenuity could convert into really desirable building sites'.[41] After the collapse of the 1900-1902 mining boom many of the villages got out of control, sanitation standards dropped and rooms became overcrowded with men who rarely, if ever, worked in the mines. As one mining company complained, 'natives in the Gold Coast simply squat in [the company's] villages and come to work when they feel inclined to do so'.[42]

The final reason for the failure of the labour stabilization strategy once again demonstrates the contradictory nature of the industry's objectives. As described earlier, the intensive nature of supervision in the mines after 1900 made an inherently unpleasant occupation even less attractive. Similarly, although the mines wanted to foster the growth of settled, stabilized communities of workers, they also insisted on maintaining very strict social control within those communities. Consequently, the authoritarian nature of the mining workplace was replicated in the authoritarian nature of the mining community, reinforcing the labour repulsive character of work in the mines.

The obsession of mining capital and the colonial state with the maintenance of law and order in the mining districts of the Gold Coast was quite understandable. Following the unsuccessful Ashanti rising of 1900, when one European mine had been captured and ransacked, expatriates feared that in any subequent unrest the Ashanti would avoid a conflict with government troops, preferring to 'drop unexpectedly on the isolated mining camps and chop all whites'.[43] The diversity of ethnic groups now living within the mining areas also gave cause for concern. In the words of one District Commissioner:

> The mushroom growth of Obuasi and the petty fights and squabbles amongst the conglomeration of natives from almost every tribe on the West Coast of Africa...may constitute a danger of a riot breaking out here, which if we had not sufficient force to cope with it, might turn into a very serious affair.[44]

Fears of disorder in the mining towns also stemmed from the observation that their inhabitants were 'more prone to commit breaches of peace than natives of the country'. Ever since the beginning of modern mining 'renegades from the coast' had flocked to towns such as Tarkwa and Obuasi, and by 1906 such towns contained 'a large crowd of determined wastrels living more or less on crime'.[45] Finally, discontent amongst the mine workers was perceived as a threat to law and order. As a later section of this chapter will show, after 1900 workers in the mines began to engage regularly in collective, and at times violent forms of protest. With many mines closing down and unable to pay wages, and with intermittent food shortages still occurring, the possibility of large-scale labour unrest was by no means remote.

In response to these perceived threats to civil order, mine management and the colonial administration introduced a strict regime of social control. Large numbers of policemen and soldiers were stationed in the principal mining towns. At Obuasi, for example, up to 200 native soldiers were stationed at the railway sidings, equipped with an armoured train that could quickly move to the heart of the town. In 1902 a Mines Police Force was formed 'specially and solely for the purpose of preserving law and order in different mining centres', and these official units were supplemented by the expatriate Gold Coast Mines Volunteer Force.[46] The judicial system also acted as an instrument of social control. Extremely harsh sentences, such as three months imprisonment with hard labour for the theft of one candle, were used to deter potential law breakers, as was the custom of having 'criminals wearing prison clothing and eating prison food paraded daily before their families'.[47]

In addition to these official forms of regulation, the mining companies also used their extensive legal rights to control most forms of social and economic activity within their concession areas. At Obuasi, the Ashanti Goldfields Corporation established a 12-man Village Council to hear petty criminal cases and to pass on offenders to the Superintendent for an appropriate punishment. The company's enthusiasm for the Council, however, was not shared by local administrators. The first two Village Council Presidents were dismissed for blackmail and rape, and the Council as a whole soon assumed juridical powers to which it was not entitled. Eventually, the District Commissioner abrogated the Council on the grounds that the Mine Manager 'thought a great deal more of the mines and the production of gold than the village or the welfare of the people'.[48] A similar conclusion could also be drawn from the Mine Managers' obsessive determination to deprive their native workers of alcoholic drinks. Having failed to impose total prohibition on the mining concessions, the mines opened their own spirit shops and were given the power to veto all applications for spirit licences from native traders in the area. In this way the mines were able to deprive 'troublemakers' of alcohol, and to withdraw the sale of intoxicating liquor completely in times of unrest. Finally, after 1900 the mining companies made a far more determined effort to prevent and detect the theft of gold. Black detectives were employed to work 'undercover' in the mining towns, while the Government was persistently encouraged to impose stricter controls over local goldsmiths, the main receivers of stolen gold. Fencing was erected around parts of the mine where theft was most common, and 'unauthorized loafers' were expelled from the area. Such precautions inevitably led to further restrictions within the workplace:

> As an essential part of a 'security system' it would be necessary to provide a change house where the natives will be obliged to leave their working clothes on quitting work, and such convenience should be provided inside the enclosure as this will deprive them of any excuse for going outside during working hours.[49]

Although these strategies of social control were far less coercive than those being used at this time in the compounds of South Africa and Southern Rhodesia, in the socio-economic and political context of the Gold Coast they could only serve to contradict the mining companies' attempt to resolve the labour question through a programme of labour stabilization. Very few individuals in the Gold Coast had been forced into the labour market by this time, and with the economy expanding, the demand for wage labourers inevitably exceeded the supply. It was a sellers' market, and very few of the men and women who wished to sell their labour power were prepared to accept the restrictive kind of living and working environment which the mining industry was seeking to impose on them. As one colonial official remarked, 'in bringing order to these districts we have not attracted the working native...The mining towns are full, not of the industrious men which the mines require, but of those who have no regard for the law'.[50] The labour question remained unanswered and mining capital was forced to look for an alternative solution.

Monopsonizing the labour market

In the first decade of the 20th Century the gold mines of South Africa and Southern Rhodesia, like the mines of the Gold Coast, were confronted with a shortage of labour and rising working costs. Short-term solutions to this crisis were found in the use of forced labour (in Southern Rhodesia) and indentured Chinese labour (in South Africa), but the long-term answer was found in the creation of a monopsonistic regional labour market. The key feature of this labour market was an agreement between the principal (white) employers of labour to avoid the competitive recruitment of scarce labour supplies, and to use the absence of competition in the labour market as a means of forcing down wage rates.

Prior to 1900 the Gold Coast mining companies had not been oblivious to the advantages which could be gained from the elimination of competition for labour. Burton and Cameron, for example, had predicted in 1883 that labour shortages would push up wages, and had suggested that only by acting together could the mines stabilize wages and introduce longer contracts. The following year, Haughton had stressed the need for 'unanimity between the various companies...for controlling or regulating the labour supply'. In 1901, when the labour question had become more serious, Dupont argued the case for monopsonization at greater length:

> Lorsque la demande viendra plus grande, le recruitement des 'boys' et leurs conditions de paiement seront facilités par le fait que tout le district est sous le control des mêmes personnes. On évitera ainsi les competitions qui on été la principal cause de la grande élevation des salaires au Transvaal.[51]

Given the new influence of South African capital and personnel within the Gold Coast mines, it was not surprising that the Mine Managers should move to put an end to the 'warfare between large employers of labour' which had now broken out, and that they should do so by attempting to establish a monopsonistic labour market in the colony.[52] In May 1901 a group of mining companies under the guidance of Percy Tarbutt and A.L. Jones submitted proposals to the Colonial Office for the creation of a 'West Coast of Africa Labour Bureau'. This non-profit-making company would undertake 'the duty of collecting and segregating labour in properly supervised and effectively managed depots, from which labour would be supplied as required to different undertakings'. The Bureau, Tarbutt explained to shareholders in the mines, would create 'a monopoly of labour engagement', and would receive the assistance of the British Foreign Office.[53] This optimism proved unfounded, for neither metropolitan nor colonial administrations were prepared to grant the Bureau the substantial powers which the scheme demanded. Seven months later the New Gold Coast Agency, a subsidiary of Consolidated Gold Fields of South Africa, made another proposal to the Colonial Office, recommending the creation of a recruitment agency which would be free to engage foreign and local labourers. This proposal, and a plan for the compulsory registration of all workers, was also rejected.

Having failed to establish an autonomous labour bureau with monopsonistic powers, the mines now turned to less formal approaches to the problem. In South Africa competitive recruitment amongst the mines had been eliminated by the creation of a powerful central organization, the Transvaal Chamber of Mines, which could impose financial penalties on mines that contravened commonly-agreed policies. In 1902 the Gold Coast mines moved in a similar direction, establishing the Mine Managers' Association, followed in 1905 by the West African Chamber of Mines, whose first Chairman was Lord Harris, former Governor of Bombay and Chairman of Consolidated Gold Fields. Like its South African counterpart, the Mine Managers' Association attempted to reduce and stabilize wage rates for mine labourers. In June 1903 a 'no poaching' agreement was drawn up and wages were fixed at 1/3 for surface workers and 1/9 for underground workers. The unanimity of the Mine Managers very quickly proved to be illusory. Within weeks (or according to one manager, hours) of the agreement being signed, some mines began to offer higher than the agreed rates, and sent out recruiting agents to lure workers away from other mines with promises of better wages and living conditions.

Simultaneously, the Gold Coast Government was making its own attempts to establish a monopsonistic labour market in the colony. Operating on a very limited budget, the Government's plans for extensive infrastructural development were being obstructed by the scarcity and high price of labour. In 1902 Governor Nathan established the Transport Department, whose principal function was to act as a labour bureau with monopsonistic powers. All natives seeking work as labourers or carriers were to register with the Department, which would allocate them to expatriate employers in return for a capitation fee. The Department would make a daily subsistence payment to each man, and the remainder of his wages were not to be paid until he had completed a 12-month contract. Using its monopsonistic powers, the Department would gradually reduce workers' wages to an 'acceptable' level. According to the Transport Officer, 'as soon as they recognized that they must take the Government wage or none at all, they must perforce yield'.[54]

In practice the Transport Department enjoyed little success in its attempt to control the labour market. In 1904 only 793 of the mines' 17,044 workers were supplied by the Department, and by 1906 the number had declined to 487. The Department did succeed in supplying the Government's own labour requirements and marginally reduced the daily wage rate for carriers, but in the mining areas the gold mines persistently outbid the Department for unskilled labour. The attempt to monopsonize the labour market had clearly failed. This failure can be explained at two levels. First, at a superficial level, it derived from the inability of the mining companies and Government to take united action on the labour problem. Second, and more fundamentally, the failure of monopsonization stemmed from the successful resistance of workers and prospective workers to this strategy of labour control.

The structure of mining capital in the Gold Coast was not at all conducive to the formulation of a coherent strategy of monopsonization. After the collapse of the 1900-02 boom, many small mines were competitively struggling for survival without the backing of the large, interlocking mining groups which had made the South African mining industry such a powerful economic and political force. The most important mine, Ashanti Goldfields, refused to join the Mine Managers' Association since its high level of profitability allowed the mine to outbid others in the labour market, while its very large concession ensured that AGC faced far less competition in its labour catchment area than the closely spaced mines on the Tarkwa-Prestea gold field. Consequently, the Ashanti Goldfields Mine Manager was able to adopt a distinctly superior tone in describing his counterparts:

> You know the difficulty of getting into cooperation with the Tarkwa managers. The Mine Managers' Association, if it had been properly conducted, was a place where these things could have been discussed and finally settled, but as you know, when they did meet and fix upon any decided action, one or other of the managers immediately contravened the general views and until they make the Mine Managers' Association on the same footing as that in Johannesburg and inflict a fine for the contravention of rules I am afraid it will never do any good.[55]

The problem of cooperation also appeared to be at the root of the inability of the mining industry and Colonial Government to take joint action over the labour question. In theory, the Transport Department scheme had several advantages for the mines, providing long-term workers on written contracts for a capitation fee which was considerably lower than the cost of recruiting a Kroo or other foreign worker. In practice, the mining industry could only only see the disadvantages of the scheme, believing that it would undermine managerial authority over the workers and prevent supervisors from using the disciplinary measures which were thought to be essential if productivity were to improve. As the Transport Officer explained, expatriates in the mines 'prefer to do as they please without anyone questioning their acts or punishments'.[56]

Resistance and the failure of monopsonization

The failure of monopsonization in the Gold Coast was not simply a result of disunity amongst the mining companies and the administration, but also stemmed from a major contradiction inherent to this strategy of labour control. As an earlier section of this chapter described, prior to 1900 workers and prospective workers in the mining areas withheld or withdrew their labour in resistance to the low wages and hard work offered by the mines. Local men could subsist without access to a cash income, and those who did wish to acquire money could do so through the production of cash crops or by entering other, more attractive, forms of wage employment. This situation had not changed by the time the Government and the mines began to think of monopsonizing the labour market. Consequently when unilateral wage reductions were made, workers and prospective workers simply refused to work. As F.W. Migeod, the Transport Officer, explained:

Whilst it remained possible to obtain many undersized men, men of poor physique and boys for that rate in considerable numbers, it was found that able-bodied men would not do a full days work for 1/6 per working day.[57]

Moreover, workers who had developed a commitment to work in the mines did not accept wage reductions passively. As the following list demonstrates, between 1900 and 1906 there was a growing tendency for discontent amongst the mine workers to be manifested in the form of overt and collective resistance.[58]

1. In July 1903, carriers on the Bekwai-Obuasi route were taking twice the allotted time and the Transport Officer reported that 'neither persuasion nor threats have been able to reduce the time taken by the natives'. In an attempt to remedy the situation one group of carriers was fined. They all deserted and after this incident all other groups of carriers refused to work on this route. The Transport Officer lamented, 'we have no means of compelling the carriers to work against their will. I have fined them, but apparently they do not mind this'.

2. In September 1903, 400 labourers at Anfargah mine went on strike. They returned the following day and proceeded to commit 'acts of open violence', breaking into the lock-up where some of their colleagues had been detained the previous day. The workers clashed with European staff and six labourers were injured in the fighting.

3. In February 1904, 80 workers at Akrokerri (Ashanti) mine went on strike after wages had been raised by 3d at the nearby mine of Ashanti Goldfields. Workers demanded parity with the Ashanti Goldfields labour force and claimed that their work was too hard. The Mine Manager stated that the strike was 'another attempt to squeeze the white man in a situation of labour shortage', and the stoppage ended after the intervention of the District Commissioner.

4. In March 1904, Ashanti Goldfields reduced the wages of skilled labourers and introduced full-day Saturday shifts. A group of carpenters, whose wages had been reduced from 4/6 and 5/6 to 3/6, sent a telegram of protest to the District Commissioner. A group of bricklayers wrote to the District Commissioner with similar complaints.

5. In July 1904, a Lagos man took out a summons against the Head Wood Contractor at Akrokerri on behalf of 60 other woodcutters. They charged the contractor with failing to pay their wages.

6. In January 1905, Ashanti Goldfields announced its intention to reduce wages from 1/3 to 1/0. The Mine Manager reported rumours that all the men affected by the reduction intended to go on strike and destroy the mine by fire.

7. In July 1905, all the firewood cutters at Ashanti Goldfields went on strike to demand higher wages. The Mine Manager asked the District Commissioner to come to the mine and give the men 'a good talking to'.

8. In August 1905, labourers at Sansu mine became restless after management failed to pay wages for two months. The Governor wrote to the Colonial Office:

> It is not impossible that in consequence of the non-payment of the labourers, disturbances such as a raid on the local markets for the purpose of obtaining food, or even an attack on the mine property itself may occur.

The following month he reported:

> An outbreak, which might have had serious consequences, was only averted by the distribution of ready money and by the personal influence of the Commissioner and the local manager.

Incidents such as these (which almost certainly represent only a small proportion of mine workers' strikes in this period) had a profound impact on the attitude of Mine Managers towards the strategy of monopsonization. While they agreed in principle with the idea of reducing wages unilaterally, in practice they recognized that to do so would provoke at best a drift of labour away from the mines and, at worst, strikes, demonstrations and other manifestations of collective resistance. For example, in January 1904 the Governor asked the Mine Manager of Prestea Mines for his assistance in cutting wage rates. The Manager replied that while he welcomed the proposal, he could not cut wages without 'risking a paralysis of mining operations'. The Mine Manager at Obuasi made the same point even more clearly. Replying to a proposal from the Gold Coast Railway that the mine should 'cooperate in a summary reduction of wages to 1/0 per day', the Mine Manager reluctantly declined the invitation:

> In case we should make a wholesale reduction in the price we pay our ordinary labour, we would have to face the possibility of an equally wholesale strike, and this we do not, at present anyhow, care to risk.[59]

The strikes of 1900 to 1906 represented an important development in the historical struggle between labour and capital in the Ghanaian gold mines. A cross-ethnic, occupational and perhaps even a class consciousness was beginning to emerge amongst the mine workers. They now recognized the power of collective action, and were prepared to use that power to thwart the strategies of labour control employed by mining capital and the colonial state. Within three years Ashanti Goldfields, the largest and most profitable mine in the colony, was to experience its first general strike, and the Mine Manager accurately predicted that 'the natives, year by year as they are becoming more educated will, I think, give us further trouble in this direction.[60] Recognizing this problem, after 1906 the mining industry, with the intermittent assistance of the Colonial Government, began to look for a new way of securing a cheap, productive and passive labour force.

Notes

1. The Mining Journal, 8 May 1884, p.575; CP, 'Report on Obuassie Gold Mine Estate', August 1895, p.31.

2. Burton and Cameron (1883) p.328; CP, ibid, p.30.

3. Skertchley (1878) p.281; LA, J. Daw, 'The Ashanti Goldfields Corporation', 1902, p.49.

4. BMA, Fritz to Basel, 18 July 1875.

5. CHP, E. Cade to AGC Directors, 10 December 1897.

6. The Mining Journal, loc cit.

7. LA, J. Daw, speaking to AGC EGM, 10 December 1898; Skertchly (1878) p.275.

8. LA, ibid.

9. Foster (1912), pp.202-3.

10. Further Correspondence Regarding Affairs of the Gold Coast, CO African No. 249, Secretary APS to CO, 2 April 1882.

11. PRO, CO96/487/14471, Antrobus minute, 22 May 1909.

12. Skertchley (1878) pp.274-5.

13. The Mining Journal, loc cit.

14. GNA, ADM45/1/1, Acting Resident Kumasi to CS, 7 July 1889.

15. AGCI, 26 February 1902.

16. Further Correspondence Regarding Affairs of the Gold Coast, Parliamentary Paper C3687, pp.98-103; AGCI, 21 August 1902; PRO, CO96/357/6056 and 8560; GNA, ADM45/1/1.

17. The Mining Journal, 16 May 1885, p.551.

18. LA, E. Cade, speaking to AGC EGM, 12 December 1898, and to AGC EGM, 21 July 1898.

19. CHP, J. Daw to AGC Directors, 10 January 1898.

20. McCarthy (1918) pp.77-8.

21. Rosenblum (1972) p.143.

22. The Mining Journal, 23 July 1892, p.817.

23. ARMD 1904.

24. CP, 'Report from Obuasi', 1895, p.6; ARGC 1894, p.9.

25. Further Correspondence Regarding Affairs of the Gold Coast, Parliamentary Paper C3687, Civil Commissioner Tarkwa to CS, 31 August 1881.

26. Skertchley (1878) p.281.

27. Eaton-Turner (1947) p.3.

28. CP, 'Report on Obbuassie Gold Mine Estate', August 1895, p.28; E. Cade to AGC Directors, 25 February 1897.

29. McCarthy (1909) p.293.

30. Further Correspondence Regarding Affairs of the Gold Coast, loc cit.

31. CP, 'Report from Obuasi', 1895, p.6.

32. CP, E. Cade to AGC Directors, 25 December 1897; LA, E. Cade, speaking to AGC EGM, 12 December 1898.

33. Quoted by Burton and Cameron (1883) p.176.

34. L. Bowler to CO, 10 July 1901, quoted by Walker (1971) p.73.

35. AGCI, 18 October 1902.

36. AGCI, 26 March 1903.

37. GNA BP228, TO to CS, 25 March 1902 and 11 October 1902.

38. RHO, 'A Man of Metal: The Autobiography of A.C. Vivian', Ms., n.d., pp.63-4.

39. AGCI, 20 May 1904.

40. AGCI, 16 July 1904.

41. Giles (1905) p.17.

42. PRO, CO96/503/33643, Gold Coast Amalgamated Mines to CO, 1 November 1910.

43. GNA, ADM12/5/112, West African Hinterlands Concessions to CO, 4 April 1902.

44. GNA, ADM53/1/1, DC Obuasi to Commissioner of Police, 25 September 1904.

45. ARA 1906, p.17; GNA, ADM53/1/1, ibid.

46. PRO, CO96/432/32969, CS to Mine Manager AGC, 10 January 1902.

47. AGCI, 14 November 1903.

48. AGCI, 7 November 1903.

49. LA, 'Report of W.R. Feldtmann', 15 July 1905.

50. GNA, ADM53/1/3, DC Obuasi to CS, 3 November 1904.

51. Burton and Cameron (1883) p.333; The Mining Journal, 8 May 1884, p.575; Dupont (1901) p.36.

52. GNA, BP228, TO to CS, 21 January 1904.

53. PRO, CO96/389/18670, West Coast of Africa Labour Bureau to CO, 29 May 1901.

54. MP, TO to CS, 19 January 1901.

55. AGCI, 3 September 1907.

56. GNAT, ADM1/24, TO to CS, 13 December 1903.

57. Quoted by Greenstreet (1966) p.36.

58. Data relating to these strikes is taken from GNA, BP228 and ADM53/1/1; GNAK, 17/20/1907; AGCO 25 January 1905; PRO, CO96/432/31746 and 33924.

59. GNA, BP228, Mine Manager Prestea Mines to Governor, 6 January 1904; AGCI, 25 and 27 July 1903.

60. AGCI, 25 January 1909.

Chapter 3

FROM LABOUR SHORTAGE TO LABOUR SURPLUS: THE RECRUITMENT AND CONTROL OF A MIGRANT LABOUR FORCE, 1906-1930

The ultimate aim of the mine managers is forced
labour in fact, if not in name.

F.W. Migeod, Government Transport Officer, December 1909.

After 1905 the Gold Coast mining companies continued to pursue
the objective which had eluded them for 30 years, to recruit and
retain an adequate number of cheap and efficient workers to ensure the profitable expansion of the mining industry. In an attempt to end their dependence on imported workers and to avoid
the use of increasingly troublesome local labour, the mines now
looked to areas beyond the Gold Coast Colony and Ashanti for a
source of compliant migrant workers. This chapter examines the
strategies used by mining capital and the colonial state to recruit
and control those workers in the period 1905 to 1930.

The Northern Territories Labour Experiment, 1906-1909

Precisely at a time when the labour question was beginning
to threaten the continued expansion of the mining industry, a
promising new source of labour became available. The Northern
Territories of the Gold Coast, the Protectorate north of the River
Volta, had only recently been 'pacified' and its boundaries fixed
by international agreement. As a potential source of mine labour,
the area appeared to possess a number of unique advantages. Recruitment there would come under the auspices of the Gold Coast
Government, which had already decided that the area had little
direct economic value. Labour recruitment in the Northern Territories (NT's) could solve the administration's own manpower problems, contribute to the expansion of the Protectorate's embryonic
cash economy, and even help to eliminate the 'tribal warfare'
which afflicted the area and which was thought to stem from the
seasonal idleness of its inhabitants. Local cooperation with such a
scheme could also be expected. Subsistence farmers in the north
had few other cash-earning opportunities, and as much of the
area was densely populated, local communities could sustain the
loss of some of their young men.

As the Mine Managers had anticipated, the Chief Commissioner of the Northern Territories (CCNT) responded enthusiastically to their first request for labour in August 1905. The Chief Commissioner promised northern chiefs that the migration of their subjects would bring prosperity to the area, and encouraged them to support his 'labour crusade'. In December 1906 30 'specially selected intelligent men from all parts of the country' were taken south to see some of the more liberally-managed mines 'in the hope that the prospect of regular work and wages would induce large numbers of their fellow tribesmen to seek employment in the mining districts'. Following the visit, the Secretary for Mines declared that northerners would make 'excellent workmen both by their strength and intelligence' and, in 1907, 271 men from the North West Province were recruited for three mines in the Tarkwa area. Early the following year a further 1,000 men were requested and, in response, the recruitment effort was intensified and extended to the North East Province.[1]

This experiment with northern labour soon ran into serious problems. In June 1909 540 recruits left Gambaga, but 200 men deserted in Tamale and a further 82 disappeared on the way to Tarkwa. By July 1st another 231 men had left the mines, and by the end of the month the remaining 27 recruits had also gone. The CCNT reported that 'it was impossible to reason with them in their quarters as their only reply to anything said was that they wanted to go home'.[2] Other groups of recruits proved equally troublesome, and either deserted en route to the mines, refused to work underground once they had arrived, or reported for duty at only a small proportion of their shifts. Meanwhile, in the north, it was reported that men returning from work in the mines had contracted venereal disease, acquired bad drinking habits, and were now refusing to accept the authority of their chiefs.

As a result of these problems, recruitment in the north was suspended in February 1910. Wolfe Murray, a senior South African labour administrator advising the Chamber of Mines, wrote that 'from the very start the experiment proved to be a failure' and that it had 'produced an incalculable amount of harm' to the prospects for future recruitment.[3] The Gold Coast Governor was quick to explain why the recruits had responded so unfavourably to their first experience of wage labour:

> There can be no doubt in my opinion that a mistake was made in the manner in which these labourers were originally recruited and sent to the mines, in large batches and without any previous medical examination or subsequent medical supervision on the journey, and this mistake was accentuated by the fact that they were unaccompanied by their wives and that insufficient provision was made for their food.[4]

While there was considerable truth in this explanation of the recruits' behaviour, Governor Rodger's despatch failed to acknowledge that many of the 'volunteers' for work in the mines were, in fact, 'conscripts'. Political officers in the north had been under great pressure from their superiors in the administration to provide the recruits requested by the mines. In the absence of sufficient genuine volunteers, these officers threatened chiefs with fines if they failed to produce enough men and offered them 5/0 head money for each labourer supplied. Not surprisingly, the chiefs then used their authority to induce men to 'volunteer' for work in the mines. As the Chamber of Mines publicly admitted, the whole experiment had ultimately depended on the use of coercion:

> The first step that a chief would take upon being approached by a Labour Agent would be to go to the DC and ask him if all were in order. Were the Commissioner to tell the chief that it was purely a matter of mutual arrangement between his people and the agent and that they must judge the merits of the latter's proposal, without interference, the efforts of the recruiter would be rendered of no avail.[5]

The treatment received by those recruits who did arrive at the mines was a further factor in the failure of the experiment. The mines had been warned by the Head Chief of Mamprusi that 'the question of future supplies of labourers would depend on the story which they would have to tell on their return... The whole success of your proposals depends on the manner in which the first few gangs are treated'.[6] Despite this warning, managers made no attempt to curb the excesses of their supervisory staff. At Abontiakoon, for example, six recruits received corporal punishment for insubordinate behaviour, two of them being 'very severely flogged' while spreadeagled on the ground by a European supervisor and African headman. Significantly, Abontiakoon had the worst record of desertions.[7] When the mining companies were threatened with legal action if such incidents were allowed to continue, their solicitor, Giles Hunt, complacently told the Colonial Secretary that 'it is necessary for the preservation of order and discipline that some summary and exemplary punishment should from time to time be inflicted on offenders'.[8]

The Chamber of Mines and the 'South African Solution', 1909-1912

Through modes of resistance such as desertion, absenteeism and refusal to work underground, the unwilling workers from the north had forced the mines to abandon their latest attempt to resolve the labour question. The industry's response to this situation was determined by several considerations. Although they continued to seek official assistance, the mines refused to entertain any scheme that might entail new financial obligations or restrict their administrative autonomy. The importation of Asian labour was still an appealing idea, but it was ruled out in 1910 when the Colonial Office stated that 'the labour difficulty is not yet so acute as to call for outside assistance'.[9] A more pressing consideration was the growing tendency of local mine workers to defend their interests through collective resistance. In January 1909 the entire labour force at Ashanti Goldfields and an unknown number of workers in Tarkwa struck to demand higher pay. Pickets were posted at the mine gates in Obuasi, but they were removed by police and the men returned to work at the old rate.

This lack of immediate success did not discourage the workers, for the general strike was followed by sectional stoppages of trammers, loco drivers, firemen, brakeboys, firewood loaders and underground miners. Confronted with such evidence of the mine workers' militancy, further attempts at wage standardization were abandoned, proposals to increase the length of shifts by two hours without a corresponding adjustment to wages were dropped, and managers decided not to implement a plan to put all labourers on a task work contract. As one manager argued, 'before this system could be started he was convinced a strike of boys would take place'.[10]

Such incidents convinced the Chamber of Mines that new strategies of labour control were urgently needed, not only to se- cure and retain an adequate number of workers, but also to de- prive them of the right and ability to engage in collective modes of resistance. A final determinant of the Chamber's policy, the in- fluence of South African mining capital, was to prove decisive in the precise choice of strategy used to achieve those objectives. In 1909 the South African mining company, Consolidated Gold Fields (CGF), took a large financial interest in nine mines on the Tarkwa-Prestea gold field. Lord Harris's position in the Chamber of Mines was immediately strengthened, and under his direction the Chamber became a forceful advocate of bringing the 'South African solution' to resolve the labour question in the Gold Coast. As suggested in the last chapter, the labour problem in Southern Africa was structurally similar to that of the Gold Coast. Low-grade mines had to minimize working costs to counteract the fixed price of gold and the rising cost of mining supplies. Local labour was in short supply, and its scarcity threatened to push wages up and increase working costs to unacceptable levels. To escape this dilemma, the South African and Rhodesian mining in- dustries employed an integrated strategy of monopsonistic recruit- ment within deliberately underdeveloped rural labour reserves, reinforced by pass laws and compounds designed to restrict the mobility of labour within urban industrial areas. While this strategy of labour control could not eliminate all modes of worker resistance, it represented a systematic and largely successful at- tempt to minimize costs, maximize profits, and reinforce the pol- itical authority of the state.

By 1909 these considerations had convinced the Chamber of Mines that the undeveloped and populous Northern Territories was still the most promising source of labour, but that to ensure the efficient exploitation of that labour it would be necessary to in- troduce the South African strategy of control. In May 1909 Giles Hunt reminded the Government of the industry's labour problems and explained in detail how very similar problems had been re- solved in South Africa. The Gold Coast mines, he argued, did not only require an additional 12,000 workers, but also needed pass laws, compounds, and a Native Labour Association to recruit and control those workers. He recognized that 'in the event of strict control and discipline being enforced it is more than likely that serious opposition from the native community may be met with'. Nevertheless, the mines would 'leave no stone unturned in their endeavours to put the question of native mining villages and the compounding of labour on a practical and definite basis'.[11] Just six weeks later, the Acting Governor consented to Hunt's proposals for a Native Labour Bureau, and a set of Draft Rules was formulated providing for the wholesale importation of the South African solution. Recruitment in the north would be undertaken by a monopsonistic agency controlled by the mining industry, and chiefs would receive head money for each labourer they supplied. At the mines, the indentured workers would be housed in communities controlled by a manager who enjoyed extensive powers of punishment and control. The recruits would work six days a week for 1/3 a day, with up to two-thirds of this amount being withheld until the completion of a 12-month contract.

The success of mining capital in persuading the colonial state to introduce the South African solution so quickly and thoroughly was short-lived. At the Transport Department, F.W. Migeod criticized the scheme for treating labourers 'much as a flock of sheep to be parcelled out as requisite and without protest':

> The natives have their likes and dislikes, some well founded, some mere whims, but both nevertheless to be reckoned with. I have known of labourers to abandon a mine in large numbers owing to some act of injustice, for a time that mine is on their 'black list' as it were...if the [Bureau] therefore anticipates that it will parcel out the labour irrespective of the natives' wishes, it will, I think, find that its anticipations were based on erroneous premises.[12]

Recognizing the truth of such arguments, Governor Rodger disowned the agreement made by Acting Governor Bryan and stated that the introduction of compounds and pass laws to the Gold Coast would be 'indefensible'.[13]

Following the rejection of the Labour Bureau proposal, the Government and mines looked more closely at the question of indentured labour. In January 1910 senior officials in the administration submitted a set of amendments to the original scheme designed to curb the powers of management and to prevent abuses in recruitment. Seven months later the Chamber of Mines produced its own report, compiled by Wolfe Murray. He admitted that men in the north were 'entirely apathetic' to the prospect of mine work, and therefore proposed the introduction of a thinly-disguised version of the scheme already rejected by the Governor.[14] Armed with Murray's report, Lord Harris renewed his campaign to gain official support for the South African solution. In January 1911 he incorporated Murray's proposals into a draft 'Coloured Labourers Ordinance' which legalized the compound system, introduced a pass law, and made offences such as desertion, absenteeism, intoxication and insubordination punishable by a prison sentence of six months. In the Colonial Office, Ellis observed that 'the thing might readily be described for political purposes as imprisonment with hard labour', while the Secretary of State told the Chamber that the Ordinance was unacceptable as it 'created many new crimes unknown to English law'.[15]

The Chamber of Mines now turned to more subtle tactics. After the rejection of the Coloured Labourers Ordinance, Ellis noted that the proposed legislation was 'only one side of the scheme by which the mines intend to reproduce the labour conditions of the Rand'.[16] The other side of the Chamber's scheme was to use the Government's mounting demands for improved health and housing conditions on the mines as a pretence for the imposition of tighter controls over labour. Confronted with 'grave evidence of the neglect of sanitary precautions' in the mines, in 1911 the Government proposed a Native Labour Health Regulations Ordinance based on the Transvaal's industrial health regulations.[17] The Chamber's enthusiasm for all things South African did not extend to this Ordinance, which imposed several new financial and administrative obligations on mine management. However, members of the Chamber soon realized that the Government's proposals could be turned to the industry's advantage. The issues of health, housing, and labour control were 'inseparable ...one whole and distinct problem',[18] the Chamber of Mines told the Colonial Office:

> It would be premature for the Government to introduce an Ordinance for the maintenance of the health of native mine labourers before an Act to govern the recruiting, engagement and control of such labourers had been placed upon the statute book.[19]

The Chamber went on to suggest that the mines would take full responsibility for the construction of new mine villages, but only on condition that management was granted total control of their administration. Once again, the Chamber had misjudged the official mood and overplayed its hand. The Government refused to relinquish control of the projected villages and abandoned its attempt to make the mines provide adequate facilities for their workers.

Having failed to gain official support for any of its proposals, the Chamber of Mines now set itself the more modest objective of an amendment to the 1893 Master and Servants Ordinance to allow the introduction and enforcement of longer-term labour contracts. In 1912 the Government agreed to amend the existing Ordinance, but the Chamber remained unhappy because responsibility for prosecuting deserters remained in the hands of the District Commissioners, who also retained the right to cancel contracts in the event of a complaint by a labourer about his conditions of work. The Mine Managers concluded that the Amendmentwould make the control of indentured workers no easier as there were 'no greater adepts at discerning the weak points in a contract', and the labourer was bound to discover that 'all he was required to do was to remain on the mine for a calendar year and loaf with impunity'.[20]

By the end of 1912 the Chamber of Mines had spent three years in intensive negotiations about its various legislative proposals, but those negotiations had proved almost totally fruitless. Reluctantly, mining capital acknowledged that the cam-

paign to bring the South African solution to the Gold Coast would
have to be abandoned. Why exactly had mining capital failed so
badly to enlist the support of the colonial state in its attempt to
assert control over the labour force? There is no doubt that the
arrogance and aggressive attitude of Lord Harris, Giles Hunt and
the mining lobby generally did little to assist their campaign, but
at a more profound level, the industry's failure to win official
support for the South African solution was rooted in the very
structure of the colony's political economy. In marked contrast to
South Africa, where mining capital had attained a position of unrivalled political and economic influence within the state, in the
Gold Coast, the future lay with expatriate mercantile capital and
the indigenous capitalist farmer. In Ellis's words:

> There is no surplus of population in the Gold Coast or its
> dependencies, there is ample land available and the people
> are having great success with cultivation of cocoa on their
> lands. The total failure of the mining industry would cause,
> at least, no more than a temporary setback to the revenue of
> the Government.[21]

In 1913 Lord Harris belatedly recognized that the Government
would not sacrifice the interests of traders and farmers to those
of the mines, and withdrew the majority of CGF's investments
from the Gold Coast. The South African solution, it seemed, could
not be used to resolve the colony's persistent labour question.

Supply and Demand in the Gold Coast Labour Market, 1912-1917

The Chamber of Mines' decision to abandon its campaign for
South African methods of labour control at the beginning of 1913
was not simply a result of the Government's intransigence on the
issue and the disappearance of CGF from the Gold Coast. It also
reflected the changing pattern of supply and demand in the colony's labour market, for between 1913 and 1917 the mining industry benefited from a period of equilibrium in the labour market, albeit a temporary equilibrium which blinded mining capital to
the approach of the most serious labour shortage in the industry's
history.

Between 1910 and 1913 the output of gold had risen steadily
as the mines completed their initial development programmes, but
from 1913 onwards production levelled off and the demand for
mine labour subsided as a result of wartime restrictions imposed
upon the industry's operations. At the same time the labour
supply situation was easing. Despite the failure of the first
northern labour experiment in the mines between 1906 and 1909, a
steady flow of migrant workers was entering the Colony and
Ashanti from the Northern Territories and neighbouring French
colonies. Such migrants now had more information about wage-
earning opportunities in the Gold Coast, and were acquiring the
taste for goods that only access to a cash income could provide.
Reflecting the growing level of out-migration from the north, in
1914 chiefs registered their first complaints about the drain of

young men from the land, while Political Officers in the area had increasing difficulty in finding labourers who were prepared to accept the low wages offered for performing public works. The mines naturally benefited from this growing flow of voluntary labour, and after 1912 workers from the north and foreign territories progressively replaced labour from the Colony and Ashanti. By 1917 migrant workers accounted for over 47 per cent of the industry's 19,000 strong labour force and over 64 per cent of the 8,600 underground employees, an increase of more than 20 per cent since 1911.

Although the new equilibrium in the labour market ended the industry's fears of serious labour shortages, there was still not the kind of labour surplus in the Gold Coast that would allow the mines to cut wages, impose greater discipline on the workers, and plan a programme of rapid expansion to compensate for the production lost as a result of the war. The absence of such a labour surplus at a time when the supply of migrant labour was expanding was indicative of the increasing demand for labour in other sectors of the economy. The principal new source of competition for labour was the cocoa industry, which in 1915 surpassed the gold mining industry as the colony's major exporter and whose rapid growth was heavily dependent on northern migrants who worked as hired farm labourers and carriers. Finding that cocoa farmers were increasing wages to attract more labour, Ashanti Goldfields lamented that 'it is a sure thing that we should not get any sympathy from the Government in any attempt we might make to suppress the cocoa planting about here'.[22] Other competitors helped to absorb the growing migrant labour force. Many workers found railway construction 'best suited to their convenience or inclination', while the rubber and timber industries were experiencing a temporary boom and therefore employing more labour.[23] The First World War also introduced another competitor to the labour market, the armed forces. Between 1914 and 1918 over 5,000 men, almost 70 per cent of them from the north, were recruited for the Gold Coast Regiment, and a much larger number of carriers were enlisted to support Britain's campaigns in West and East Africa. Although the loss of northern labour to the armed forces was partially offset by an influx of French subjects escaping conscription in their own territories, the activities of Political Officers recruiting for the army made life very difficult for the African labour recruiters working for the mines. Moreover, in a repetition of the events of 1898, when military recruiters entered the mining towns many mine workers rushed out of the area to avoid enlistment. Finally, the war introduced one other private competitor to the labour market. In 1914 high-grade manganese deposits were discovered at Nsuta, just five miles south of Tarkwa. Manganese was regarded as a strategically important mineral, and the new industry received full assistance from the Government, including the services of political officers in the north who were instructed to recruit workers to be sent to Nsuta.

Although the problem of labour supply and control was not a major issue for the mines between 1912 and 1916, four features of the pattern of supply and demand in the labour market in that period were to assume particular significance in the post-war era. Firstly, migrant workers from outside the Colony and Ashanti had become the largest regional group in the mines labour force. Consequently, when the equilibrium of the labour market was upset after the war, it was to the Northern Territories and French colonies that the mines looked for new workers. Secondly, the period had witnessed the rise of the cocoa industry and its determinant impact on the colony's labour market. Shortly after the war the full extent of that impact was to be revealed. Thirdly, in recruiting for the armed forces the Colonial Government had revealed its willingness to use compulsion to compensate for an insufficient number of volunteers in a crisis. Finally, for the first time since 1910 the Government had used Political Officers to recruit labour for a private enterprise. These were to be pertinent considerations when between 1918 and 1920 the Gold Coast, and particularly the mining industry, experienced the most serious labour crisis in its history.

The Post-War Labour Crisis, 1918-1920

In the immediate post-war period several factors combined to destroy the equilibrium which had existed in the Gold Coast labour market since 1912. In 1918-19 an influenza epidemic swept through the colony, killing 60,000 people, including 28,000 in the Northern Territories. The epidemic not only reduced the number of potential migrant labourers, but also killed a considerable number of mine workers and caused a flight of people out of the mining towns. Simultaneously, a rapid escalation of cocoa prices on the world market was stimulating a massive new demand for labour and forcing cocoa growers and brokers to pay up to 15/0 a day for the services of an unskilled worker. Neither the Government nor the mines could respond to these wage rates, and labourers naturally flocked into the cocoa industry to seek their fortune.

The impact of the influenza epidemic and cocoa boom on the mines' labour supply was exacerbated by Governor Guggisberg's Ten Year Development Plan, announced in November 1919 and emphasizing labour-intensive infrastructural projects. The Government calculated that it required 27,000 extra labourers for the Plan to be implemented, and a Central Labour Bureau was established in Kumasi to regulate the flow of migrant labourers to government departments and private employers. The Bureau was unable to cope with the demand for labour and failed to get permission to recruit in Nigeria and French West Africa. With no end of the cocoa boom in sight, in January 1920 Guggisberg decided to reintroduce a formal recruitment scheme in the Northern Territories. Despite the evidence of compulsion and desertion which had accumulated since the failure of the first experiment with northern labour, Guggisberg chose to recruit through the chiefs and Political Officers. The new scheme was introduced in January 1920, and the District Commissioners of the Northern Territories immediately began to issue instructions to chiefs specifying the number of men they were expected to supply for the Government's development programme.

While the Government was taking these steps to ensure its own supply of labour, the situation in the mines was growing progressively worse. The mining lobby repeatedly pressed the colonial and metropolitan administrations on the question of labour shortages, but received an unsympathetic hearing. Despite the Colonial Government's own low wage policy, it told the mines that if they were to offer better pay and conditions, they would experience no problem in attracting labour. For the mining industry, insult was added to injury by the official recruitment programme in the north. Guggisberg refused to make a proportion of the new recruits available to the mines, on the grounds that mine work was so unpopular that any such agreement would inevitably result in the use of compulsion. This observation was confirmed after July 1920, when the mines were allowed to send their own recruiting agents into the north. These agents had very little success, and were totally incapable of competing with the District Commissioners recruiting for the Government. As the Financial Times explained, 'if Government through the Political Officers calls for labour they will get what there is to be got and civilian recruiters - be they ex-officers or native headmen - will fail'.24

The post-war problem of labour shortages very quickly became intertwined with the problem of controlling wages. Since 1912 the mining companies had been able to keep wage levels static, but now that policy was coming under growing pressure. The shift from food to cocoa production had pushed up market prices in the mining areas, while the payment of mine workers in a new, widely disliked and undervalued paper currency had exacerbated the decline in the purchasing power of their wages.

One response of the mine workers to these hardships was to maintain their standard of living by turning to crime. In 1918 the administration explained that the growing number of thefts in the Western Province was directly related to the high cost of food in the area. Gold stealing in the mines also increased, and prompted the Commissioner of Police in Sekondi to establish a new organization of mine detectives. A more effective, and a more significant response to declining real incomes, was to strike for higher wages. In June 1919 AGC ran short of its usual gelignite supplies and asked the hammer boys to drill wider holes. According to the Mine Manager:

> The boys organized themselves and picketed the mine forcibly, preventing willing workers from going to work. Many scrummages occurred and some blood was shed. Several arrests were made by the police.

In response to this 'symptom of a more general unrest' management agreed to pay an extra 3d a day to the hammer boys. Four months later, when the Mine Manager attempted to reintroduce the smaller drills and to reduce wages to their former level, the hammer boys struck again. Shortly afterwards, other underground workers stopped work to demand payment in 'hard' rather than paper currency, and in December 1919 the Corporation attempted to stem the rising tide of resistance by paying all its workers in gold. Further symptoms of discontent soon appeared. In February 1920 there was 'a big strike' at Tarkwa, and workers successfully demanded a 3d wage rise. Three months later, following strikes by government workers in Accra, Sekondi and Kumasi, the Government raised its wage rates and workers at AGC began to make similar demands. 'As soon as we began to get into our stride again and to shake up working conditions to normal activity one gang of boys after another petitioned for higher wages and threatened to go on strike'. The Manager preferred not to risk another disruption of production and granted a wage rise of 3d.[25]

In the following three months workers at AGC made further demands for up to 9d a day extra, and in August 1920 workers at the Central Treatment Plant and some other sections stopped work for 12 days. The Corporation's Directors decided that it was 'impossible on economic grounds to yield to these too frequent section strikes'. A lock-out was threatened and workers were laid off. This action persuaded the workers to return on the old terms, but the Mine Manager thought that labour was 'suspiciously quiet' and he reported rumours of a general strike if an extra 3d was not paid at the end of the month. Two weeks later lead strips and other equipment were stolen from the Assay Office. The Mine Manager wrote:

> The strips by themselves are useless to anyone so the theft is evidently an act of spite. We have had quite an epidemic of thefts here recently, several white staff bungalows being broken into and many things stolen.

Discontent was also expressed in more covert ways. In the words of the mine's Consulting Engineer:

> Apart from these sectional ebullitions, with which it is possible to deal, there has also been the far less tangible form of unrest which manifests itself in a passive form, i.e. simply in abstention from work. This, of course, is more difficult to remedy.

No strike took place at the end of the month, but workers continued to demand increases. In October 1920 workers were told by management that they would be granted a rise of 3d but that they would no longer be paid in gold. There was a 'storm of protest' at the announcement and workers presented an ultimatum threatening that if they did not receive an extra 3d and payment in gold, or an extra 6d and payment in paper currency, they would strike. Younger workers made 'derisory gestures' at older men who were prepared to wait for the rise, and arranged for pickets to stop work at the mine. Management submitted to the threat and agreed to pay an extra 6d. The workers returned to the mine promising 'plenty work, no palavers'. The Mine Manager could not' believe that workers would act like this of their own accord, and suggested that a white foreman had 'evidently spread some of his Bolshevist doctrines among his boys and told them they ought to be getting higher wages and that they should strike for them'.[26]

The shortage of labour and resultant militancy of the workers had a severe impact on the mining industry. Between 1917 and 1920 the tonnage treated by the mines fell by 43 per cent, and in the last six months of 1920 alone, the average wage on the mines increased by 6d or 7d to 2/6-2/8. Total working costs had risen by as much as 250 per cent since 1912 and 175 per cent since the end of the war. The Government reported that 1920 had been a year 'of unremitting difficulty and anxiety for the mining industry owing to the high price and scarcity of labour'. More dramatically, the Financial Times observed that 'the whole industry is threatened with collapse'.[27]

Coercive Recruitment in the North, 1921-1925

Mining capital did not accept the rapid decline of the industry passively, but lobbied vigorously in the metropolis and colony to win official assistance in resolving the growing problems of labour shortages and rising wages. Initially such assistance was not forthcoming, as the Colonial Office believed that 'the mines are to some extent (probably a considerable extent) to blame for their own difficulties':

If the mines think we are going to take any action which will have the effect of compelling the natives to do mining they are mistaken (and nothing else will really please them).[28]

This intransigent attitude was gradually eroded by mounting evidence of the crisis in the mines. At the Colonial Office even Ellis, an inveterate opponent of the mining lobby, was assuming a more cooperative position. He had 'reason to know that the Governor dislikes the mines and wishes they were not there', but added, 'this is not an attitude we can adopt - especially during the existing gold famine'.[29]

Guggisberg's policy soon changed to reflect Ellis's pragmatic realization that a profitable industry with powerful supporters in the metropolis could not be allowed to collapse for lack of official support, however socially and politically disruptive that industry might be. In February 1921 Guggisberg stated that he now believed the mines should receive assistance in recruiting labour, and cabled the CCNT in Tamale, saying, 'Mines in desperate straits shall send them equal labour as railway'.[30] Having agreed to help the mines, Guggisberg supported their efforts to recruit more workers with characteristic enthusiasm. He acceded to the mines' longstanding request for legislation requiring all labour to be placed on written contract, while Political Officers in the north were left in no doubt about the need to satisfy the industry's demands for labour:

> Strict orders have arrived from His Excellency the Governor that 1,000 labourers are to reach the mines by Christmas at least...80 is all that will be required as your share. Do your utmost to get them down on time.[31]

As in earlier periods when they had been involved in the recruitment process (1906-10 and 1914-17), the Political Officers had little option but to obey these orders and passed on such requests for labour to the chiefs. Likewise the chiefs, whose political authority was increasingly dependent on the administration, had no choice but to find the number of 'volunteers' they had been asked to provide.

As Guggisberg had argued before his change of policy in 1920-21, few northerners were keen to work in the mines, and the inevitable consequence of giving official support to recruitment for them was the use of compulsion. Contrary to its later protestations of innocence, the administration was aware of the use of coercion in the recruitment of mine labour from a very early date. Even before the end of 1920 the _Financial Times_ reported that 'there is a feeling on the coast...that the recruited labour is not quite so voluntary as it appears'. Six months later the Acting DC in Bole reported that 'if I am ordered to send men I can do so of course - but it will be forced labour'. The chiefs, fearing a total loss of popular support, informed the Government that 'no one would voluntarily enlist for labour', and even the CCNT admitted that 'he knew most of the boys do not want to work for the mines'. He nevertheless continued to transmit demands for mine labour to his officers in the north. Not surprisingly, when in February 1924 the DC in Yendi interviewed 50 'volunteers' presented by a chief, he discovered that only two really wanted to work in the mines.[32]

Further evidence of compulsion came in the form of resistance to recruitment. Northerners were in fact fighting a battle against forced labour on two fronts. On one hand, they were opposing the right of their chiefs to call on them to perform unpaid communal labour, both by mass migrations across political boundaries and by a simple refusal to do such work. In the words of one DC:

> As you know, the people are willing enough and they work contentedly to a certain point. That point reached, then their natural obstinacy sets in and nothing short of a bullet is of any use... Is the Government prepared to go to the utmost limit - namely to shoot these people if they refuse to work?[33]

Now, the northern men also had to fight against their compulsory enlistment for work in the mines, a fight which they engaged in with some success. The DC at Kratchi, for example, reported that:

It is impossible to make work on the mines popular amongst the people in this district. The recruiter has only to mention the word 'mine' for the applicants to fade away.[34]

As in the period 1906-09, desertion became a major problem for the mines. In the year ending March 1923, 2,524 men were sent to the mines, but 483 of that number absconded before they had reached the south. For some groups of recruits the desertion rate was considerably higher. In November 1922 no less than 48 of 90 recruits from Savelugu deserted before starting work in the mines. Those men who did actually arrive in Tarkwa and Prestea resisted in alternative ways. Many 'had to be driven down the shaft' after refusing to work underground, while others would not work with machines, refused to be transferred from one task to another, insisted on six rather than nine-month contracts, and demanded to be paid all their wages immediately rather than collecting them once the contract had expired.[35] There is no evidence to suggest that the unwilling workers from the north organized any strikes at the mines, but this was a form of resistance used by a group of recruits brought from Southern Nigeria in 1922-23. Their spokesman, Ajeyigbe, wrote to the DC at Oyo, and provided a rare example of how workers perceived conditions in the mines at this time:

We have reach here and undertake the business that we was engaged for. Though the work is hard we do not mind it but the treatment giving to us here is very bad and even no food was given to us. Most of us fell ill through starvations. We beg your honour to consider us and see that this cruel act be subside and that the manager here give us sufficient money for chop. There is not a single day for us to recruite our health and this course a sickness on us oftenly.[36]

The unpopularity of work in the mines amongst the northern recruits slowly forced the administration to admit to the use of coercive tactics in enlisting labour. In 1922 Guggisberg observed that although the DC's in the north had been instructed not to use any form of compulsion, 'there is, however, a very thin dividing line between that and the influence of Political Officers in a country such as the NT's'. The following year the CCNT told his superiors less ambiguously:

The recruitment system must necessarily leave the impression in the minds both of the chiefs and the labourers that it is by a Government order that they go down...it is extremely possible that a certain amount of compulsion is exercised to induce labourers to come forward.[37]

Ultimately it was not the recruits' resistance or concern over the use of compulsion per se that forced the Government to reconsider its policy, but evidence of extremely high mortality rates amongst the indentured northern labourers. In 1923-24 the death rate per thousand ranged from 31.34 at Prestea to 65.73 at Abontiakoon, and at Abosso reached a staggering 104.32. It was hardly surprising that migrant workers in Kumasi believed that any man who went to the mines would be 'finished in six months', or that a northern villager, on being recruited for the mines, stated that he wanted to cut his throat since 'he might as well end it at once'.[38]

While the CCNT believed that the recruits were treated 'extremely well...almost too well', the Colonial Office would not allow recruitment to continue while such high mortality rates persisted. Ellis recommenced his attack on the mining lobby, complaining that 'they have been pressed to improve the sanitary conditions for years past, even before the war, and have got out of it with one excuse or another'.[39] Indeed, the managerial attitude towards health and safety was one of consistent apathy. Since 1913 the mines had been obstructing the Government's attempts to make pulmonary tuberculosis a notifiable disease, while deaths caused by accidents were complacently regarded as 'a very difficult thing to control and always liable to occur if the men are being the least bit pushed to produce tonnage'. When the Chamber of Mines eventually agreed to the introduction of ex gratia payments to the relatives of dead workers, it was only done under considerable pressure and 'really for the purpose of propaganda and not so much out of consideration for the boy's relatives'.[40]

In retrospect, the Colonial Government and the mining industry acknowledged the link between compulsory recruitment and the high mortality rate of northern workers. As one mine admitted:

> Chiefs, in selecting the natives for work in the mines, had chosen, probably to be relieved of weaklings, very largely those in a poor state of health, and in numerous cases those actually suffering from disease.[41]

The Mine Managers were much less ready to admit that the conditions they allowed to exist in the mines had also contributed to the high death rate of recruits. Previous failings were explained away with pathetic excuses. Pneumonia injections had not been introduced because they would 'tend to drive workers to apply for work elsewhere'. Latrines had not been renewed due to 'lack of funds', and cloakrooms not provided for the workers because of their 'thieving habits'. The Chamber of Mines even alleged that the official mortality figures had been miscalculated, while one Mine Manager argued that natives with diseases deliberately went to work in the mines to use their superior medical facilities.[42] Such excuses were rebuffed by a lengthy report written by the eminent physician Sir William Simpson, who insisted that recruitment in the north should not be permitted again until conditions had been improved and the Government had assumed much greater powers of inspection in the mining industry. In 1925 the Government acted on this advice and introduced the Mining Health Areas Ordinance, a piece of legislation that finally put an end to the mining industry's hopes of achieving total administrative control over their concession areas.

Resistance, Migration, and Underdevelopment, 1925-1930

The period 1920 to 1924 had been a significant one for the Gold Coast mining industry. The colonial state had demonstrated its very ambiguous relationship with mining capital, both assisting it in the recruitment of forced labour and obstructing it by the introduction of new and relatively stringent health regulations. Mining capital had brought its activities into public disrepute and assistance in the future. Most significantly, the mine worker in the south of the colony and prospective worker in the north had, according to Guggisberg, 'learnt to pick and choose, <u>and to know his own value in the labour market'</u>.43 Consequently, when recruitment in the north was allowed to recommence in 1925, the Governor warned the mines that their reputation was 'like mud amongst the natives', and in the first year of the new recruitment scheme only 80 men were enlisted.44

The inability of the mines to recruit northern workers did not produce another crisis as they had anticipated, for throughout the period of compulsory recruitment between 1921 and 1924 the earlier equilibrium in the labour market was steadily reestablished as the cocoa industry moved into a period of depression. Ashanti Goldfields, situated closer to the cocoa belt than the Tarkwa-Prestea mines, was the first mine to feel the benefit of this trend. In February 1922 AGC began a wage-cutting campaign and reduced the pay of the hammer and shovel boys. Encouraged by this success, management reduced wages at the mill and cyanide plant, an action 'not taken without a certain amount of hesitation as the natives concerned are better organized than in other departments and know very well that they can hold us up by striking'. In the event there were no strikes, but management discovered that 'many of the natives however are still very independent and promptly left work on being reduced'. Within a year the drift of workers away from the mine had forced the Mine Manager to end the wage-cutting campaign, and by May 1924 shortages of hammer and shovel boys were forcing pay levels back to their earlier position. A series of strikes at the mine made the pressure for wage rises even greater, culminating in a five-day general strike for 3d a day extra pay in July 1925. The strike was unsuccessful, and the workers returned to the mine after the local DC had bound over the village and mine headmen to keep the peace. The Mine Manager predicted:

> The moral effect of the failure of these strikes will, we think, do a great deal of good. It is almost certainly the semi-educated 'clerk' who poisons the others by telling them about strikes going on all over the world. Unfortunately it seems impossible to catch these men.45

The Tarkwa-Prestea mines did not enjoy the luxury of a surplus labour population at this time, and without a supply of cheap indentured recruits from the north, were forced to look for an alternative means of overcoming labour shortages and stabilizing working costs. The strategy employed to achieve these objectives was to reduce the unit cost of labour by paying much closer attention to 'economy, efficiency, and the introduction of labour saving machinery'.[46] The most important innovation was the jackhammer drill, a South African invention which could do the work of 50 labourers drilling by existing methods. Initially the use of the jackhammer was less than a total success. Some workers refused to use the new machines, while others used the extra wages paid for jackhammer work to 'buy' extra leisure. As the Mines Department reported, 'a driver earning 6s on one day will not turn out on the next. It is this spasmodic effort which lowers the output...neither will monetary inducements stimulate him to further efforts'.[47] Such a lack of commitment was symptomatic of the attitude of the mine workers generally:

> Akoon mine puts down the mine over 1000 boys every working day. Take the round figure of 1000 boys going down the mine on Monday. On Tuesday 10% of the boys who went down on Monday will be replaced by others who did not. On Wednesday a further 10% of the boys who went down on Monday will be replaced by those who did not. On Friday only 60% of the boys who went down on Monday will be at work... The waste of manpower is obvious.[48]

Several attempts were made to eliminate these limitations to efficient production. Some mines refused to pay their labourers until they had worked a total of 36 shifts while others paid a bonus to any labourer working every shift in a month. Managers frustrated by what the Secretary for Mines described as 'the happy complacency of the habitual loafer' introduced the 'loafer ticket', a system used in South Africa to prevent slack work.[49] Ashanti Goldfields, who employed an 'efficiency engineer' to improve labour productivity, attempted to introduce that symbol of the capitalist work ethic, the time clock. Over 100 surface workers went on strike to protest against this innovation, and warned management that if the clock was not removed they would collect their pay and leave the mine. The Mine Manager wrote that 'as their attitude was unreasonable and a direct challenge to the Corporation we took up a resolute stand'. Extra police were brought to the town, and after three days the strike collapsed.[50]

While the mines were attempting to reduce their labour requirements by using new techniques to increase productivity, the labour supply situation was steadily easing. Between 1924-25 and 1929-30 the number of migrants crossing the Volta increased by no less than 400 per cent, and the size of this flow was such that the supply of labour to the gold mines became 'not only adequate but actually plentiful'.[51] This sudden movement in the balance of supply and demand in the Gold Coast labour market was the result of several socio-economic trends. The completion of railway construction projects and the introduction of the light Ford truck released large numbers of carriers and labourers for other work, helped to spread information about employment opportunities, and facilitated the geographical mobility of labour. At the same time, rising taxation levels, recruitment campaigns, conscription and compulsory crop cultivation in the French territories were all pushing men off the land and into the Gold Coast labour market. With the onset of an international economic depression, the demand for labour in the commercial and agricultural sectors was declining, and the net result of these trends was the creation of a labour surplus in the mining areas and the Gold Coast generally.

Underlying these trends, however, the long-awaited resolution of the Gold Coast labour question would not have been possible were it not for the subordinate role that the Northern Territories had been forced to play in the political economy of the colony. In 1899 Governor Hodgson had announced that the Northern Territories had little value. He would, therefore, not spend 'a single penny more than absolutely necessary for their suitable administration and the encouragement of the transit trade'.[52] When Guggisberg took office in 1919, the tone of official policy changed dramatically. The new Governor claimed to be a 'faddist' on the question of northern development, even an 'over optimist':

> I should like to send a message to the Northern Territories that I hope within the next few years to see trains loaded with groundnuts, shea-butter, corn and cattle steaming south across the Volta. The career of the Northern Territories as Cinderella of the Gold Coast is nearing its end.[53]

Referring to the proposed Northern Territories railway which had been constantly postponed by earlier governors, he wrote:

> I am doubtful if the agricultural poverty of the country was a reason for the decision to postpone the railway. Rather it was due to the policy which has openly obtained of starving the Northern Territories of the means of development. That time is now passed.[54]

The road to underdevelopment in the Northern Territories was paved with the good intentions of administrators such as Guggisberg. In fact, the development of the north was incompatible with the whole logic of the colonial economy. The commercial and industrial development of the south which served metropolitan needs could only be achieved if expatriate and indigenous employers had a cheap source of labour to draw on. The only area where such labour could be found was in the Northern Territories. Migrants from the north were quite literally, in Guggisberg's words, 'worth their weight in gold', and any economic changes in the area which might restrict the flow of out-migration were therefore not welcomed.[55] As one DC in the north argued, the colonial economy was designed to benefit 10 per cent of the population, while the other 90 per cent were left 'slowly rotting in the bush'.[56] In order to escape this fate, young men left the area in search of a cash income, new goods, and new experiences in life, a movement that was officially condoned on the grounds that it represented 'the first steps towards this country coming to a further state of civilization'.[57] In fact, out-migration completed the cycle of poverty in the northern economy, forcing more migrants to the south to serve the interests of foreign and domestic capital. In 1937 the DC in Yendi made a plea for a more constructive policy. 'The Protectorate has its own economic destiny to work out', he argued, 'and that destiny is not solely to provide a reservoir of labour for the commerce and industry of the Gold Coast and Ashanti'.[58] It was a plea that was to be systematically ignored throughout the colonial period.

Notes

1. GNA, ADM56/1/3, CCNT to Acting CS, 18 May 1906; ARMD 1911; ARGC 1906, p.50; PRO, CO96/455/6833, 'Report by the Quoted by Prah (1976) p.23.

2. Quoted by Prah (1976) p.23.

3. PRO, CO96/503/33643, 'Report by G.W. Murray', 24 August 1910.

4. PRO, CO96/493/5862, Governor to SS, 3 February 1910.

5. Quoted by Berg (1960) p.232.

6. Quoted by Walker (1971) p.99.

7. GNAT, ADM1/24, Acting DC Tarkwa to CCWP, 28 June 1909.

8. Giles Hunt to CS, 24 June 1909, in _ibid._

9. PRO, CO96/494/6772, 'Minutes of a Meeting', 12 March 1910.

10. COM, 7 June 1910.

11. PRO, CO96/486/37605, Giles Hunt to CS, 30 May 1909.

12. MP, TO to Acting CS, 4 April 1910.

13. GNAT, ADM1/24, Governor to SS, 30 October 1909.

14. PRO, CO96/503/33643, loc cit.

15. PRO, CO96/503/374, Ellis minute, 9 January 1911; CO96/513/14360, 'Notes of an Interview', 1 May 1911.

16. PRO, CO96/513/23428, Ellis minute, 24 July 1911.

17. Further Correspondence Relating to Medical and Sanitary Matters in Tropical Africa, pp.108-9.

18. PRO, CO96/525/25823, WACM to CS, 13 August 1912.

19. WACM to CO, 13 March 1911, in Further Correspondence Relating to Medical and Sanitary Matters in Tropical Africa.

20. ARCM 1911-12, p.119.

21. PRO, CO96/513/23428, Ellis minute, 24 July 1911.

22. AGCI, 10 April 1914.

23. PRO, CO96/545/21358, Governor to SS, 10 June 1914.

24. The Financial Times, 21 December 1920.

25. AGGI, 20 June 1919, 13 October 1919, 8 January 1920, 21 February 1920.

26. GNA, ADM53/5, District Record Book entries, 5 August to 29 August 1920; AGGO, 10 August 1920; AGGI, 7 and 20 September 1920, 16 and 18 October 1920.

27. ARA 1920; The Financial Times, 21 December 1920.

28. PRO, CO96/612/29844, CO minute, 16 July 1920; CO96/612/25183, CO minute, 4 June 1920.

29. PRO, CO96/619/12844, Ellis minute, 9 March 1920.

30. GNA, BP298, Governor to Governor's Deputy, 27 February 1921.

31. GNA, ADM56/1/256, CCNT to DC Yendi, 2 November 1922.

32. The Financial Times, 21 December 1920; GNA, ADM 56/1/256, Acting DC Bole to Provincial Commissioner Southern Province, 7 July 1921; PRO, CO96/644/5136, Acting CCNT to CCNT, 9 November 1923; GNA, ADM56/1/58, 'Notes of Interview', 17 February 1921.

33. GNA, ADM56/1/278, DC Northern Mamprusi to Provincial Commissioner Northern Province, 12 July 1921.

34. GNA, ADM56/1/256, DC Kratchi to COM, 10 August 1923.

35. COM, 14 January 1922.

36. GNA, BP351, Nigerian labourers to Comissioner Oyo, n.d.

37. Guggisberg (1922) p.72; GNA, ADM56/1/256, CCNT to Acting CS, 20 November 1923.

38. COM, 23 February 1921, 25 January 1922.

39. COM, 25 January 1922; PRO, CO96/644/5136, Ellis minute, 6 February 1924.

40. AGCI, 2 March 1923; COM, 8 March 1924.

41. PRO, CO96/651/5103, T and A Consolidated to SS, 1 February 1924.

42. GNA, BP622, 'Notes on a Visit to Obuasi', 28 October 1925; COM, 4 July 1924; PRO, CO96/651/16798, Fanti Consolidated to SS, 4 April 1924.

43. Quoted by Thomas (1973) p.93.

44. COM, 4 June 1925.

45. AGCI, 19 June 1922, 7 July 1922, 1 July 1925.

46. ARMD, 1924-25, p.3.

47. ARMD, 1925-26, p.9.

48. ARMD, 1926-27, p.4.

49. GNA, BP351, SM memorandum, 19 November 1925.

50. AGCI, 5 December 1924; GNAK, File 199, Assistant Mine Manager AGC to DC Obuasi, 4 December 1924.

51. ARMD 1928-29.

52. Quoted by Bening (1975) p.76.

53. Quoted by Wraith (1967) p.112, and Der (1975) p.132.

54. Quoted by Bening (1975) p.78.

55. Quoted by Songsore (1975) p.326.

56. GNA, ADM56/1/256, DC Bole to CCNT, 19 August 1924.

57. DC Lawra, quoted by Goody (1956) p.9.

58. GNAT, ADM1/167, DC Yendi to CCNT, 21 July 1937.

Chapter 4

THE GROWTH OF CONSCIOUSNESS
AND ORGANIZATION OF RESISTANCE, 1930-1947

> If we go back with nothing in our hand or without any prom-
> ise whatsoever for these boys and just ask them to go back
> to work, it might result in loss of life.
>
> S. Cleland, Obuasi Branch Secretary, Mines Employees'
> Union, October 1947.

Between 1870 and 1930, mining capital in the Gold Coast had been engaged in a constant struggle to recruit and retain an adequate number of workers to keep the industry in full production. Resistance within the mines had caused fewer problems. Strikes had occurred throughout the 60 years of modern mining, but they were sporadic, organized on an ad hoc basis, and were therefore relatively easy to suppress. In the 1930's this situation changed dramatically. Strikes began to take place more frequently and on a much larger scale, forcing mining capital and the colonial state to introduce completely new strategies of labour control. As this chapter demonstrates, those strategies failed to obstruct the development of the mine workers' consciousness and organization, and actually created the preconditions required for them to participate in the first national mines strike.

Discontent and the Dynamics of Resistance, 1930-1937

The Gold Coast mining industry experienced wildly fluctuating fortunes in the 1920's and 1930's. The disastrous slump of 1920 was prolonged by the scarcity of labour, a static gold price, and the rising cost of mining supplies. By the end of the decade many mines had 'either relapsed into a moribund condition or disappeared altogether'.[1] In contrast, after 1931 a 70 per cent increase in the price of gold following Britain's decision to abandon the gold standard prompted a spectacular revival in the industry. Labour shortages no longer acted as a constraint on expansion, investment was available for the purchase of new mining technology, and the completion of many infrastructural development projects initiated by Guggisberg allowed new mines to be established quickly and cheaply. By 1940, the value of gold produced in the colony had increased by approximately 500 per cent.

The rapid expansion of the gold mining industry had a profound impact on mining capital, mining labour, and on the relationship between capital and labour. With the colony's dominant agricultural and commercial sectors moving into recession, the mining sector suddenly assumed a new degree of importance and influence in the colonial political economy. The strength of the mining industry and its relationship with colonial and metropolitan governments was reinforced by the restructuring of mining capital into a small number of mining houses linked by a complex network of interlocking directorships. The mining houses were effectively organized by the important South African companies, Consolidated Gold Fields and Anglo-American, who brought the Ashanti Goldfields Corporation into the Chamber of Mines for the first time. A powerful London Advisory Committee (LAC) was formed to represent the Chamber's interests in London, while in Tarkwa the Chamber's new headquarters was placed under the administration of Lieutenant-Colonel Bamford, the colony's former Inspector General of Police.

The strengthening of mining capital between 1930 and 1940 was matched by a growth in the consciousness and collective action of the labour force, which expanded rapidly from 12,500 men in 1930-31 to around 40,000 in 1938-39. As the table on the following pages demonstrates, there were at least 12 major strikes in this period. Four of these stoppages involved the entire labour force of a mine and another three involved the majority of underground workers. Seven strikes lasted for more than one day and one continued for 11 days, at this time the longest strike ever recorded in the industry. Most of these incidents were accompanied by serious acts of violence against managers, blacklegs and the police who were sent to break the strikes. These examples of collective resistance were also more successful than earlier stoppages, and more than half of the stoppages forced management to grant concessions to the workers.

Although it is not possible to provide a full description of these remarkable events, the following report of a strike by firewood labourers in Obuasi in December 1934 conveys something of the militancy and solidarity of the mine workers at this time:

About 7 a.m. Mr. R.M. Bushell, Fuel Superintendent of the Ashanti Goldfields Corporation came to me and reported that about 40 labourers at his department at Ofinasu about 9 miles from Obuasi had gone on strike on the 26th December 1934 and would not allow new labourers employed in their stead to work but assaulting them. Mr. Bushell added that the presence of couple of police may prevent molestation of the new labourers by the old ones... While I was in District Commissioner's Court report came through to the effect that the labourers on strike at Ofinasu behaving so riotously that the 3 constables sent out were defeated and threatened with assault by the old labourers if they interfere.

STRIKES IN THE GOLD MINES, 1930-1937

No.	MINE	DATE	PARTICIPANTS	GRIEVANCES	WORKERS' ACTION
1	ARISTON	15.09.30	All workers	Non-payment of wages. Behaviour of European timekeeper	Picketing. Blacklegs flogged. Timekeeper forced to take refuge in Village Office
2	AGC	3-7.02.34	Machine, rockdrill and hammer boys, and some other underground workers. Total 1,000	Low wages. Dangerous work. Fines. Native timekeeper taking bribes	Picketing. Blacklegs flogged. 30-40 strikers patrolled town with offensive weapons
3	TARQUAH AND ABOSSO	30.08.34	Drill sharpeners	Low wages. High rents	No data available
4	AGC	26-28.12.34	32 firewood loaders 9 firewood stackers 5 line pickers 25 lumber boys 55 track maintenance boys 100 formation boys	Low wages	Blacklegs assaulted armed strikers. Railway trucks derailed and track blockaded. Police attacked. Train carrying arrested workers boarded by strikers
5	AGC	2-12.03.35	Jackhammer, machine and spanner boys, then all workers	Low wages. Long hours underground	Picketing and intimidation. Police station stoned by workers after arrest of headman
6	ABOSSO	23.01.35	Pumpboys, greasers and loco drivers	Low wages. Long hours. Fines	Picketing
7	AGC	1.06.35	All workers	Low wages. Long hours underground. No sick pay. Intimidation by European staff	General strike threatened but not called. Workers engaged lawyer to present grievances
8	CENTRAL WASSAU	1-3.12.36	Underground workers	Low wages	Procession marched to meet Mine Manager
9	ABONTIAKOON	15-16.01.37	Hammer and drill boys	New system of pay	Picketing of shaft. Blacklegs beaten up
10	MARLU	7.10.37	Shovel drivers and moulders	Low wages. One fitter on each shovel requested. Bonus requested	No data available
11	ARISTON	21-24.11.37	All underground workers, some surface workers	Low wages. Change of shift system. Rakeoff	Intimidation. Demonstrations against police
12	BIBIANI	3-13.11.37	All workers	Low wages	Stones thrown at police. European staff stoned. Armed strikers surrounded courthouse where three strikers were held. Stewards and cooks of Europeans molested

MANAGEMENT RESPONSE	OFFICIAL RESPONSE
European staff shot and wounded seven workers while trying to rescue timekeeper	Police reinforcements sent to mine. Official enquiry into shooting but no prosecutions. Compensation ordered
Wage rises granted - 3d to underground workers, 1d and 2d to unskilled and skilled surface workers. Some dismissals after strike ended	Police reinforcements sent to mine. DC spoke to strikers with Mine Manager
Mine Manager refused to listen to workers' representatives until strikers returned to work. Dismissals threatened	No data available
Workers dismissed and new labour engaged. 1d increase to track maintenance boys	10 extra police sent to protect strikebreakers. Police Superintendent and DC called on strikers to return. Five headmen arrested and sent to assizes. Sixty workers arrested and fined 13/- each
New labour engaged. Blacklegs paid double. New hoisting system introduced to reduce hours underground. Bonus introduced after strikers returned	Sentries posted at vital installations. 24 extra police sent to mine. DC asked Tribal Heads to inform on strike leaders. 2 mine headmen arrested and given one and 3 months jail and hard labour
Fines stopped	Police reinforcements patrolled village
No data available	CID men sent to Obuasi to report on unrest and workers' meetings
Police reinforcements requested. Shift boss who had promised extra pay dismissed	12 extra police sent to mine
All workers' demands met, all unpaid wages met, old pay system returned, underground workers' pay adjusted	DC called on Wangara headmen and Serikin Zongo to persuade men to return
Strike leaders dismissed	DC spoke to strikers on behalf of Mine Manager and threatened legal action against them. Chief of Bogusu asked to prevent villagers helping strikers. CID men sent to mine
Strike leaders dismissed. Police reinforcements requested	60 policemen marched through mine village as 'show of strength'
Tribal Heads and Serikin Zongo approached for help	3 strikers arrested and charged. 100 extra police sent to protect blacklegs

I arrived Ofinasu with Mr. Bushell and found 80 labourers collected at the Firewood Railway Station looking very excited. I delivered the message from the DC to them. Their answers were, we are not going to Obuasi. If the DC wishes to see us he must come to Ofinasu. We are not going to work and we are not going to allow any new labourers to work. We shall flog them if they attempt to work and shall not allow the locomotives to run between Obuasi and Ofinasu carrying firewood unless our pay increase by 3d. They were so truculent and with some difficulties I got them to allow the locomotives to go to Obuasi light. They derailed the trucks carried by the locomotives by forcing woods and stones into the wheels in my presence. There were empty trucks in the middle of the road between Ofinasu and Obuasi and I told the new boys to load these trucks...There were picquets [sic] along the line and as soon as the new boys started loading...a gang of about 30 men arrived at the scene in full force assaulted the loading boys and drove them into bush with stones...The Senior Superintendent of Police returned to Obuasi and reported to me that the strikers were extremely truculent and were armed with thick sticks with bolts screwed to the ends...The rude labourers were called to assemble and were spoken to at length by the Commissioner but would not listen to anything said to them, insisted upon assaulting the new boys and damage the trains unless their wages are increased.

The Assistant Commissioner of Police, the Senior Superintendent of Police, thirteen Escort Police and myself proceeded to the 9-mile station and I addressed the five headmen against whom the police had warrants, and four more headmen of the gangs who had just struck...They repeated their demand for an extra 3d and stated their boys would not go to work without it...The crowd was plainly in favour of preventing the work being carried on, and the warrants were then executed. The prisoners were conveyed by train to Obuasi. A large part of the crowd attempted, by jostling the police, to interfere with the entraining of the prisoners and many jumped on the train and travelled to Obuasi on it. At Obuasi 67 were taken into custody and charged with interfering with the police in the execution of their duty and 13 men were charged under Section 264 of the Criminal Code.

I attribute the reluctance of the strikers to cease intimidation and put their grievances or reasons for their conduct before Government to the fact that by the time I had been informed of what was happening they had taken what they thought was an irrevocable step in striking without notice, and were convinced that the only hope of keeping their employment, labour being plentiful, was to adopt an uncompromising attitude and force the employers to meet their demands.[3]

Why did the mine workers act so militantly in this period? As the list of strikes demonstrates, demands for higher pay featured amongst the workers' demands in nine of the twelve stoppages recorded. This is not surprising, as an examination of the movement of real earnings in the mining industry after 1930 reveals that the mine workers were suffering a serious deterioration in their standard of living. In 1920 the average wage on the mines stood at between 2/6 and 2/8. Between 1929 and 1932 the emergence of a labour surplus allowed this figure to be reduced to 1/10, and by the end of the 1930's wages were still at the same level. The impact of the first wage cuts after 1929 was softened by a decline in the cost of living, but from 1932 onwards, rising living costs and static wages combined to reduce the real income of the labour force.

Several features of life in the mining towns contributed to this trend. Between 1932 and 1938 food prices rose by up to 200 per cent as a result of the contraction of the domestic economy. In Tarkwa, which was already 'notorious for the high price of foodstuffs', a 'close and powerful ring' of traders charged the mine workers prices that were 'out of all proportion to wages' and forced them to adopt an unbalanced and deficient diet.[4] The housing shortages which accompanied the rapid expansion of the mining industry pushed up rents and led to the growth of large, uncontrolled 'mushroom villages' owned by local chiefs who had no interest in the improvement of public amenities and populated by many 'hangers on', 'whose main object is to baton on to the miner and obtain his money'. The crux of the whole problem was, as the Medical Department reported, that 'the policy of the large majority of the companies has been to obtain the labour first and to consider the question of housing at leisure'.[5] The administration also had no doubt about the relationship between poor housing and the workers' discontent. In 1935 a medical officer complained about managers who 'failed to appreciate the fact that satisfactory quarters and a contented and fixed labour force are closely related'. Similarly, three years later the newly-formed Labour Department argued that 'sporadic strikes in mining areas...can be reduced to a minimum if the problem of the mushroom village is effectively tackled without delay'.[6]

The influx of aspirant wage earners into the booming mining towns had other negative consequences for the mine workers. Chain migration on the basis of kinship and ethnicity meant that established workers had to provide food and housing for newly arrived dependents while they looked for work. Moreover, the labour surplus in the mining towns allowed the African headmen who controlled the hiring of mine labour to demand a 'rake-off' from anyone wanting to get or keep a job. In the words of the Acting DC in Obuasi, 'very few if any persons can find work here unless they have several pounds to support their application'.[7]

This examination of the declining real income of the mine workers provides a general explanation for the growth of discontent and collective resistance after 1930. However, a sense of grievance amongst the members of any social group is never automatically transformed into collective remedial action. To understand the particular dynamics of the mine workers' resistance between 1930 and 1937 it is necessary to explain the relationship between the socio-economic status and the socio-economic structure of the labour force. In the 1930's that labour force comprised three relatively discrete strata. First a group of skilled artisans, primarily from the south of the colony, earning between 3/0 and 10/0 a day, and working without close supervision. Second, a group of educated clerical workers on similar rates of pay, and also from the Colony and Ashanti. Third, the mass of manual workers earning between 1/0 and 3/0, under direct European supervision. Amongst this group there existed a high degree of overlap between regional origin and employment. In 1933-34 the Colony and Ashanti supplied just under 50 per cent of the surface labour force, but only 20 per cent of the underground workers. In contrast, over 75 per cent of all underground workers came from the Northern Territories and French colonies, but under 40 per cent of the surface labour came from these areas.

There was a clear relationship between this structure and the pattern of participation in the strikes of 1930-37. None of these stoppages involved clerical workers and only one involved artisans. Seven of the twelve involved only underground workers or were initiated by underground workers. Six of the seven strikes which lasted for more than a day were led by the underground workers, and in each of those stoppages the strikers engaged in picketing, intimidation of blacklegs, and other forms of violence. In contrast, no violence occurred in two of the three surface workers' strikes. On the basis of this evidence, it appears that underground workers (and therefore northerners) exhibited a higher degree of militancy than their colleagues on the surface and from the south. This feature of the mine workers' resistance derived from four characteristics of the underground labour force in the 1930's.

Firstly, although the annual rate of labour turnover in the mines was as high as 80 per cent at this time, as early as 1931 expatriate observers noticed a growing tendency for some migrant workers to settle in the mining areas rather than going home on a seasonal basis and risking a period of unemployment on their return. By 1937 more women were joining their husbands in the mines and having children who 'knew no law and have no country except the pithead and the mines village'. Four years later, Doctors Murray and Crocket found that although only 6 per cent of the underground workers had been employed continuously by one mine for five years or more, for skilled categories such as machine, hammer, and blast boys, the proportion was 26.9 per cent, 12.6 per cent, and 22.39 per cent respectively.[8] Thus the underground labour force contained a core of committed mine workers, entirely dependent on their cash wage, and reluctant to resist against declining real earnings by simply leaving the mines.

Secondly, these workers enjoyed a unique degree of bargaining power by virtue of their key role in the production process. As a result of their skills and their ability to bring an immediate halt to mining operations, the machine drivers, blast boys and hammer boys became a self-conscious elite in the labour force. Thus in January 1940, when the AGC London office proposed a Christmas bonus for the clerks, the Mine Manager replied that the machine and loco drivers 'consider themselves socially superior to the clerks' and that any attempt to deprive them of a similar bonus would 'foster serious discontent amongst our labour and might even lead to a complete shutdown of the mines'.[9]

The third determinant of the underground workers' militancy and solidarity derived from the common dangers they experienced in the workplace. Several major accidents occurred during the period of rapid mining expansion after 1930, claiming the lives of 349 underground workers but only 39 surface workers. In the worst of these accidents 41 workers at the Ariston mine were killed. Colonial Office files reveal that prior to the disaster a European engineer had advised the company that the shaft where the accident took place was too dangerous to use. As he complained, 'the Company Chairman's main idea was to get rich quickly and make as much money as possible while the going was good'. Despite repeated pleas by coroners, DC's, the Colonial Government and Colonial Office, the Chamber of Mines rejected the idea of accident compensation. As one official in the Gold Coast remarked, 'it is quite clear that the mining companies are only interested in the mining of gold and do not care for the safety of their employees'.[10] Eventually the Chamber decided to introduce a standard compensation scheme in order 'to forestall Government's intentions in the matter'. The scheme paid 'considerably less' than the amount recommended by the Government, and the Chamber's justification for this move provides a revealing insight into the mentality of mining capital:

I suggested it might be wise to go slowly with legislation of this nature as it was impossible to say what effect an innovation of this description would have on a comparatively primitive people such as the mines employees on the Gold Coast ...These were a primitive people with a history of raiding, looting and slavery during the whole of their existence. The number of convictions of these people in the Gold Coast Colony for crimes of violence (especially murder and robbery with violence) was out of all proportion to their numbers as compared with the other inhabitants...To the majority of the inhabitants of these territories a sum of £200 or £300 is equivalent to a winning ticket in the Irish Sweep to an English labourer. Consequently the average native is worth more dead than alive to his 'brothers' and once the effect of this legislation is realized by the northern natives there is a serious risk that accidents in the mines will become more and more frequent.[11]

Underground workers were also most likely to suffer from the respiratory diseases endemic to all mining communities. In 1930-31 the percentage of deaths from pulmonary tuberculosis in the mining towns of Tarkwa, Abosso and Prestea was three times higher than the percentage in the colony as a whole. Pleas from the Medical Department and International Labour Organization to take action about tuberculosis and silicosis were ignored, while the Chamber of Mines publicly claimed that the mining companies were giving workers from 'illiterate bush communities...the opportunity to learn the value of sanitation and hygiene and to appreciate the amenities of civilized life'.12

Finally, although the core of skilled underground workers had particular cause to be discontented and formed a self-defined elite within the labour force, they were in no sense a labour aristocracy, socially or economically divorced from the other mine workers. They experienced the same hazards as other underground workers. Their wages of between 2/0 and 3/0 a day were not significantly greater than those of the unskilled worker, and anyway, had to support more dependents than other employees. They also had no prospect of promotion to salaried or supervisory posts as the mines were firmly opposed to the training of skilled African mining engineers. Ties of kinship, ethnicity and communal residence cemented the solidarity of experienced and inexperienced workers, while underground they laboured together in small, close-knit gangs where differences of status and income were eroded by a common antagonism to authoritarian white supervisors. Indeed, while the underground workers used collective modes of resistance to restore the value of their income, they also participated in strikes to defend their ability to engage in informal modes of resistance. In September 1930, for example, the Ariston workers demanded the dismissal of a timekeeper who described himself as 'a sort of detective' who was hired 'to find out attempts by labourers to defraud the company by forged tickets, tickets showing an excess number of days worked etc.'. Similarly, AGC management hired a firm of South African consultants to study ways of boosting productivity. Once they had left the mine, the Manager reported that 'the mine officials are relieved that the business is ended, because the natives were getting restive at being watched and rumours of a strike have been prevalent'.13

The strikes of 1930 to 1937 represented an important stage of development in the mine workers' struggle. Most significantly, those strikes witnessed the emergence of a distinct pattern of collective resistance, a pattern that was rooted in the actions of the militant and frequently violent core of experienced underground workers. This part of the labour force was able not only to mobilize sectional stoppages, but also to lead the large number of newly arrived underground and surface workers in strikes of a much larger scale. They did not need the assistance of a formal organizational structure such as a trade union to mobilize such resistance, and to avert the risk of intimidation they did not rely on prominent individual strike leaders. Thus, although these strikes appeared superficially to be 'spontaneous' in nature, even expatriate managers were prepared to concede that stoppages were 'well organized and frequently planned'.[14]

This period also witnessed a new sophistication in the political consciousness of the mine workers, a growing understanding of the forces ranged against them and the relative success of different modes of resistance. The alliance between mining capital and colonial state could, of course, hardly escape the workers' attention. Managers could shoot their employees without fear of prosecution, police reinforcements were always on call when a strike broke out, the judicial system was used to punish workers who dared to withdraw their labour, and even tribal heads and chiefs were coopted by government and management to undermine the solidarity of the labour force. Such alliances between mining capital and other institutions of authority generated an awareness of the need for united and large-scale resistance on the part of the workers. By 1937 the Chamber of Mines sadly acknowledged that coordinated action by workers from several mines would inevitably soon replace the isolated stoppages of earlier years. The mine workers were, therefore, beginning to identify themselves as an occupational community with common interests and common enemies, even if they did have different employers. Moreover, they were beginning to express their collective identity in the language of class and class conflict. In the words of a petition sent by AGC workers to the Government in June 1938:

> We are the working class. We suffer but there are no rewards. We demand justice and equality. We do not find any justification why we should not be paid the same as our Brother Miners in England or the United States of America. We are the same as they. But our time will come when we will rise up and take what is our rightful due.[15]

Finally, the mine workers' strikes of 1930-37 were significant because they were perceived as a serious threat to the authority of mining capital and the colonial state. As such, they forced the Mine Managers and Government to consider the introduction of entirely new strategies of labour control, designed to curtail the willingness and ability of the labour force to engage in collective resistance.

Responses to Resistance, 1937-1944

Between 1930 and 1937, as in earlier periods, official and managerial responses to the mine workers' resistance were essentially negative. A combination of coercion, intimidation and persuasion was used to break strikes and preserve order, but little systematic thought was given to the problem of collective labour resistance and its control. Throughout this period of unrest the Colonial Office urged the Government in Accra to adopt a more vigorous policy towards the inspection of labour conditions and the elimination of industrial conflict, but the administration insisted that Gold Coast workers enjoyed good wages and living conditions, and that labour relations in the colony were 'creditably harmonious'.[16]

The colonial state, security, and the origins of the Labour Department, 1937-39

The Government's complacency was briefly interrupted by the growing militancy of the mine workers, and in April 1934 District Commissioners were instructed to collect full information about the strikes that were taking place. Anticipating the Chamber of Mines' reaction, the Government reassured the industry that it remained unwilling to 'inspect, enquire, and generally pry into the affairs of employers'. There was, the Colonial Secretary noted, 'little to be said for the establishment of a separate Labour Department in the Gold Coast, and a great deal against it'.[17] Between 1934 and 1936 the colonial administration was forced by events beyond its control to adopt a much more interventionist policy. A series of violent strikes in the West Indies prompted the Colonial Office to exert much greater pressure on governments which had proved reluctant to implement its earlier recommendations on the subject of labour administration. In October 1937 the Gold Coast Government finally acknowledged that:

> The recent spread of labour unrest through the British Colonial Empire points to the necessity of an organization, and accurate knowledge of labour conditions should the day come when we have to face serious labour disturbances in the Gold Coast.[18]

That day came sooner than anticipated, for between October 1937 and April 1938 the Government was confronted with the colony's third and most serious cocoa hold-up, a strike of lorry drivers, and, at the same time, strikes at the Marlu, Ariston and Bibiani mines. The latter two were both general stoppages, lasting three and eleven days respectively, and were both characterized by an unusually explicit and violent anti-European mood amongst the workers. For the first time, the colonial administration faced the prospect of a broad front of urban and rural mass opposition.

The fears which these events generated amongst government officials and mine management were reinforced by their suspicion that the mine workers' strikes had been organized by political agitators. Ever since nationalist politicians Kobina Sekyi and J.B. Blay had expressed concern about the plight of the mine workers in 1933, official and managerial paranoia about the presence of political activists in the mines had reached a new level of intensity. Every stoppage was thought to have been mobilized by 'imported agitators and bolshie advisors' or other 'politically minded individuals'.[19] In 1937 such suspicions were not entirely unreasonable, for the strikes came at a time when the itinerant political organizer, I.T.A. Wallace-Johnson, was engaged in an intensive campaign to enlist the mine workers' support for the West African Youth League (WAYL). Wallace-Johnson had made a special study of conditions at the Ariston mine where the 1934 mining disaster had occurred, and in January 1937 he warned the Mine Manager:

> The League is determined to leave no stone unturned in its efforts to see that a fair and humane treatment is meted to African labourers and workmen engaged in the above mines and that better recognition is given to dignity of African labour in general by mining companies.[20]

Later that month the Chamber of Mines reported:

> There is no doubt that the 'Youth Movement' is gaining strength and may in time become menacing. It is most desirable that the schedule of wages should be treated very confidentially, particularly in view of the labour agitation which has recently occurred...It is quite conceivable that the Youth League may be behind these labour troubles.[21]

In fact, the vast majority of mine workers were not persuaded to give their support to Wallace-Johnson's movement. As one government official noted:

> The cry of 'agitators' has been raised after all recent strikes and there are some about...but it is yet to be proved that the presence of any prominent member of the WAYL has been the immediate cause of a strike or even of unrest on any mine.[22]

Nevertheless, the activities of the WAYL, the strikes of October and November 1937, and the cocoa hold-up combined to provoke mining capital and the colonial state into a frenzy of activity to tighten security on the mines. Mine Managers persuaded the police to ban and seize copies of radical newspapers such as Africa and the World and the African Sentinel. Only authorized individuals were allowed to enter the mine villages, and the Government was urged to allow the introduction of 'modified village control', a thinly disguised compound system, and to give powers of arrest to the mines' security watchmen.[23] Meanwhile, the administration itself forced Wallace-Johnson out of the colony and began to take a keen interest in the activities of any mass organizations with vaguely unorthodox ideas. The Watchtower Church, for example, was said to be selling pamphlets in the mining town of Marlu which 'argue against all established forms of Government, democracies, hierarchies, monarchies, dictatorships etc'. The Governor proposed the extension of radio relay services to the mine villages 'to make dificult the path of the professional agitator' and, like the Chamber of Mines, the administration became concerned about the strength of police in the mining areas:

> Strikes are in the air and not only in the mines. The 'anti-pool' feeling and its possible repercussions make it more than ever desirable that if trouble starts on a mine or mines the police authorities shall not be obliged to denude other parts of the country of police.[24]

Governor Hodson examined the problem of security personally, and told Ashanti Goldfields that:

...he attaches much importance to each mine establishing a Rifle Club, the nucleus of which would be invaluable in the case of any rising as the members of the club would be in a position to protect and defend the vital points of the mine, especially the Power House, until the government could send troops.[25]

Such panic amongst government officials and Mine Managers was reinforced by a crime wave which coincided with this period of labour unrest. The Government reported that 'a feature of the year [1937-38] has been a large increase in the mining areas of cases of stealing and gold stealing in particular'. On the Bibiani to Dunkwa road two Europeans escorting gold worth £12,500 were ambushed by armed thieves. AGC management complained about the number of 'bandits and bushrangers' in the Obuasi area, while in Tarkwa a European mine contractor was attacked by workers armed with cutlasses after a dispute over deferred pay.[26] Under pressure from Lieutenant-Colonel Bamford, the Government allowed Mine Managers to become Justices of the Peace, empowered to issue search and arrest warrants, and introduced new legislation which put the onus on anyone found in possession of gold to prove that it was acquired legally.

While these short-term security measures were being implemented, metropolitan pressure on the Gold Coast Government was mounting. The events of 1937-38 had demonstrated that the administration's _laissez-faire_ approach to the handling of industrial conflict was inadequate and that a more constructive policy was called for. At the end of 1938 the Governor finally bowed to this pressure, and conceded to the Colonial Office that 'nothing short of a Labour Department will be adequate to the needs of the Gold Coast'.[27] In theory, this admission represented the beginning of a new phase in the history of labour control in the mining industry. With the creation of a Labour Department the colonial state, which had always played a supportive, intermittent, and coercive role in the elimination of labour resistance, was now pledged to take direct, regular, and constructive responsibility for that task. Belatedly, the Colonial Government had recognized that to ignore grievances and suppress resistance could be counter-productive. In the future it would control labour by institutionalizing industrial conflict through the provision of recognized channels of communication between workers, management and the administration.

In practice, the creation of the Labour Department did not have an immediately radical impact on the strategies of labour control used in the mining industry. The Government was still, as one expatriate observed, 'unduly deferential' towards the mining lobby, and therefore chose as the first Commissioner of Labour J.R. Dickinson. He had once served as a DC in Obuasi, where he had quickly learned that it was, as he said, 'essential to fit in with the Ashanti Goldfields Corporation'.[28] Dickinson's concern to appease the mining lobby was reflected in his attitude towards the handling of industrial conflict. Governor Hodson explained the new strategy of institutionalization to the mining companies, stating that:

He thought it would be a very good thing for us to have one person to deal with, whom we could pat on the back and tell him how glad we were to see him, and send him away in effect to plead our cause.[29]

Dickinson quickly reassured the mines that the Governor had no intention of encouraging the intervention of trade unionists or other agitators in labour disputes. Indeed, with growing evidence that the mine workers were becoming 'one and all detribalized', Dickinson insisted on the need to reinforce 'traditional' allegiances:

The easiest and most satisfactory way of dealing with Africans in the aggregate is through their chiefs and headmen, and the latter's position is enhanced when it is seen that they have the support and respect of Europeans.[30]

At the same time, Dickinson attempted to encourage those Europeans to 'consider the African from the psychological point of view'. He produced a booklet which provided advice on how unnecessary disputes could be averted and resolved. It taught expatriate miners (who according to the Governor were 'entirely ignorant of the Africans' customs and mentality') the rudiments of personnel management:

Try to understand the African. Take a real interest in him and help him in every way you can...He is usually a very sober person and his lapses during customs can be regarded leniently. In any case, nothing can be done with Africans when they are celebrating customs.[31]

Finally, Dickinson urged the Mine Managers to appoint full-time Welfare Officers who could deal with workers' grievances:

It is common in England for large undertakings to employ at least one Welfare Officer and it has been found to be well worthwhile, for contented labour is just as necessary from the point of view of efficiency as up to date machinery... After all, if he can only prevent a strike of one day he saves his pay for the year.[32]

Wage control and labour legislation, 1939-41

Dickinson's insistence that the Labour Department should 'build on what is done now and on native custom' allayed the mining lobby's fears of extensive official intervention in managerial matters, and for a year the Chamber of Mines and the Department enjoyed a harmonious working relationship.[33] By the end of 1939 however, the Government had been forced to abandon its cautious policy of labour administration and to introduce a series of measures which ran directly counter to the perceived interests of mining capital. In March of that year the Governor privately admitted that it was 'almost impossible to justify the low wages at present paid to labourers'.[34] When the railway workers struck for higher pay two months later, the Governor responded by introducing a minimum daily wage of 1/3-1/4 for government employees. This had no immediate impact on the mines, as most workers in the industry earned more than the new minimum wage. In December 1939, however, further strikes by public sector workers forced the administration to announce a 20 per cent increase in the minimum wage. Workers in four of the gold mines immediately submitted demands for a comparable increase. The mines attacked the 'thoughtless precipitancy' of the Government's actions, and to avoid any unrest awarded an increase of 3d to all workers earning less than 2/6 a day.35

To complement its new policy of preventing strikes by means of wage regulation, the Government also adopted a much more vigorous approach to the policy of institutionalization. Again, in response to metropolitan pressure, in 1941 the administration introduced the Trade Union Ordinance, the Conspiracy and Protection of Property (Trade Disputes) Ordinance, and the Trade Disputes (Arbitration and Inquiry) Ordinance. This legislation gave a legal basis to picketing and the formation of trade unions, but also banned strikes by government employees and strikes in sympathy with workers in different industries, and outlawed intimidation on picket lines. Despite the introduction of these ordinances, Dickinson remained firmly opposed to the encouragement of unionization. 'In view of our system of Native Administration', he said, 'it is not a particularly urgent matter'. Stressing the importance of maintaining good relations between the administration and the traditional elite, he recommended that as the chiefs were accustomed to representing their people, they should also act as the representatives of workers living within their areas of jurisdiction. With an alarming degree of naivety, he believed that this system would have 'all the effect of the Trade Union, and comes to the same thing in the end'.36 This was not a view shared by the Colonial Office, the Governor, or indeed the mine workers, and Dickinson's proposal that chiefs should be used to act as brokers between labour, management and government was quickly abandoned.

The Colonial Office policy was that the role of broker should be assumed by trade union officials, but that safeguards should be introduced to ensure that those officials did not become the mobilizers of labour resistance. Pursuing this policy, from 1940 onwards it posted 22 'trade union advisers' to the colonies, experienced British unionists whose task was 'to direct our embryonic Trade Unions in the way they should go, and help them to avoid the pitfalls which might beset them'.37 Such 'pitfalls', of course, included any kind of activity which went beyond the safe ones of grievance-handling and the negotiation of incremental benefits for union members.

One of the two trade union advisors posted to the Gold Coast was I.G. ('Taffy') Jones of the South Wales Miners' Federation. Jones was by no means a puppet of the administration and he brought a refreshing realism to the Labour Department. Just eight months after his arrival he reported on conditions at Ashanti Goldfields in a tone of unprecedented criticism:

The wealth that this mine has produced and the conditions of the surrounding town does not reflect any credit upon us but stands as an indictment against our trusteeship...If one examines the wages paid in the light of the fantastic profits made by this company, a simple calculation shows that in 12 years 1925-37, shareholders, assuming that they bought their shares in 1924 at par, have received back nine times the value of their original investment, the wages are deplorably low and cannot be justified.[38]

Despite such criticism, Jones and his fellow trade union advisor, Oswald Kitching, were in the words of another Labour Department officer, 'obviously very carefully chosen men'.[39] They shared the British TUC's preference for colonial trade unions which were radical by local standards, but which discouraged spontaneous rank-and-file action. Moreover, they were strictly advised by the Government that they had 'no freedom to air their personal ideologies and sympathies in their contacts with workers'. The trade union advisor, according to the Colonial Office, 'must obviously be in sympathy with the trade unionists but he must always remember he is a government official and temper his words accordingly'.[40] To the relief of the Chamber of Mines, Jones took note of these warnings and spent the first two years of his appointment assisting with the organization of the relatively skilled and educated railwaymen who had proved so troublesome since 1939. Jones was allowed to contact the clerks and artisans in the mines with a view to the creation of a trade union, but he was warned by the Commissioner of Labour about the 'undesirability of fostering Trade Unions involving inarticulate and illiterate labour' in the mines.[41]

Mining capital and the policy of paternalism, 1941-44

The Government's new strategies of labour control were described as 'a catastrophe' by the Chamber of Mines.[42] The new policy of wage regulation in the public sector could only encourage the mine workers to demand pay rises, while the legislative innovations made in 1941 would inevitably generate pressures for the creation of one or more trade unions in the mining industry. Unions were considered totally inappropriate for mine workers who had no understanding of the 'theoretical democratic basis' of unionism, and who were 'almost entirely controlled by native custom, superstition, and fear'. In the opinion of a senior member of AGC management, unionism 'should either not be allowed or so hedged around by legislation that its effectiveness in fomenting labour troubles should be reduced to a minimum'.[43] A despatch from the AGC London office summed up the gloomy mood of mining capital:

We think that we are now on the threshold of a profound change in colonial administration, which, under pressure of political and public opinion, made sharper and more sensitive by the war, will tend more and more to subordinate the interests of organized commerce and industry to those of the owners of the soil and the native workers.[44]

Between 1941 and 1944 the mining industry was given plenty of evidence to substantiate this statement. With the outbreak of war in 1939 the influence of mining capital in the Gold Coast steadily declined as production fell, working costs rose, and the price of gold remained static. This trend was reinforced in 1941 by the Government's introduction of an Excess Profits Tax on the mines, and in the following year by the Colonial Office's Mines Concentration Scheme, which closed four of the mines and financed their maintenance costs through a levy on the seven that were allowed to continue in production. Simultaneously, Governor Burns introduced a programme of political reform which paved the way for a process of orderly decolonization. The mining industry considered this to be a totally unnecessary concession to the colony's embryonic nationalist movement, and a policy that would inevitably threaten the very existence of the expatriate mining sector.

Mining capital was now confronted with an acute dilemma. Given the peculiar cost structure of the gold mining industry, the only determinant of profit levels which the mines could influence directly was the cost of labour. However, the growing militancy of the colony's workers and the Government's new policy of wage regulation and legislative reform ensured that any attempt to reduce wage levels would fail. The mining industry's response to this dilemma took the form of a new strategy of labour control, that of paternalism. By means of this strategy the mines hoped to check the decline of the mine workers' real earnings, to increase the workers' 'job satisfaction', and thereby counteract the strikes and the upward pressure on wages that were threatening the industry's profitability.

During the war the cost of living, which had risen steadily throughout the 1930's, continued its upward movement. Population growth, urbanization, the presence of large military units in the colony, and the continued contraction of the domestic economy exacerbated the existing shortage of local foodstuffs and pushed market prices up rapidly. The Government attempted to reverse this trend through several price regulation schemes, but these had very little success. Between May 1939 and December 1941 local food prices increased by 65 per cent, while the total cost of living for the lower wage earner rose by 51 per cent. The District Commissioner in Obuasi reported that most labourers in the town were forced to live on credit and were consequently accumulating large debts. In Tarkwa the DC reported a similar trend, and observed that 'at present scarcity prices are being demanded, and if this is allowed to continue there will, I am afraid, be labour unrest'.[45]

To prevent such a development, the mines agreed that:

Any measures to be taken to meet the increased cost of living must be by joint action of all the companies concerned, and particularly should be the result of a decision arrived at voluntarily, not in response to demands which might later be made by employees.[46]

These measures were of three principal kinds. Firstly, workers were encouraged to grow more of their own food requirements. Free land was provided for this purpose, and propaganda posters were displayed in the mine villages informing the workers of their employers' generous gesture. What the employers had failed to recognize was that very few men who worked down a mine for six days a week would have the energy or inclination to spend their spare time farming. As a result, only married workers who had the use of free family labour took advantage of the scheme. A more effective means of stabilizing the cost of living was to sell food to the workers at or below cost price. In February 1940, for example, AGC announced its intention to take on the role of 'benevolent wholesaler' to retailers in Obuasi, and to supply basic foodstuffs such as rice direct to the labour force at subsidized prices. The mine's London office was reassured that the subsidy provided good value for money. 'We have a very contented labour force', wrote the Mine Manager, 'and if by chance a demand were made for an all round increase in wages, we could not expect it to be less than 1d a day'.[47] The cost of such an increase would be far in excess of the sum spent on subsidizing food supplies.

After the very limited success of its first two attempts to reduce food prices, from 1943 the mining industry resorted to the tactic of providing free food for the mine workers. Cocoa drinks, made from surplus stocks purchased at a nominal fee from the Government, groundnuts, biscuits, kenkey and sugar were all distributed to workers as they began their shift. This had the additional advantage of improving productivity levels. The Acting Chief Inspector of Labour, noting the success of one free food scheme, commented:

> The resulting improvement found in the standard of work derived from the provision of this ration, and the consequent economic advantage to the mine will no doubt cause the extension of the practice to other mines.[48]

These efforts to curtail labour resistance through the reduction of food prices were just one aspect of a broader strategy of paternalism initiated by the mines in the early 1940's. Ashanti Goldfields, the most profitable and innovative company, had in fact been experimenting with this strategy ever since the three major strikes which hit the mine in 1933 and 1934. The London office instructed the Mine Manager:

> I should advise you to extend the hutment accommodation and see what can be done in improving their social amenities such as a native club, and I do not know whether we could give them some amusement in the way of a cinema etc. I think we need to look ahead...and see how we can make our labour more dependent on us for social services. I believe we can do more to retain our labour and make it contented to be in our employ by means of this kind than by inducing them to stay with us by increased pay.[49]

This paternalistic strategy was taken up by the other, less profitable mines as the importance of curtailing collective labour resistance became evident. The longstanding housing problem was finally tackled through the building of new estates to replace the old mushroom villages. Electric lighting was provided for a nominal fee, and rents were pegged at a level considerably lower than those charged by private landlords in the mining towns. Higher-grade workers such as artisans and clerks were provided with superior, two or three-roomed houses, in contrast to the small one-room compound houses allocated to manual labourers. In this way the natural cleavages in the labour force were reinforced, and the possibility that unionization or political activism amongst the artisans and clerks might spread to the mass of workers was reduced.

The mining companies also made a belated attempt to meet the Medical Department's criticisms of health conditions in the mines. New hospital accommodation was constructed, and free treatment extended to the dependents of employees. Ventilation in the mines and sanitation in the mining villages were improved, while workers were encouraged to spend their leisure time in healthy pursuits through the provision of African Clubs equipped with sporting and recreational facilities. Sports teams, bands and clubs were established by newly-appointed Welfare Officers, the purpose of which was to develop the workers' attachment to and identification with their employer. At the same time, the mining companies made efforts to establish closer ties with the local community. Land and buildings were provided free of charge for churches and mosques, while mission schools and other voluntary associations also benefited from the new-found concern of the mining companies for their exployees' extra-curricular activities.

With the political tide rapidly turning against mining capital, the industry was naturally keen to publicize its humanitarian interest in the workers. As one mine claimed, 'the welfare of the African employees has been the unceasing and untiring concern of the Directors and Management since the inception of the Company'.[50] In fact, such statements were deliberately designed to obscure the real purpose of the paternalistic programmes introduced at this time. These programmes were in no sense altruistic, but were consciously used as a means of asserting greater control over labour. Sports, entertainment, and recreation were used to 'develop corporate institutions and the team spirit' in the mines. The Welfare Officer 'would provide excellent cover for any activities as intelligence officer which we might desire him to undertake'. Workers were provided with better housing because 'if we show this extra interest in building good quarters for them, we will be in a stronger position in the event of any unrest'. In addition to its role in controlling the wages and political activity of the mine workers, paternalism was also used as a means of controlling their productivity and the supply of labour. Apparently generous benefits such as gratuities and pensions were invariably conditional upon a worker's record of attendance and obedience, and therefore acted as a simple form of incentive payment for regular work and good behaviour. The payment of gratuities and travelling expenses to workers on their retirement was only introduced because without such benefits they would become troublesome 'hangers-on without any visible means of support', whose presence in the mining towns 'might eventually seriously affect the future of labour from the Northern Territories'.[51]

Many of the improved amenities granted to the workers after 1940 were not even given voluntarily, but came in response to the growing criticism of the mines by various government departments. At AGC for example, the decision to construct new housing in 1940 was only taken when management realized that if this were not done there might be an influx of health inspectors 'who might insist on somewhat drastic methods. It will be much better to attend to it ourselves'. Similarly, pensions and gratuities were granted only when the Mine Manager acknowledged that 'the time is coming when employers of labour in this country will, under pressure of political and public opinion...be made to provide some scheme of pensions (or gratuities) for their African employees'.[52]

Finally, the publicity given by the mines to their paternalistic efforts failed to reveal the financial constraints placed upon welfare spending. For example, the mines refused to admit any responsibility for the high level of pulmonary tuberculosis amongst the labour force, and insisted that workers with silicosis would only receive compensation if they had worked for more than two years in the mines. A two-week leave scheme introduced for long service workers was based on the assumption that:

It would have a salutary effect on the health of the natives and would be reflected by an increase in their efficiency, and at the same time considerably reduce the payments which the Benevolent Fund is called upon to make.[53]

Even more cynical was the Corporation's publicly stated concern for education and infant welfare in the mining towns, while in the mine itself boys under 14 were employed on firewood trains for 6d a day, and girls of the same age earned 1/0 for carrying 25 barrels of sand or 100 kerosene tins a distance of over 400 yards.

The Chamber of Mines was consistently evasive when confronted with questions about the mines' welfare expenditure. For example, Colonel Bamford deviously proposed that any statement on this subject should include the amount spent on both African workers and European staff. Thus the account of welfare expenditure submitted to the Government in 1940 surreptitiously included all the money spent on the Takoradi hotel used exclusively by white staff on local leave. This reluctance to provide accurate figures was understandable given the negligible amounts actually spent on welfare in relation to profits. At AGC, for example, a total of £57,889 was spent on African welfare between 1929 and 1939, of which £32,225 was spent on housing The remaining £25,664 represented under 0.3 per cent of the profits made by the mine in the same period.

Unionization and the First General Mines Strike, 1944-1947

The new strategies of labour control introduced by mining capital and the colonial state after 1937 met with only a very limited degree of success. Despite the efforts made to appease the mine workers and to prevent their grievances from escalating into collective modes of resistance, strikes continued to plague the industry. Between 1938 and 1944 there were a total of 17 stoppages in the gold mines, over 44 per cent of the colony's total. Demands for higher pay featured in ten of these strikes, and as in the period 1930-37, declining real incomes were the principal source of the mine workers' discontent. The purchasing power of the unskilled government labourer's wage decreased by no less than 34 per cent between May 1939 and November 1941, and by November 1944 had recovered by only 7 per cent. As this chapter has already suggested, the mining companies' efforts to shield their employees from these trends by the provision of cheap and free food were largely unsuccessful.

While the frequency of strikes was not reduced after 1937, the new strategies of labour control did have some success in curtailing the scale of collective resistance. The trend towards longer and more inclusive strikes was reversed, and all 17 strikes between 1938 and 1944 were sectional stoppages involving relatively small numbers of workers and lasting for two days or less. It is, of course, impossible to determine whether the reduced scale of resistance was a direct result of the new procedures of grievance handling introduced by management and government, but the Labour Department's Annual Reports for this period do suggest that the speedy intervention of District Commissioners and Labour Officers did help to contain the scale and length of stoppages. Significantly, the antagonism of workers towards government officials, which had escalated markedly between 1930 and 1937, subsided now that those officials replaced repression with mediation. By the early 1940's Mine Managers were reporting that workers regularly took their grievances and demands to members of the Labour Department and Mines Department. There is no evidence to suggest that the tribal heads were as readily accepted in their role of mediator between labour and management.As one group of tribal heads admitted during a strike in Tarkwa, 'it is beyond our capacity to do anything by ourselves'.[54] Despite several attempts to boost their authority after 1937, the tribal heads remained an impotent component of the structure of authority established in the mining industry.

The creation of the Mines Employees' Union

Another objective of the new labour control strategies was to obstruct the unionization of the mine workers. There already existed enormous natural obstacles to such a development. Horizontal and vertical cleavages in the labour force, the isolation of the mines from each other and the main centres of political activity, the high turnover of unskilled workers, and fears of managerial victimization had combined to prevent the creation of a mine workers' union even after 70 years of struggle in the industry. The Government, despite its nominal commitment to the institutionalization of industrial conflict, was only too pleased to perpetuate and augment these obstacles. This policy naturally received the strong approval of mining capital. As one influential mining engineer observed in August 1944:

> Jones has already been of considerable assistance in the settlement of labour disputes on one or two of the gold mines, and he is by no means 'pro-native'. He is not going to advocate prematurely the formation of labour unions and I think we are particularly fortunate in having a man of his type appointed.[55]

In fact, at the time this statement was made the first steps towards the unionization of the mine workers had already taken place. Just two months earlier, workers at the Electric Shop in the Abosso mine had gone on strike in protest against harassment by a young expatriate foreman. The man was forced to resign, and encouraged by this success the workers agreed to create a more permanent form of representation. On June 4th 1944 workers from the Electric Shop and other departments elected an Executive Committee, and at two subsequent meetings, workers from Abosso and other nearby mines created the Gold Coast Mines Employees' Union (MEU). In the latter half of 1944 the MEU General President, J.N. Sam, launched a campaign to recruit new union members. I.G. Jones tried to persuade Sam to abandon the idea of a general union and to establish a separate union for manual workers at each mine and an industry-wide union solely for clerical workers. Sam and his colleagues rejected this advice, and in the words of a contemporary observer, Jones 'was compelled to accept their terms of amalgamation and to forward their application for registration'.[56] The application went ahead, and the MEU was registered with a membership of 1,780.

The small proportion of the 24,000 mine workers who joined the MEU in 1944 was indicative of the socio-economic cleavage which separated the union's leadership and its potential members. The MEU was the creation of educated, literate artisans from the south of the colony. J.N. Sam was a Fante carpenter who had been a teacher before joining the mines. S.M. Bissah, the MEU Secretary, also a former teacher, was an Nzima electrician. As this chapter has already suggested, in the 1930's the mass of workers, especially the northern underground workers, had established a strong tradition of independent resistance, while the artisans had been reluctant to take action against management. Between 1937 and 1944 this cleavage was marginally reduced by a growing militancy amongst the artisans. Coming under the influence of the nationalist movement, they were now more prepared to stand against their expatriate employers, and were responsible for three of the 17 strikes in those years. Nevertheless, there was still a distinct lack of trust between the artisans who founded and led the MEU and the mass of manual workers who formed its potential membership.

For the first two years of its existence, the MEU was further weakened by the Government's efforts to control its activities. Having failed to prevent the creation of a mine workers' union, the Labour Department was determined to ensure that the MEU became an instrument of labour control rather than a vehicle of labour resistance. I.G. Jones was given the responsibility of ensuring that the union pursued moderate and apolitical objectives, and the union leaders, who were neither politically radical nor industrially militant, were happy to accept his advice. Thus in 1945, when a non-union strike of winding-engine drivers began at Bondaye, Jones 'persuaded the union to use all its influence to get the strikers to return to work'. MEU officials agreed to do this, and told the workers involved that the stoppage was 'wholly unconstitutional'. The men agreed to return to work, and the local Labour Officer commended the union, making 'a personal remark of its future prospects if it continued to direct its affairs in these constitutional lines'.57

While Sam, Bissah, and their union colleagues valued such recognition, they began to appreciate that the purely regulative role allocated to the union by the Government was inimical to the MEU's objectives. These were threefold: to maximize the union's membership, to establish the union as the recognized representative of the labour force, and to use its resultant bargaining power to secure improved conditions of service for the mine workers. Between mid-1944 and mid-1946 it became clear that the union would have to take the initiative in securing better conditions of service for the workers before it could hope to win mass support and become the recognized voice of the labour force. Evidence for this conclusion came in two forms: in the passive form of the workers' continued reluctance to join the union, and in the active form of informal and collective resistance mobilized independently by the labour force.

Independent resistance and the MEU, 1944-46

After its foundation in June 1944, the MEU made slow progress in winning the allegiance of the mine workers. The original union membership of 1,780 represented 5.9 per cent of the total labour force. By 1946-7 the figure had risen to 2,050, but this still only represented 6.5 per cent of its potential maximum. At the same time, the mine workers were showing very little inclination to channel their grievances through the MEU and its officials. As in earlier periods of unrest, workers resorted more frequently to informal modes of resistance. Gold thefts increased rapidly after 1944, to such an extent that by December 1945 there were 97 goldsmiths working in Obuasi even though gold was not officially available through the banks at this time. To counter this trend the Chamber of Mines established a new Mines Detective Organization, while at AGC the rabidly conservative Chairman, General Spears, attempted to reduce the mine's annual security bill of £9,500 by importing 24 'large and powerful dogs trained in aggressive tactics'.58

A more readily quantifiable mode of informal resistance used by the workers in this period was that of restricted output. In 1940 an expatriate observer had remarked that some Mine Managers:

> ...hardly know whom they employ, or perhaps even care. To these I venture to suggest that it is fairly certain that their workers, faced by managerial unconcern and indifference, 'get their own back' by negligent work, poor attendance, and studied indifference on their own part.[59]

In the first two years after the formation of the MEU, such informal modes of resistance became even more widespread and were clearly reflected in the mines' production figures. For example, the average tonnage milled per underground man-shift at the five largest mines, which had risen from 44.4 in 1940 to 44.6 in 1944, slumped badly to 39.0 in the following three years. The overall tonnage milled per shift, which stood at 195 in 1943, dropped by 17.4 per cent to 161 in 1947. According to AGC management, 'the African's attitude to his work is changing, and he is no longer prepared to put his back into it as formerly'. The worker, it was regretted, was now 'more enlightened and less willing to exert himself'.[60] The machine drivers, for example, worked at a self-determined pace which was well below their potential maximum. According to one Mine Manager:

> Sixteen holes is not a standard laid down by the mine, but appears to be considered by the men as a fair days work... and sixteen holes of the average depth required occupies approximately half a shift under normal conditions.[61]

Naturally, management attempted to correct this situation, but soon discovered that 'labour is quick to resent efforts to improve their performance, the usual reaction being a simple refusal to accept changed conditions'.[62]

For the founders of the MEU, struggling to establish the credibility of their union in the face of managerial and official antipathy, the most worrying form of independent resistance was not gold stealing or restricted output, but strikes taken without the consent, approval and participation of the union. Two such strikes in particular revealed the uncertain status of the MEU. The first occurred at Ashanti Goldfields. In September 1945 the Mine Manager reported 'restlessness amongst the boys' as a result of food shortages and high prices in Obuasi. On October 9th the mine was said to be 'very near a general strike' and later that month a series of sectional stoppages took place, forcing management to concede wage rises within the limits laid down by the Chamber of Mines pay schedule.[63] In early November the Mine Manager was growing increasingly nervous. General Spears was due to arrive for his annual visit to the mine, and a general strike timed to coincide with his visit was a distinct possibility.

These fears were confirmed when on November 23rd, shortly after Spears' arrival in Obuasi, 200 machine boys led all 6,700 of the mine's workers out on strike for higher pay. Spears opposed the intervention of the local Labour Officer, believing that the mine should not negotiate or make any concessions, but should win an outright victory over the workers. After two weeks, during which the District Commissioner and tribal heads unsuccessfully called for a return to work, the strike was still going strong. The Mine Manager lamented that there was no sign of division amongst the strikers, and that the police had been unable to discover anything about the organization and leadership of the stoppage. Only when Spears had threatened to dismiss strikers and to review the wages of the men who returned to work did the strike end. Negotiations ensued, and wages were again increased within the Chamber's schedule.

The second significant strike for the MEU leadership took place in May 1946. In 1944-45 a Gold Coast Mines Certificated Winding-Engine Drivers' Union had been formed and registered with 139 members. In mid-1945 this union of skilled workers made demands for wage increases 'to an absurdly high level', and in September the London Advisory Committee of the Chamber of Mines agreed to grant wage rises to the men in order to prevent a threatened strike.[64] No further unrest amongst this group of workers was reported until May 1946, when winding-engine drivers at Ariston went on strike in protest against the Government's ruling that they should undergo regular medical inspections. The strike spread to four other mines, where it left many workers trapped underground. The stoppage continued for seven days, and only ended when its leaders were prosecuted for taking strike action against a government order.

These two strikes, in conjunction with the other evidence of the mine workers' growing discontent, taught the MEU leadership a number of lessons. The unionization of the winding-engine drivers and their general strike of May 1946 demonstrated that coordinated action by workers at different mines was possible, and that in the absence of an attractive and dynamic general union, smaller unions might emerge to represent different categories of worker. The experience of the MEU during the Ashanti Goldfields strike was similarly instructive for the union leadership. It proved once again that if the MEU did not take up the initiative in the struggle for better wages and conditions, then the mass of workers would simply have to defend their interests in the ways familiar to them, ignoring and by-passing the union structure. Moreover, the punitive actions of General Spears during that strike, which included threats of instant dismissal to MEU officials and a refusal to allow Sam and Bissah to address the workers, proved that management would not recognize the union unless it was forced to do so. Again, this objective was not served by pursuing the passive policies advocated by the Labour Department. All these considerations pointed to the need for the MEU to adopt a much more aggressive stance in its relationship with management. By doing so, the union would win the support of the mine workers and the recognition of the mining companies, and it could then proceed to press its claims upon the Chamber of Mines in a peaceful manner. Only if management still proved reluctant to concede its demands would the union be forced to defy the Labour Department by threatening or using the weapon of an industry-wide strike of mine workers.

Sam and Bissah's awareness of this situation was clearly reflected in the more assertive nature of MEU policy from mid-1946 onwards. In April the daily wage rate of the unskilled government labourer was increased by up to 3d, the first rise since 1941. The Chamber of Mines refused to follow the administration's example, a response which represented a clear-cut and timely challenge to the MEU. The union's leaders could use this opportunity to take the initiative against the Chamber, irrespective of the MEU's current membership and organizational strength, and hope that this initiative would win the workers' support. Alternatively it could continue with its attempt to increase membership and strengthen organization before launching a campaign for higher wages, hoping that in the meantime, the workers did not take independent action to win a pay rise. On June 7th 1947 the MEU's decision to adopt the former policy was revealed. Bissah wrote to the Chamber of Mines, requesting a meeting to discuss new conditions of service. The MEU, he stated, demanded new minimum surface and underground rates of 1/9 and 2/0, and a general increment of 1/0 per day 'to stand in substitute of the war bonus ignored the African miners since the outbreak of the war'.[65]

Mining capital on the defensive 1945-46

Since the formation of the MEU in June 1944, mining capital had been confronted with mounting evidence of the discontent amongst the mine workers. Now, an educated, literate section of the labour force was threatening to give coherence and direction to this discontent, and to do this in a manner that was entirely legal within the framework of labour legislation introduced by the Government in 1941. The Chamber of Mines' initial response to this threat was almost entirely negative. On August 9th 1946 it finally agreed to meet MEU officials in the first joint conference of the two organizations, but on September 25th the Chamber informed the union that its members 'find it impossible to meet your demands as presented'.[66] The Chamber's belated and negative response to the union's wage claim was intended to delay the process of negotiation. It had taken the important step of recognizing the union's ability, if not its right, to represent the mine workers, but before negotiations proceeded any further the Chamber wanted to allow time for new, defensive strategies of labour control to take effect. These strategies had three objectives: to undermine any popular support that the union's new policy had attracted; to counteract the financial impact of any wage concessions forced upon the industry; and to reduce the workers' willingness to pursue their wage claim by means of collective resistance.

The first strategy was used primarily by Ashanti Goldfields, and was designed to eliminate the union's potential role as a vehicle of labour resistance. The Chamber of Mines had been trying to do this since the creation of the union in 1944, and had made repeated efforts to persuade the Government to provide it with minutes of all the meetings held between MEU officials and the Labour Department. The administration had rejected this proposal, arguing that such an arrangement would inevitably destroy the union leaders' confidence in the Government and its policy of encouraging moderate unionism. Most members of the Chamber recognized the validity of this argument, and by January 1946 the Chamber's Chairman had conceded that the MEU would not easily be eliminated:

> Members were all aware of how 'bush' the so-called unions were, but they had the support of Government, and whether members like it or not they had come to stay, and he felt it was in the best interests of the Chamber to cooperate with the Labour Department in trying to guide the unions into the correct channels rather than going into opposition.[67]

General Spears was not convinced by this argument, and he continued to wage a bitter campaign against the MEU branch in Obuasi. 'It is certainly our determination to get rid of these disturbing elements', he stated, and expressed the hope that the police 'would be able to help in chasing out these disturbing elements'.[68] In an attempt to render the union branch superfluous, he instructed the Mine Manager to establish small departmental committees of workers, supervisors and managers at which grievances could be ventilated and discussed. The Colonial Office and Colonial Government were scathing about Spears' hostility to the official policy of labour administration. In London a Colonial Office official wrote that the general strike at AGC had been 'no more than an attempt to get him to listen to the men's complaints with which [the Mine Manager] had declined to deal'. Referring to the new 'Group Committees', he stated that 'the Gold Coast Government is certainly not going to be dictated to by Spears on this important matter of the organization of labour representation'. I.G. Jones, now Acting Commissioner of Labour, held a similar view:

> It is questionable in view of the previous quoted expressions of Spears, that the motive is not the delay of the development of free Trade Unionism in the real sense of the term and the creation of a company union. Such a form of organization is a travesty of Trade Unionism and could have disastrous effects upon the growth of organized workers' representation in this country.[69]

The second response of mining capital to the new militancy of the MEU was to counteract the financial impact of any wage rises it was forced to concede by reducing the unit cost of labour through an improvement in productivity levels. This strategy took a number of forms. The mining companies explored the potential of new plant and machinery as a means of reducing labour requirements. At AGC, for example, a new treatment plant costing £500,000 was opened in 1947 with the specific aim of 'counteracting the effect of the continued pressure of the past few years for increases in rates of pay'. The mines also acted individually and collectively to investigate 'the latest developments in manpower efficiency', and contacted South African mining consultants for advice about their new 'efficiency schemes'. As a result of such contacts, the mines created new Time Offices in order to establish 'an increased measure of control' over the movements of the labour force. New accounting procedures were introduced to provide 'a better index of departmental efficiency', and greater attention was given to 'improved layouts, transportation, tools and techniques'.[70] These innovations coincided with a new attempt to clamp down on informal modes of resistance such as absenteeism and malingering. Bonus schemes were extended to a larger proportion of the labour force, and a series of experiments was initiated to determine which bonus schemes were most effective as a means of encouraging higher output.

The third response of mining capital to the growing threat of union-led strike action was to reduce the mine workers' willingness to withdraw their labour through an intensive campaign of paternalism. Early in 1946 a member of the Ross Institute was invited to recommend improvements to the mines' medical services, and further plans for the construction of new housing were announced. Recreational facilities and entertainments were expanded, allowing some lucky mine workers to listen to a mechanical piano playing officially approved tunes such as 'Thanks Mr. Roosevelt' and 'I Like to Walk Behind a Man Who Smokes a Fat Cigar'. More vigorous efforts were made to inculcate a sense of 'company loyalty' amongst the workers through inter-mine competitions, the distribution of good conduct badges, and the transfer of workers who had given 'long and loyal service' to salaried status. In the words of General Spears:

> These and various other measures were being undertaken with the object of ensuring that the African workers, who are today a happy and contented community, would find ever stronger reason for being attached to the mine.[71]

At the same time, the mines were making desperate efforts to reduce the cost of living for their workers. The Chamber of Mines introduced a new scheme for the bulk storage and distribution of foodstuffs, and later extended this programme to non-food items such as cloth, soap and fuel. The reopening of the mines which had been placed on a 'care and maintenance' basis during the war exacerbated the problem of food supply, and in response, the District Food Price Committees in the mining areas were persuaded to restrict the export of foodstuffs to other areas until local requirements had been satisfied. In March 1946 the Chamber of Mines decided to go even further and to establish canteens at all the mines, charging 4d for a meal which cost up to 11d to produce. In the words of the AGC Mine Manager, the canteens were 'the best antidote to inflationary prices and the inevitable demands for increased wages which would follow.'[72]

Mine labour on the offensive, 1946-47

It did not take long for mining capital to discover that the strategies it had hurriedly introduced to counteract the growing militancy of the mine workers and the MEU were achieving few positive results. The slump in productivity levels which had started in 1944 continued unabated and despite the workers' demand for higher wages, they were not prepared to increase their income by working harder. For example, bonus payments were normally paid to a worker only if he maintained an attendance qualification of 23 shifts per month, but the absenteeism rate for underground workers was so high that 25 per cent were disqualified from receiving any extra payment. The Chamber of Mines complained:

> The Mining Industry would like the African employees to place on increased wages a value similar to that they place on the extra leisure gained from task work... In order to operate a bonus scheme satisfactorily full cooperation of the men must be obtained and so far this condition has not been satisfied.[73]

For mining capital, the failure to produce immediate improvements to productivity levels in 1945-47 was regrettable, but was not nearly so serious as the failure to prevent the MEU from persisting with its claim for large wage increases. In December 1946 the Chamber attempted to make a preemptive award to the workers, increasing surface wages to 1/6-2/0 and underground wages to 1/9-2/3. It was a clever manoeuvre which put the ball back in the MEU's court, and the union's National Executive was left with the difficult task of choosing an appropriate response. Their choice was determined by several considerations. As the union leaders had hoped, their decision to take the initiative against management earlier in the year had bridged the gap between themselves and the mass of workers. Branch union officials reported that although the workers were still reluctant to join the MEU, they were prepared to give their conditional support to the union's campaign. Sam and Bissah recognized the fragile nature of that support, and were therefore keen to reflect popular opinion in their response to the Chamber's new wage schedule. Discussions with workers demonstrated that they had been 'gravely provoked by the conduct of the Chamber' and did not believe that its offer should be accepted.[74] The MEU, therefore, decided to turn down the wage rises that had been offered. Sam realized that the union had still not got the support or organizational strength it required for a credible strike threat to be issued, and therefore believed that negotiations should be pursued further with the Chamber of Mines. The final consideration bearing on the union leaders' response to the new offer was their reluctance to provoke an industry-wide confrontation between labour and capital. Despite the new militancy of the union, its founders still regarded the strike weapon as a last resort, only to be used in extreme circumstances. Indeed, Sam explicitly rejected the radical potential of the labour movement:

People without a knowledge of the working of a union view and misinterprete trade unionism to be revolutionary organization, but it is a preservative movement. It does not make trouble, but rather removes it. It does not create class feelings but on the contrary reduces it.[75]

The union Executive's actions between November 1946 and March 1947 represented an attempt to reconcile these considerations. Firstly the Chamber's invitation to discuss the new schedule was rejected on the grounds that more time was required for consultation between national officers, branch officers and workers. Sam then 'preached patience to the workers', assuring them that further action would be taken after the union's Annual Conference in March 1947.[76] At the Conference Sam reaffirmed his commitment to peaceful negotiations, and the delegates attempted to avert the impending confrontation with the Chamber of Mines by calling on the Government to establish an enquiry into conditions of service in the mining industry. The administration rejected the request and told the union officials that it would not intervene in the dispute until bilateral negotiations had proved fruitlesss.

Events now moved rapidly towards a climax. In June 1947 Sir Alan Burns left the colony and an inexperienced caretaker governor took office. In July the Korsah Committee's report on the wages of unskilled government employees recommended a minimum wage of between 2/0 and 3/0 and retrospective rises to January 1st 1946. Following this announcement the MEU Executive Committee formulated a new set of demands which included a minimum surface wage of 2/0-3/0 and a minimum underground wage of 2/6-3/6, a general increment for all other workers based on the Korsah Report, retrospective payment of all increases for two years, and the direct deduction of union dues from the wage sheet. On August 15th the Chamber and MEU met again and the union was asked to await the results of negotiations taking place in London on the question of mining taxation before the Chamber could make a response to the new demands.

The union's acceptance of the Chamber's request for a postponement of negotiations proved to be a tactical error. By this time the workers had refrained from taking independent strike action for over a year while they left the MEU to pursue negotiations with the Chamber. Government employees had now been given a substantial increase but the union had accepted yet another delay in securing a rise for them. The workers were now 'very angry' and 'infuriated' with both the Chamber and the union.[77] Rumours spread that the Executive had been bribed by the Chamber:

'If they had not been corrupted by the authorities why should they fail to deliver the goods all this time', became a popular question. 'What is at the Chamber that has made them mute', they asked.

Some workers believed that the union officials had accepted £500 'hush money' from the Chamber, and one rumour circulated that angry workers planned to assassinate the union leaders for their treachery.[78]

Faced with the possibility of a total loss of support, the Executive had little choice but to confront the Chamber again with its demands. On September 5th 1947 the two sides met again, and the Chamber increased its offer to 2/6-2/9 for underground workers and 2/0-2/3 for surface workers. The new offer still failed to satisfy the workers, who were 'very angry' and 'resentful' about the Chamber's intransigence. The Executive realized that to retain the support and confidence of the workers, the offer would have to be rejected. 'Patience had been exhausted, the worst must happen'. On September 8th Bissah presented an ultimatum to the Chamber stating that unless the demands made on July 11th were granted, a general strike of mine workers would be called at midnight on September 29th.[79]

The Chamber refused to make further concessions, and believing that the MEU was incapable of organizing a general strike prepared for the stoppage. On the day the ultimatum was due to expire Jones met the Executive in a last bid to prevent the strike:

> The meeting of the Executive of the Mine Workers during which they declared a general strike is to me unforgettable. Imagine a small room, very badly lit, filled with the representatives of the union, some dressed in European clothes and others in the artistically coloured cloth that enhances the natural dignity of the African. The meeting opened with a prayer, and the hymn which is sung at the beginning and end of all mine-workers' meetings. The President, a man of considerable character, bearing and personality, called on me to speak. I arose and through the Labour Inspector, who was my interpreter, I began. My purpose was to avoid the strike, sincerely believing as I did, that the owners were prepared to discuss once again with the Union wage scales and every means to avoid a stoppage of work. For two hours my voice and that of my African colleague rose and fell with the intensity of argument. The vote was taken and our advice was not accepted.[80]

The next day the Executive agreed that no branch unions would negotiate a separate settlement with management and that work would resume only on the instructions of the national officers in Abosso. On October 1st I.G. Jones arrived in Abosso after escaping from Tarkwa where he had been threatened by angry workers. Jones was unable to persuade the union officials to call off the strike and on October 10th the Commissioner of Labour promised that if the workers returned the Government would establish an independent arbitration enquiry. Four days later William Gorman KC arrived in the colony to act as arbitrator. The MEU insisted that the enquiry should be conducted while the strike was in progress, and recognizing the solidarity of the workers, the Chamber was forced to agree.

At preliminary talks held on October 18th Sam made it clear to Gorman that the MEU had been pushed into the strike by the strength of rank-and-file opinion. He stated that he and his fellow officials represented 'a very angry mob and any decision we make on their behalf must be a sensible one otherwise we may lose our lives when we get back'. Another union official, J.B. Borquaye, said at the formal proceedings of the arbitration enquiry:

> If the employers knew how much help the union was giving them they would grant this request without the union having to ask. There are many of the NT boys who have stated that but for the intervention of the trade union they would have demanded increases in pay and back pay with cudgels and cutlasses.[81]

While it is a common bargaining tactic for union officials to announce their inability to control the rank-and-file, these statements were more than an attempt to call the bluff of the Chamber of Mines and William Gorman. As the preceding narrative has shown, the MEU's negotiating strategy was consistently determined by the nature of rank-and-file opinion and the workers' unwillingness to give anything more than conditional support to the union leadership. Moreover, as later chapters will show, this interpretation of the union's behaviour is supported by the subsequent pattern of union/worker relations in the gold mines.

The strike continued while the Chamber's counsel, Sir Roland Burrows, and the MEU President, J.N. Sam, put their case to Justice Gorman. European managers made attempts to intimidate the strikers and force them back to work. At Bremang, for example, the Mine Manager threatened union officials who arrived at the mine, brandishing a revolver and shouting 'You bastard Africans with your fucking union'.[82] Despite such hysterical reactions, support for the strike remained unanimous and no violence occurred. Workers survived by hunting and gathering in the bush, and by accepting occasional gifts of food from shrewd market women who were only too keen to see the workers win their demand and thereby increase their purchasing power. On November 3rd 1947, five weeks after the strike had been called, the Arbitration Award was announced and the strike was terminated.

The arbitration enquiry was the greatest humiliation ever experienced by mining capital in the Gold Coast. The Chamber had been forced to accept the enquiry, to participate in it while the strike continued, and to defend publicly its wages and welfare policy. Gorman's Award, while carefully avoiding a complete capitulation to the union's demands, undoubtedly confirmed the validity of the union's claims. It awarded minimum underground wages of 2/6-3/0 and minimum surface wages of 2/0-2/6 retrospective to April 1st 1947, a 45 hour week, an overtime rate of one and a quarter, 14 days annual paid leave to workers with a year's service, up to 30 days paid sick leave per year and a gratuity scheme for workers who left the mines through ill health or voluntarily after five years' service. In the words of an

American observer, the strike represented a 'complete surrender' by mining capital to the demands of the workers.[83]

The dynamics of the 1947 strike

The general mines strike of 1947 was by any standards a remarkable event. There was little evidence in the sporadic strikes of the 1930's and early 1940's to suggest that the mine workers would be able to undertake a strike of such scale and length at such an early date. Even with the creation of the MEU in 1944, the mine workers' lack of enthusiasm for the union justifiably led managers, government officials and even union officials to believe that the strike was doomed to failure. It is necessary, therefore, to explain this rapid transition in the scale of the mine workers' resistance, and to locate the strike of 1947 more clearly within the historical dialectic of resistance and control in the gold mining industry.

The origins of the 1947 strike are to be found primarily in the strategies of labour control introduced by mining capital and the colonial state in response to mine worker and other mass protest in the 1930's. Instead of curtailing the collective expression of discontent by the labour force, those strategies actually established the objective preconditions ('organization') and the subjective preconditions ('consciousness') required for the mine workers to engage in a coordinated and protracted struggle with mining capital in September to November 1947.

Prior to the mid-1930's the objective conditions required for a national confrontation between mine labour and capital did not exist. Organization and control of the mines was decentralized, Mine Managers were competing for the scarce commodity of labour, and the Chamber of Mines was insufficiently representative or united to act as the sole spokesman of mining capital. Consequently, conditions of service for the labour force were determined at a local level, and struggles for improved conditions were confined to individual mines. The sporadic and isolated nature of resistance was reinforced by the state's attitude towards labour administration. Workers' organizations were illegal and the expression of discontent, even in peaceful forms, was repressed. Formal bargaining between workers and management was therefore impossible, even at local level.

In the late 1930's and early 1940's these objective conditions changed sufficiently to allow collective bargaining between representatives of labour and capital at national level. The expansion of the mining industry concentrated capital, eliminated competition between the mines and established the Chamber as a representative and united institution. The members of the Chamber, attempting to reduce and stabilize wages, progressively introduced unified conditions of service for their workers. Simultaneously, in response to working class and rural protest in the colony, the Government adopted a more permissive attitude towards worker representation and the expression of discontent. Trade unions were legalized and the Government was powerless to prevent the creation of a union claiming to represent the whole of the mines labour force. The Chamber was forced to recognize the legitimacy of the union and to enter into negotiations with its leadership. By the mid-1940's collective bargaining at national level had been initiated and the organizational preconditions for a full-scale confrontation between labour and capital had been established.

These organizational changes encouraged workers of different grades and at different mines to develop a consciousness of their common fate and of the need to participate in a united struggle against mining capital. The Government's attempt to curtail strikes in the public sector through the introduction of a rising minimum wage reinforced this trend by intensifying the Chamber's resistance to wage demands and by providing a common point of reference for the wage expectations of all workers in the mines.

Although the organizational preconditions for a general strike had been established, and the mine workers had developed a consciousness of their common interests, one final precondition was required for the workers to engage in a coordinated and protracted struggle. A general mines strike was impossible until the consciousness and the organization of the workers were fused. In practical terms this fusion necessitated a commitment by the mine workers to the MEU and its negotiating strategy.

The successful fusion of union and workers in 1947 was not the result of any efforts made by MEU officials to mobilize that labour force against mining capital. As the narrative presented earlier in this chapter has already suggested, in 1946 the union was forced to adopt a more aggressive negotiating strategy because of its failure to win support amongst the workers. Once this support had been gained it remained strictly conditional and union leaders were prevented from accepting a negotiated settlement by the strength of rank-and-file opinion. Eventually the union's need to retain popular support pushed it into presenting the general strike ultimatum of September 1947. Thus the general strike was the result of an interaction between the historically rooted militancy of the rank-and-file workers, particularly the northern, underground workers, and the organizational skills of artisans committed to the forms of representation and negotiation introduced by expatriate strategies of labour control. As the following chapters will show, the 1947 strike disguised but did not eliminate the tension between these two political cultures. The workers' support for the MEU was entirely dependent on the union 'delivering the goods'. When it failed to do so, the workers quickly abandoned the union and reverted to familiar, pre-union modes of resistance.

Notes

1. _West Africa_, 21 February 1931, p.194.

2. The data in this table is drawn from the following sources: GNA, CSO162/34, ADM56/5/44; GNAK, File 653; GNAS, File 786; PRO, CO96/742; COM, October and November 1937, _passim_; AGCI, January 1934 and January to March 1935, _passim_: DAT, 'Annual Report on Wassaw-Aowin District 1937-38'; Enquiry into the Wounding of Eight Africans at Prestea on 15th September 1930.

3. GNA, CSO162/34, Acting DC Obuasi to CCA, 2 January 1935, and Senior Superintendent of Police Obuasi to Commissioner of Police Ashanti, 31 December 1931.

4. Cardinall (1931) p.233; ARMedD 1937-38, pp.4, 79, 104.

5. GNA, ADM11/1865, Deputy Director Health Services minute, 23 April 1945, ARMedD 1938-39, p.37.

6. PRO, CO96/720/31034, Deputy Director Health Services to Director Medical Services, 3 January 1935, ARLD 1938-39, p.9.

7. GNA, BF3708, Acting DC Obuasi to CIL, n.d.

8. DAT, Annual Report Wassaw-Aowin District 1937-38, p.22; Murray and Crocket (1941) p.13.

9. AGCI, 11 January 1940.

10. PRO, CO96/720/31005, Ayton minute, 8 October 1934; CO96/725/31005, COM to SM, 8 February 1936.

11. COM, 29 April 1938; AGCO, 7 May 1937.

12. ARCM 1933, p.12.

13. Enquiry Into the Wounding of Eight Africans at Prestea on 15th September 1930; AGCI, 22 May 1937.

14. ARWP 1937-38, p.74.

15. Quoted by Gutkind (1974) p.25.

16. GNA, CSO1481/30, Governor to SS, 15 May 1931.

17. CS minute, 16 April 1936, in _ibid_.

18. CS minute, 2 October 1937, in _ibid_.

19. AGCI, 14 February 1934.

20. GNA, CSO716/33/1, Wallace-Johnson to Manager Ariston Gold Mine (1929) Ltd., 14 January 1937.

21. GNAS, File 786, COM to SM, 23 January 1937.

22. GNAS, File 322, 'Memorandum on Labour Troubles', n.d.

23. RHO, Creech Jones Papers, Box 18/3, passim.

24. GNA, CSO162/34, DC Wassaw-Aowin to Commissioner Western Province, 19 October 1937; GNAS, File 786, 'Minutes of a Meeting', 3 July 1937; GNA, CSO777/31, CS minute, 2 December 1937.

25. AGCO, 6 October 1938.

26. ARWP 1937-38, p.41; AGCI, 11 February 1938.

27. GNA, CSO1481/30, Governor to SS, 15 October 1937.

28. Meek et al. (1940) p.59; GNAK, File 398, DC Obuasi to Acting Commissioner Eastern Province Ashanti, 7 August 1929.

29. AGCI, 2 December 1937.

30. Dickinson (1939) p.5.

31. ibid.; PRO, CO96/758/31216, Governor to SS, 25 January 1939.

32. AGCI, 15 December 1939.

33. GNA, CSO162/34, CIL to CS, 12 November 1938.

34. GNA, ADM13/1/14, 'Executive Council Minutes', 28 March 1939.

35. AGCI, 15 August 1941.

36. ARLD 1938-39, p.12.

37. Acting Governor, Gold Coast Legislative Council Debates, 17 February 1942.

38. GNA, BF1211/23, 'Report on Conditions of Labour', 3 October 1942.

39. RHO, Ms. Afr. 31435, 'Interview with G.N. Burden by K. Bradley'.

40. LDA, 3166/6, CL memorandum, 10 July 1947 and SS memorandum, 24 June 1947.

41. GNA, BF2250/1, CL to CS, 10 January 1944.

42. COM, 9 December 1938.

43. AGCI, 2 December 1937.

44. AGCO, 25 June 1943.

45. GNAK, File 1509, DC Obuasi to CCA, 27 October 1939; GNAS, C184, DC Tarkwa to Director of Agriculture, 19 July 1941.

46. AGCO, 12 January 1940.

47. AGCI, 6 November 1940.

48. GNA, BF1211/12, Acting CIL to CS, 17 February 1942.

49. AGCO, 6 March 1934.

50. In the Matter of the Trades Disputes (Arbitration and Inquiry) Ordinance 1941, and in the Matter of a Trade Dispute Between the Gold Coast Mines Employees' Union and the Gold Coast Chamber of Mines. Award of Arbitrator, [Gorman Award], p.51.

51. AGCI, 8 December 1941, 2 January 1943, 3 June 1943, 19 August 1944; AGCO, 7 January 1938, 25 June 1943.

52. AGCI, 18 January 1940, 19 August 1944.

53. AGCI, 5 July 1938.

54. GNAK, File 1509, Tribal Headmen to DC Obuasi, 8 March 1935.

55. AGCO, 29 August 1944.

56. Blay (1950) p.15.

57. ibid, p.18.

58. GNA, BF5117, Senior Veterinary Officer to Department of Animal Health Tamale, 12 April 1947.

59. Meek et al. (1940) p.58.

60. AGCI, 10 April 1947, 10 May 1947.

61. Gorman Award, p.72.

62. AGCI, 18 October 1946.

63. AGCI, October to December 1945, passim, Gold Coast Government File DC5449, notes kindly provided by Jon Kraus.

64. ARLD 1946-47, p.8; COM, 8 and 17 May 1946.

65. Gorman Award, p.25.

66. ibid., p.59.

67. COM, 18 January 1946.

68. COM, 17 December 1945.

69. PRO, CO96/779/31359, Gurney-Williams minute, 18 May 1946, and Acting COL to Governor, 11 March 1946.

70. LA, 'AGC Mine Manager's Report', 30 September 1947; AGCI, 8 August 1944, 27 November 1945; AGCO, 2 May 1947.

71. LA, General Spears, speaking to AGC AGM, 25 April 1946.

72. ARCM 1947, p.16.

73. Gorman Award, pp.74-5.

74. Blay (1950) p.23.

75. SAM, 'Address at Obuasi', 23 March 1947.

76. Blay (1950) p.23.

77. Gorman Award, p.7.

78. Blay (1950) p.30.

79. ibid., p.32; Gorman Award, p.7.

80. Jones (1949) p.23.

81. Blay (1950) pp.141 and 228.

82. SAM, MEU Secretary, Bremang Gold Dredging Company to General Manager, 8 October 1947.

83. USA, 848n504/10-1647, US Consul Accra to SS Washington, 24 October 1947.

Chapter 5

WORKER MILITANCY AND UNION RESPONSE, 1947-1956

If the mines are losing money, then let them close.

D.K. Foevie, General President, Mines Employees'
Union, April 1952.

The post-war decade was a period of momentous political and socio-economic change in the Gold Coast. The rise of mass nationalism, the politicization of the trade union movement, a boom in the colony's economy and the growing opportunities for social and geographical mobility offered to the population all generated important structural changes and conflicts within the political economy of the country. The mining industry was inevitably affected by these developments, which combined to produce a period of intense and complex conflict between the mining companies, the mine workers and their trade union, and the various fractions of the colonial state. This chapter examines that conflict and demonstrates how it culminated in a second general strike of mine workers in 1955-56.

Mining Capital and the MEU under Pressure, 1947-1950

In the three years which followed the first general mines strike, mining capital was subjected to growing economic and political pressures. Since the late 1930's the industry had been caught in a vicious circle of rising working costs and taxation, a static gold price, and declining investment. The 1947 strike and Gorman Award exacerbated these trends by increasing the labour component of total working costs and by discouraging the substantial investment required to equip the mines for increased and more efficient production. The prospects for improvement were not good. The industry had no control over the price of gold or cost of stores, and so recovery could only come about by means of reduced taxation and a stabilization of labour costs. These objectives became increasingly elusive as a result of the mining industry's declining influence vis-à-vis the colonial state and the mines labour force. After the 1947 mine workers' strike and the civil disturbances which shook Accra and Kumasi in February

1948, nationalist politicians began to press for immediate constitutional reforms. In October 1949 the Coussey Report proposed
a form of semi-responsible government which substantially reduced
the influence of the mining lobby in the Legislative Assembly.
This attempt to defuse the nationalist movement failed, for three
months earlier Kwame Nkrumah had left the moderate United Gold
Coast Convention to form the more radical Convention Peoples'
Party (CPP). The new party rapidly won the support of rural
and urban masses and forced the Government to introduce more
fundamental reforms. In February 1951 the CPP won the colony's
first national election and Nkrumah, who had been detained after
an abortive general strike in January 1950, was released from
prison to become 'Leader of Government Business'.

Mining capital was horrified by the 'poisonous doctrines' of
the nationalist movement and the 'grave mistakes in official policy'
which had taken place, both of which threatened the industry's
ability to secure tax concessions and to attract investment.[1]
Simultaneously, the objective of stabilizing labour costs was becoming more elusive. After the Gorman Award many other private
sector workers struck for increased wages and back pay. The
success of these strikes and the growth of the colony's wage-
earning population during the post-war boom encouraged the formation of new unions and the strengthening of established ones.
The labour movement, led by the TUC, Trade Councils and the
Railway Union, became increasingly politicized, culminating in the
'Positive Action' strike for immediate self-government in January
1950. The Colonial Government and Chamber of Mines agreed that
these developments were undesirable, but differed on how the
growth of radical trade unionism might be curtailed. The Government believed that to regain control of organized labour it was
necessary to encourage apolitical, moderate unionism while reducing working class discontent by a policy of wage regulation in
the public sector. Both policies ran directly counter to the perceived interests of mining capital, which responded to the mine
workers' militancy and the Government's strategies of control by
introducing a wide range of measures designed to reduce the
MEU's ability to mobilize collective resistance, to end the mine
workers' willingness to support such action, and to offset wage
rises through increased productivity.

Mining capital launches an offensive

Immediately after the 1947 strike, mining capital launched an
offensive on the mine workers and their trade union in a desperate attempt to prevent any repetition of that stoppage. The
mining companies undertook a thorough intelligence-gathering
operation to identify the leading activists in the MEU, and then
attempted to dismiss them under the guise of retrenchment programmes. The most celebrated example of this strategy occurred
at AGC where the Branch Secretary, 'a competent and reliable
worker', was laid off.[2] This provoked a strike by 200 workers,
and the man was reinstated. Less prominent union officials were
not immune from such punitive treatment. Following a 23-day
strike at Nanwa Gold Mines in January 1950, no less than 17

union officials were ordered to leave the mine. In cases where the evidence against unwanted men was less concrete, the Mine Managers were not beyond arranging for stolen gold to be found among their possessions, an offence which ensured automatic dismissal. The rank-and-file were also encouraged to desist from collective resistance. In March 1949 the Chamber of Mines devised a poster to be displayed in the event of a strike threat, warning workers that anyone who participated in the action would be in breach of contract and liable to lose all his accumulated benefits. Simultaneously, the Chamber was trying to encourage the MEU to settle disputes peacefully and without disrupting production. Thus in June 1948 the two parties agreed to the formation of Local Negotiating Committees at each mine and a Central Joint Council to discuss general grievances and conditions of service. As the Colonial Office Labour Advisor argued, 'by regular meetings you can keep misunderstandings to a minimum. If you only meet when there is a misunderstanding it may take months to clear it'.[3] Thus mining capital adopted a strange combination of intimidation and institutionalization in an attempt to curb the militancy of the MEU and its members.

On an ideological level, in an attempt to influence the attitudes and behaviour of the literate mine workers, Ashanti Goldfields began to publish its own newspaper, the Ashanti Times. Although it purported to be 'a medium whereby factual news and its correct interpretation could be made available to local inhabitants', it was in fact a propaganda vehicle for mining capital, designed to counteract the growing current of nationalist and socialist ideas in the colony.[4] The paper's role as a subtle instrument of social control was made explicit in a directive sent to the editor by General Spears, who was personally responsible for the creation of the paper:

> The Ashanti Times has not so far fulfilled its function. While it may be a fact that direct propaganda might not be desirable there can be no disadvantage in at least containing far more news directly concerning the mine than it has to date. Nor can there be any disadvantage to a definite editorial policy in regard to mining affairs. It is well known that the selection of news is one of the most powerful weapons of propaganda and by selecting and emphasizing the right sort of news and by editorials, which while not being direct propaganda would influence opinion in the right direction, much can be done to fulfil the essential purpose of this newspaper which is to build up a body of opinion interested in and loyal to the mine...In so far as the newspaper is not able to do anything to build up the morale of the workers or to strengthen the cooperation between the management and the workers or to enlighten public opinion about the problems facing management, it is not justified in its existence. World news and features should be the sugar on the pill.[5]

The efforts of mining capital to control the mine workers by ideological means were reinforced by an expansion of the paternalistic programme initiated in the previous decade. This programme had taken a severe blow after the 1947 strike, when the MEU organized a successful boycott of the mine canteens on the grounds that cheap food was no substitute for a living wage. Management failed to convince rank-and-file workers that the boycott only benefited the wives of union officials who were food traders and caterers, but remained certain about the need 'to get good food by one method or another into the underground workers'.[6] The mines therefore expanded the range of free foodstuffs distributed to the workers to include nutritious substances such as yeast, sugar, bread, guinea corn and porridge. The threats that the mines had made during the 1947 Arbitration Enquiry to abandon all their welfare schemes were quickly forgotten, and new plans for improved mine townships were drawn up. At Bibiani, for example, northern workers were provided with compounds that were 'a home from home' and which put 'some brightness in their lives'. As a result, these workers were said to be 'the most contented of any...and consequently little worried by labour disputes'.[7]

The final aspect of the offensive launched by mining capital in this period was a new campaign to offset higher wages with increased productivity. Earlier experiments with the use of bonus schemes, gratuities, and other forms of incentive payment were extended in an attempt to improve the motivation and performance of the labour force. Simultaneously, discipline was strengthened in the workplace and sanctions such as dismissal and suspension were employed more widely to penalize and reform workers whose output was inadequate. More adventurously, the mines made some tentative efforts to organize the labour process in a more systematic manner. New Planning Departments were created to devise ways of improving training techniques, patterns of labour allocation and underground excavating efficiency. Mechanization was used as a means of reducing labour complements and increasing the scale of production, while drilling efficiency was improved by the introduction of vented jackhammers and the extended use of tungsten carbide drill steel.

Rank-and-file reactions

How successful were these attempts to reassert control over the mine workers? In terms of controlling the productivity of labour, mining capital enjoyed a fair measure of success. Between 1947 and 1950 output per man-shift increased by just under 31 per cent, while the tonnage produced per underground worker increased from 140.28 to 179.16, a 28 per cent increase. While total working costs grew from 3/6 to 5/10 per ton, the labour component of those costs remained static at approximately 38.75 per cent. Nevertheless, there was little doubt amongst the Mine Managers that further improvements could be made. Increased gratuities failed to reduce the overall rate of labour turnover, which remained at between 80 and 90 per cent, while incentive bonuses could not convince all the workers to perform their tasks more efficiently and regularly. Thus in 1948-49 a third of the workers who were able to earn bonuses failed to do so on account of their absenteeism and low output.

While the strategies used by mining capital to improve labour productivity were a qualified success, the campaign to curtail the mine workers' collective resistance was a complete failure. Between mid-1948 and mid-1951 there were 26 strikes in the gold mines, in which a total of 70,522 man-days of production were lost. The strike-propensity of the mine workers, measured in terms of m.d.l. per 10,000 employees, was over twice that of the colony's average. Such statistical evidence of the mine workers' continued militancy prompts three related questions: why did they strike so frequently? What issues provoked those stoppages? What role did the MEU play in the mobilization of those strikes?

The 1947 strike provided conclusive proof of the efficacy of the strike weapon and acted as a great catalyst to the evolution of the mine workers' political consciousness. As the American Consul in Accra had predicted in October 1947:

> Many believe that this abject surrender to the miners was a great mistake, and would lead the natives to believe that they could at their whim hold up their employers.[8]

This proved to be an accurate prediction, and despite the gains made from the Gorman Award, the mine workers seemed to one Labour Officer 'always to be seething with discontent'.[9] In J.N. Sam's words:

> The provoked employee brooding over his pains and sorrows pays no attention to the entreaties of such officers, and in critical times they are harrassed, hooted at and branded as traitors.[10]

Indeed, the mine workers' flippant attitude towards strikes was a source of great frustration to the Labour Officers. One reported that 4,000 workers in Prestea had struck for five days and won no concessions, 'yet consider the strike a successful one, having exhibited their solidarity and cohesion'. Strikes, he lamented, were considered to be 'a good picnic, with a finale of drinking and drumming'.[11]

A greater insight into the militancy of the mine workers in this period is provided by a breakdown of strike issues. Strikes for higher wages accounted for half the man-days lost in all the mines (gold, diamond, bauxite, manganese) and just under 40 per cent of man-days lost in the gold mines. As these figures suggest, the wage rises provided by the Gorman Award did not satisfy the workers. Local food prices were still increasing faster than pay, causing one observer to note in July 1948 that prices 'are now high enough in the majority of local commodities to nullify the effects of the increases payable under the Gorman Award'.[12] Underground workers were particularly disillusioned by the Award, believing that the importance of their work should be reflected in a minimum underground wage that was higher than the maximum surface wage. Significantly, a series of wage strikes at AGC in October 1949 involved only the underground workers, while a general strike at Ariston in June 1949 was led by the underground labour force. These strikes and the Government's implementation of the Lidbury-Gbedemah Award to public sector workers forced the Chamber of Mines to concede an average wage increase of 17 per cent in October 1949, but even this increase failed to offset the increased cost of living, and real incomes continued to decline.

Over 40 per cent of the man-days lost in the gold mines in this period, and 12 of the 26 strikes, were accounted for by stoppages in protest against disciplinary actions (suspensions, dismissals and demotions) imposed on workers guilty of faulty work and misconduct. The significance of this feature of the mine workers' resistance is threefold. Firstly, it indicates that despite increased wages and improved conditions of service, workers continued to clash with management over issues of workplace authority, and continued to take collective action to resist the extension of managerial control. Secondly, it provides further evidence of the mine workers' enhanced solidarity after the 1947 strike. Seven of the discipline-related strikes involved between 250 and 1,200 workers, suggesting a growing consciousness of the fact that an attack by management on one worker or group of workers was tantamount to an attack on all. Finally, these statistics provide evidence that the new managerial strategies designed to boost productivity were not accepted passively by the labour force. In addition to the 12 strikes against disciplinary actions, three were undertaken by workers seeking higher bonuses or different methods of bonus calculation. Four strikes were protests against retrenchments and transfers following the introduction of labour-saving machinery and work methods, and two were organized to protest about the behaviour of individual supervisors. Thus in attempting to curtail the informal resistance of the mine workers, management actually provoked workers to participate more frequently in collective modes of resistance.

Tensions within the MEU

The 1947 strike and Gorman Award immediately boosted the popularity of the MEU. Prior to the strike only 2,050 workers, 5.6 per cent of the labour force, were paid-up union members. By 1947-48 this figure had jumped to 15,000 (39.9 per cent) and by 1948-49 to 15,500 (42.2 per cent). Although half the mine workers remained outside the union, the Government admitted that the MEU had 'an influence which extends beyond that of its membership'.[13] Encouraged by the union's new popularity, Sam and Bissah made no radical changes to MEU policy after 1947. The strike weapon was still regarded as a last resort, and the leadership acknowledged that 'since our cry is for better pay we must also put out our best and spend our energy to increase production'.[14] Sam and Bissah continued to avoid political affiliations, and were congratulated by the Labour Department for their 'exemplary behaviour' and 'consistent and responsible policy' during the civil disturbances of February 1948.[15] This moderate, productionist and apolitical policy was to come under attack from three sources between 1947 and 1950: from rank-and-file workers who wanted to use the strike weapon more freely than the union leadership; from workers and branch union officials who wanted the MEU to play a more active role in the nationalist movement; and from politicians who also sought to enlist the union's support in the quest for self-government.

The problem of rank-and-file autonomy within the MEU became clear almost immediately after the implementation of the Gorman Award. In January 1948 underground workers went on strike at the Central Wassau Mine over a mistake in the calculation of back pay, and walked around the mine armed with sticks ignoring the branch union's advice to work normally. The following month 400 workers at Amalgamated Banket Areas (ABA) went on strike to demand the dismissal of the Mine Doctor. The Mine Manager reported that there existed 'a certain group of people against the union, and in ABA is losing ground'. Similarly, at AGC the Mine Manager observed that the branch union was 'not nearly so strong as it was'.[16]

The most dramatic manifestation of rank-and-file independence occurred not at a gold mine but at the Nsuta manganese mine, where two unofficial strikes took place in January and February 1948. The first strike, which was about the dismissal of a shovel driver for inefficiency, was organized by a group of workers calling themselves 'The New Order of Youngbloods'. Sam and Bissah condemned the strike but failed to convince the workers to ignore the breakaway organization. The second strike followed the branch union's decision to support managerial warnings issued to two masons accused of unsatisfactory work. The New Order persuaded 1,000 men to withdraw their labour, and the Branch President and Secretary of the MEU were beaten by strikers who accused them of failing their duty. The Tarkwa Labour Officer reported that the New Order was establishing its own organization, appointing officers, and asking members to swear an oath of allegiance. This was not a completely isolated incident, for earlier that month the Governor had reported that other discontented mine workers were 'fostering the growth of dissident bodies with the object of breaking away from the union'.[17] Confronted with such evidence of rank-and-file militancy, branch officials began to ignore the advice of Sam and Bissah and to support the lightning strikes that workers were organizing. Local union officials, the Tarkwa Labour Officer complained, were unduly influenced by workers who used 'intimidation and hooliganism' to support their demands, and needed 'strong official coaching if there must be an end to these unreasonable strikes'.[18]

The rash of unofficial and branch union strikes that occurred in this period were indicative of the failure of the 1947 strike to forge a lasting alliance between the southern surface workers who dominated the union hierarchy and the northern underground workers who formed the rank-and-file of the labour force. As I.G. Jones remarked:

The NT labourer could be a very obstinate individual, and he had evidence to prove that action taken by the so-called southern executives had very often been determined by the NT boys.[19]

Concerned by the inordinate degree of influence being wielded by the underground workers at branch level, Sam and Bissah attempted to prevent local strikes by encouraging branch unions to coopt northern and underground representatives on to their Executive Committees and by imposing fines on union officials who organized or supported strikes without prior permission from the MEU headquarters.

The full range of tensions within and between the labour force and the MEU was revealed more clearly in the prelude to the 'Positive Action' strike of January 1950, when the TUC used an obscure dispute between the Government and Meteorological Workers' Union as the occasion for a full-scale confrontation between organized labour and the colonial state. The strike, which lasted for 13 days and involved over 35,000 workers, was belatedly supported by Nkrumah and the CPP but ended in failure, martial law, and the arrest of prominent TUC and CPP leaders. After the strike, the Government, Chamber of Mines and even the MEU declared that the mine workers had remained loyal, refused to strike and therefore ensured the failure of the action. In fact the role of the MEU was far more ambiguous, and this ambiguity crystallized the growing tensions within the union at this time.

Between August 1949 and January 1950 the MEU and the mine workers were presented with the opportunity to take national strike action over both 'industrial' and 'political' issues. In August 1949 the Government awarded a 15 per cent cost of living allowance to lower-paid public employees. The London Advisory Committee instructed the Chamber of Mines that any claim for a similar increase by the MEU should be rejected on the grounds that the Government had refused to grant the tax concessions requested by the Chamber. While this wage dispute was taking shape, tensions were emerging amongst the mine workers and MEU officials. The Accra riots and their political aftermath had drawn some of the southern mine workers and branch officials into the nationalist movement and the CPP, and in March 1949 the Chamber expressed its first fear that the MEU might embark upon a strike for 'political reasons'.[20] It was agreed that while the underground workers would go on strike for higher wages, they would adamantly refuse to participate in a political strike. Those from the north of the colony had little awareness of the Gold Coast as a political entity, and those from French West Africa evidently had little to gain by supporting the nationalist movement. The interests of the union's national officers differed from those of both the southern surface workers and the northern underground workers. Although sympathetic to the CPP and its objectives, Sam and Bissah were concerned that if the MEU adopted an overtly political stance it would lose the support of the Government, which sanctioned its status as a bargaining unit, and of the underground workers, who gave the union its industrial strength and bargaining power.

In the last quarter of 1949 the 'industrial' and 'political' choices confronting the MEU became increasingly intertwined. In September the price of gold increased by 44 per cent, allowing the Chamber to abandon its policy of confrontation and to concede a wage increase of 17 per cent. The MEU insisted that the new gold price allowed the mines to make more substantial concessions, but the Chamber refused to consider a demand for the retrospective payment of these increases. Negotiations proved fruitless, and by December 1949 a second national confrontation between labour and capital seemed increasingly likely.

At exactly the same time as the MEU moved towards a clash with the Chamber of Mines, the national trade union movement was heading for a confrontation with the Colonial Government. Following the dismissal of 60 Meterological Department workers for staging an illegal strike in October 1949, Anthony Woode, TUC General Secretary, threatened a general strike. The dispute continued throughout November and December, and the TUC and Trade Councils grew in their determination to confront the Government with a demand for the immediate granting of Dominion status to the colony.

By December 22nd the MEU had resolved to call a strike in support of its demand for 12 months' back pay. Afraid that the northern workers would identify this decision with the TUC's strike threats, Sam instructed branch officials to tell workers that the union's strike threat had nothing to do with the Positive Action campaign. The Chamber of Mines, recognizing the incipient conflict of interest between southern and northern workers, invited a group of prominent northern chiefs to the mines, who told the northern workers to ignore any strike call because it was made by southern union officials who were pursuing purely political objectives. One Mine Manager was informed that these appeals had been successful, and that the northern workers would fight any pickets posted to stop them working. Sam and Bissah received similar information but were undeterred and continued to urge workers to prepare for a strike over the back pay issue. Meanwhile, Anthony Woode had arrived in Tarkwa to mobilize support for the TUC's general strike.

By the first week of January, Sam and Bissah had decided that they could not afford to commit the MEU to support the TUC'sstrike, but they were having 'great difficulty in restraining the more ardently political members of some branch unions'. On January 6th the Positive Action strike was launched. The next day the Acting Commissioner of Labour met Sam and Bissah 'and they gave me their assurance that if there was a strike in the mining industry it would be on industrial grounds and have no political reasons'. He continued:

In view of the known strength of the CPP in the Tarkwa area, and the fact that a vocal proportion of members of the various branch executives are known to be adherents of that party, it would appear that they have done their best to honour that undertaking.[21]

However, he was not confident of Sam and Bissah's ability to continue with their apolitical policy in the face of pressure from branch union members and officials. It was, he said, significant that 'this union – perhaps the only one which could have covered a political strike with the appearance of an industrial dispute – has refrained from striking during recent weeks'.[22] This suspicion that the MEU was attempting to reconcile the conflict of interests within its own ranks by disguising political action as industrial action was reinforced four days after the Positive Action strike began on January 6th. On January 10th and 11th Nkrumah and Pobee Biney, the railway workers' leader, visited Tarkwa in an attempt to enlist the support of the mine workers and the MEU. Before leaving the town both made speeches which indicated that they expected the MEU to join the strike.

On January 16th 20 members of the MEU National Executive Council (NEC) met with Sam and Bissah, and at 5 a.m. the next morning they agreed to present an ultimatum to the Chamber, expiring at midnight on January 21st. Copies of the ultimatum were typed and distributed to the delegates. News of the ultimatum was leaked to the General Manager at Tarquah and Abosso Mine (T and A), who circulated the news that in the event of a strike Sam, Bissah and prominent headmen would be dismissed. On hearing this threat workers in the drill shop, power house and mill met in their workshops and resolved not to support any strike called by the union. The National Executive was recalled and met to discuss this latest development. Strike action now seemed less advisable. The T and A workers had been expected to spearhead the strike, and without their support the whole plan seemed doomed. The executives were now less confident that the northern underground workers would support the strike. The northern chiefs invited to the mines the previous month had achieved some success in turning opinion against the union and its allegedly political activities. Moreover, in a desperate bid to avert the MEU's participation in the general strike, the Government had persuaded the Chamber to make its latest pay offer retrospective to October 1st 1949. The wording of this announcement gave the impression that the union had dropped its demand for 12 months' back pay, the demand upon which the MEU depended to capture the support of the northern workers. In view of these considerations Bissah advised the other MEU officials not to send the ultimatum. Copies of the letter were burned and a conciliatory reply to the Chamber was drafted. The Tarkwa Labour Officer reported:

> The efforts to call an immediate strike in support of Nkrumah's positive action campaign, albeit on supposed industrial grounds, have been thwarted.[23]

This sequence of events between September 1949 and January 1950 revealed the somewhat illusory nature of the 1947 general mines strike. While there were many issues which united the mine workers and the MEU against mining capital, the solidarity exhibited in the 1947 strike had obscured some of the tensions and conflicts within the labour force and the union. In January

1950 the national officers of the union had given equivocal support to the TUC and CPP's general strike in response to pressure from the 'more ardently political' surface workers and branch officers. In doing so they had alienated the northern underground workers who, since the formation of the union in 1944, had consistently demonstrated that their support for the MEU was strictly conditional. In the absence of what they regarded as appropriate action from the MEU, they would reject it and defend their own interests in the ways most familiar to them.

Conflict in the Workplace, 1950-1954

By 1950 it was quite evident that the response of mining capital to the political and economic pressures confronting it since the 1947 mines strike had failed. After 1950 these pressures became even more acute, and prompted mining capital to look for new solutions to its problems. The Colonial Government's accelerated timetable for decolonization was perceived by the mining companies as a direct threat to the industry's existence, while the labour policy pursued by the administration after the Positive Action strike of 1950 was viewed with incredulity by the Chamber of Mines. Contrary to the Chamber's wishes, the Government did not use the strike as a pretext for the abolition of the trade union movement, but persisted with its policy of guiding the unions 'into a sound and responsible movement able to play its organic part in the democratic structure of the territory'.[24] The Government therefore refused to consider the Chamber's proposals for legislation against unofficial strikes, and frustrated by the Chamber's inability to negotiate without constant reference to the LAC, even threatened to establish a Wages Board to determine pay levels in the mines. Confronted with this evidence, the Chamber recognized that it could not rely upon the Government to stabilize wages or curtail labour organization in the mines. New and independent strategies of labour control therefore had to be found.

Mining capital in search of a strategy

The first such strategy introduced after 1950 was a new campaign of labour recruitment in the Northern Territories. The rapid expansion of the colony's economy during the post-war boom, the wartime break in migratory flows from French West Africa and the growing demand for labour in the Francophone area had combined to restrict the supply of labour to the gold mines. While this had no immediate impact on wages, which were now determined primarily by the Government's own incomes policy, it was obstructing the industry's attempts to increase the productive capacity of the mines, and thereby benefit from economies of scale. Initially, the Chamber of Mines established a Migrant Labour Committee to investigate schemes that might 'consolidate friendship with the NT's and encourage the flow of recruits'.[25] Northern chiefs and Roman Catholic missionaries were asked to act as informal labour recruiters, and when these arrangements failed to produce many new workers a formal recruitment programme was initiated. This was based at a Transit Welfare Centre situated at Bolgatanga and which employed local African recruiting agents working on a commission basis. Meanwhile, at the Government's labour camp in the town, the Chamber was allowed to display photographs of the mines illustrating 'the happy time which NT boys enjoy, both at work and at play'.[26]

In the mines, new strategies were introduced to curtail the activities of the MEU and to reinforce the tensions within the labour force which had been manifested during the crisis of January 1950. Union officials were systematically denied promotion on the grounds that it was 'morally inconsistent...to place an active trade union leader or official in a position of trust in an industry where he may become liable to be delegated supervisory powers'.[27] J.N. Sam also complained that 'union officials had often met with discriminatory attitudes from the managements...to the extent of debarring council members from attending meetings'.[28] At AGC and Bibiani, management continued its attempt to by-pass the union and to encourage divisions within the labour force through the Group Committee system. As the AGC Mine Manager happily reported, 'they were a threat to the union executive, and we should do everything in our power to encourage the Group Committees as much as possible'.[29] Similar results were achieved through the creation of new Salaried Staff Associations:

> ...the main object of which was to separate the salaried staff who were mainly supervisory categories from the daily paid employees who were members of the GCMEU. It was made a condition of employment on a salary...that the employee joined the Salaried Staff Association and agreed not to take part in strikes nor to be a member of the MEU.[30]

Workers who refused to be bound by these conditions were immediately demoted and moved out of their staff bungalow to the labourers' compound.

The Chamber of Mines had been delighted by the split between northern and southern workers which emerged in 1950, and was very keen to reinforce and perpetuate this division. I.G. Jones warned that it would be 'a ghastly mistake to encourage a split between the NT and southern workers...the MEU should continue to exist, the age of headmen has gone for ever'.[31] This advice was ignored by some mines, which surreptitiously encouraged northern workers to form independent organizations to rival the MEU. In June 1951 the Gold Coast Northern Territories Welfare Association was formed in Tarkwa. The Secretary insisted that the new body 'has no interference with labour unions' but the Labour Department was not convinced:

> It is improbable that the members of the Association could afford to contribute regularly to both organizations monthly, and the possibility that interest in the new Association would be greater than that in the mines union is also apparent.[32]

On examining the complicated 38 articles of the Association's constitution, the Deputy Commissioner of Labour commented, 'I am tempted to believe that they were not drawn up by a Northern Territories mine worker'. Similar developments occurred at Bibiani, where an Association of Underground Workers was established in 1952 and whose existence, management admitted in 1954, 'might have accounted for the drop in union strength'.[33]

Although the mining companies expended a great deal of time and effort in such anti-union strategies, they were aware that these strategies met with strong disapproval in official circles, and that even the destruction of the MEU would not necessarily diminish rank-and-file pressures for increased wages. Moreover, non-wage variables in the industry's cost structure, such as the gold price, taxation levels and the cost of stores, would not be influenced by the weakening of the MEU. With all these considerations in mind, mining capital recognized that there was only one strategy for survival that could be undertaken with any hope of success, and that was 'to counteract the constantly rising spiral of costs...by means of increased productivity and the elimination of waste in all its forms'.[34]

The introduction of scientific management

The mining industry's efforts to boost productivity between 1947 and 1950 had enjoyed considerable success, but the Gold Coast mines lacked the specialized personnel and knowledge required to realize the full potential of the labour power at their disposal. Consequently, in 1950 they turned for assistance to Southern African consultants who specialized in the reorganization of mining operations in accordance with the principles of 'Scientific Management'. This set of productivity-boosting techniques had been devised in the late 19th Century by an American engineer, F.W. Taylor, and had popularized the use of innovations such as time study and work study, ergonomics, aptitude testing and payment-by-results. Such techniques were applied with some success to the regular and repetitive operations of manufacturing industry, but it was not until the 1940's, when rising working costs and labour shortages were threatening the mines of South Africa and Southern Rhodesia, that Scientific Management was systematically applied to the mining of gold.

The Southern African consultants who arrived in the Gold Coast in 1950 quickly recognized the extent to which management had hitherto failed to assert control over the productivity of the mine workers. According to two Rhodesian consultants, productivity in the Gold Coast mines was only half that achieved by the mines of South Africa. Labour in the colony was 'periodically in acutely short supply', and the MEU 'had at times been difficult'. The workers were 'not well disciplined, well trained, nor of a physically high standard'. Overmanning was rife, the theft of gold endemic, and employees worked at well below their potential performance. Absenteeism rates of up to 25 per cent and turnover rates of up to 90 per cent were common, and a reflection of the workers' 'indifference to the obligations of employment'. These obstacles to efficient production were reinforced by the backward character of management. European supervision was 'extremely dilute because of the difficulty of attracting good men to the tropics'. Those Europeans who were prepared to work in the Gold Coast were 'lacking in knowledge of Africans and unused to supervising men'. The political environment of West Africa exacerbated the situation, since 'labour was not compounded as elsewhere in Africa, and consequently neither feeding nor attendance could be controlled'. Finally, management had unacceptably low expectations of the labour force. 'It was considered that the West African native could not be taught in the comparatively short time he was on the mine to carry out carefully planned standard instructions', nor would he 'respond to incentive pay or payment by results'. Despite this gloomy analysis, 'the initial reaction of the survey...was that these obstacles could be overcome, at least sufficiently to justify the cost involved', and four related strategies were introduced to boost productivity.[35]

Firstly, the mine workers were encouraged to improve the quantity and quality of their work by the introduction of new incentive bonus schemes. According to consultants Fraser and Somerset:

> With primitive labour on simple daily pay...bad tools or bad working conditions are treated with complete indifference. Broken shovels, dull saws, faulty switches are accepted with philosophic detachment.

However:

> When every workman is conscious of the necessity for and has a pecuniary interest in maintaining the conditions and in the planning which will enable him to take home a substantial increase in earnings, the task of management in discipline and organization is greatly simplified and its hand is greatly strengthened.

Unlike earlier bonus schemes, the new incentive payments were calculated on the basis of 'scientific' measurements of work performed. Time study analysts examined each task in the mine and calculated the time a worker or labour gang would require to complete the task if they worked at a 'standard rate'. A 'rest factor' was added, and the final figure was termed the '100 per cent performance', expressed in terms of the 'standard minute':

> This is a unit of work analagous to a horsepower...used to describe the credits allowed a workman for the performance of specified tasks...The relationship between the credits earned in standard minutes and the total minutes in the working shift indicate the man's percentage effectiveness.[36]

Bonuses were available to all employees whose work was quantifiable in this way, and payments started once a 50 per cent or 75 per cent 'effectiveness rating' had been attained.

Secondly, to encourage efficient work and to assist the mine workers to qualify for the new bonuses, the consultants trained the labour force in the use of new working methods. The basic operations of scraping rock, loading it and tramming it along underground tracks, which had always been performed largely by manual methods, were progressively replaced by mechanized techniques. At the same time, existing equipment was used more efficiently as a result of 'planned preventive maintenance' schedules designed to eliminate mechanical breakdowns. The consultants used aptitude tests to match individual workers with specific tasks in the mine, and using a combination of time study and work study, ascertained the most efficient method of performing each task. This method was described in words and pictures in a 'manual of standard practice' which described 'precisely how management requires operations to be done in any given set of circumstances' and covered 'the detail of every activity from stoping to clerical returns and from sampling to grass cutting'.

The third innovation of the consultants was to instruct Mine Managers in new methods of labour distribution. Using the standard minute as a unit of work, the consultants calculated the number of man-shifts required to complete an operation if all employees maintained a '70 per cent efficiency rate'. This procedure enabled management to reduce labour complements and eliminate overmanning, to transfer surplus service workers to more productive tasks, and to ensure that all workers were kept fully occupied. Labour distribution was made the responsibility of new Labour Control Departments, which operated 'a properly designed specific plan, by which the daily distribution of labour is controlled according to predetermined standards'. The plan enabled management to hire, fire and transfer labour according to changing conditions, to compile more detailed records of production and productivity, and to keep a much closer check on the location, task and performance of each worker and gang.

Finally, to ensure the success of these three strategies, the consultants took steps to improve the quality and quantity of supervision in the mines. The ratio of white supervisors to African workers was increased from 2.4 per cent in 1949 to 3.2 per cent in 1954, and considerable attention was paid to the selection and training of African supervisors. Trainees were informed that their interests were quite different from the men they controlled. 'As a supervisor a man is no longer simply a worker, he is an executive, he has improved his status'. His task was to 'undertake the skilled functions of directing, coordinating and controlling the actions of other people', and he was induced to perform such tasks effectively by the provision of incentive payments of up to a third of his basic salary.[37] Ultimately this depended on the effective imposition of discipline in the workplace, to eliminate all the productivity-restricting modes of resistance which had been identified by the consultants in their surveys of the mines. In the words of the AGC training manual:

The value of a good headman to the mine is in direct proportion to his ability to maintain discipline. Discipline is the first essential quality required by supervisors, and can only be enforced if the supervisor is amenable to discipline himself.[38]

Productivity, protest, and the MEU

Between 1950 and 1954, as in the preceding three-year period, the efforts of mining capital to assert greater control over the activities of the mine workers and the MEU achieved few positive results. The measures introduced to increase the flow of labour from the north of the colony soon ran into serious problems. The chiefs who were invited to assist the recruitment drive were becoming increasingly critical of conditions in the mines, and Mine Managers found to their horror that on their visits to the south the chiefs were actually 'allying themselves with the union' and making demands for higher wages.[39] The Transit Welfare Centre was totally incapable of competing with African labour recruiters working for cocoa and food farmers, and who used a variety of legal and illegal ploys to attract workers away from the mines. In the 18 months after May 1950 the Centre recruited an average of only 42 men per month, and many of these simply used the Centre's offer of free transport to the mines as a cheap means of reaching other jobs in the south of the colony.

The attempts made by management and consultants to boost productivity levels appeared far more successful. Between 1950 and 1954 overall tonnage per underground worker jumped from 185.87 to 265.80, an increase of 43 per cent, while at one of the mines reorganized by Fraser and Somerset, productivity measured in this way increased by no less than 64 per cent. The tonnage produced by the mine's 3,500 workers in 1954 would have required 6,000 workers to produce at 1950 productivity levels, an improvement which saved the mine £250,000. At another mine, tonnage per shift increased by 65 per cent between 1949 and 1954, although only an additional 5 per cent of the rock-face was worked. At a third mine, labour was reduced by 25 per cent while tonnage increased by 30 per cent, representing an 80 per cent increase in tonnage per shift. Such substantial improvements to productivity levels successfully countered the rising level of wages. Between 1950 and 1954 average earnings (wages, bonuses, overtime) per shift increased by 59 per cent, but overall expenditure on labour rose by only 19 per cent. In the same period, expenditure on other working costs rose by 27 per cent.

The real significance of these figures only becomes apparent when they are examined in conjunction with the industry's strike statistics for the same period. Between 1951 and 1954 there were no less than 44 strikes in the gold mines, totalling 117,885 man-days lost, 40 per cent of the colony's total. The number of man-days lost per 10,000 employees was over three times the national average. By any standards, therefore, the mine workers were in an exceptionally militant mood. This quantitative increase in the level of collective resistance was matched by significant qualitative changes. Twenty-two strikes (83,990 m.d.l.) were organized in protest against dismissals, suspensions, fines and demotions imposed on workers accused of various kinds of misconduct. This represented over 70 per cent of the total m.d.l., compared with around 40 per cent in the preceding three year period. Another 16 per cent of the total were accounted for by strikes over bonus payments (1,136 m.d.l.), retrenchments and transfers (4,480 m.d.l.), new working methods (4,912 m.d.l.) and supervisory behaviour (8,384 m.d.l.). In the same period, the proportion of man-days lost in wage-related disputes slumped from over 37 per cent (1947-50) to a mere 4.3 per cent of the total.

The very clear pattern of collective resistance expressed in these strike statistics is a reflection of two features of the mine workers' situation between 1950 and 1954. Firstly, the reduced level of resistance in connection with wage demands is indicative of the beneficial impact of the pay increases forced upon the Chamber of Mines in 1952 and the simultaneous downward trend in market prices which stemmed from the slump in the price of cocoa. Significantly the diamond and bauxite mines, which refused to grant wage increases at the same time as the gold mines, provoked three massive strikes amongst their normally passive workers. Secondly, the rapid growth in the level of resistance associated with workplace conflicts demonstrates that the introduction of Scientific Management provoked, in the words of two expatriates, 'serious opposition by workpeople' and 'a major confrontation with labour'.[40]

The origins of this confrontation are to be found in the very nature of Scientific Management as devised by F.W. Taylor. According to Taylor, the 'greatest evil' of modern industry was what he described as 'soldiering'. By this he meant absenteeism, restricted output, malingering, sabotage and bonus cheating - the covert and individual actions of workers described in this book as 'informal resistance'. The task which Taylor set himself was to find a means of 'doing away with slow working and soldiering in all its forms, and so arranging the relations between employer and employee that each workman will work to his very best advantage and at his best speed'.[41] In other words, Scientific Management is a direct manifestation of the struggle between labour and capital, a strategy which seeks to maximize the surplus value appropriated from labour by depriving the worker of any autonomy within the labour process.

The true nature of Scientific Management is revealed more clearly by an examination of its impact on the mine workers at the point of production. Theoretically, there was no upper limit to the amount of bonus that could be earned under the new incentive schemes. In practice, however, bonus levels were subject to constant manipulation. Workers who earned very high incentive payments soon discovered that their production targets were upgraded, forcing them to strive after even higher levels of output if they wished to maintain their higher earnings. Although basic wages were guaranteed under the new schemes, bonus payments could be reduced or withheld as a punishment for any kind of misconduct. Moreover, workers who consistently failed to qualify for a bonus were liable to be dismissed. Thus the 'carrot' of a bonus also acted as a 'stick' with which workers who obstructed the objectives of mining capital could be beaten. Similarly, although the new manuals of standard practice were purportedly introduced to teach workers the simplest method of performing any task, an employee who preferred to ignore the manual's instructions and to work in his own way was again liable to be punished. Thus the worker, irrespective of his experience, level of skill and knowledge of local conditions, was deprived of the right to make any choice about his own working method. In every other respect, the introduction of Scientific Management represented an assault upon the workplace freedoms that the mine workers had hitherto established and defended. Shaft tops were sealed off, making it impossible for workers to come and go as they pleased, while new clocking-on and changing facilities made it far more difficult for them to arrive at work late, to leave early or to linger in the mine to steal gold. Above all, the mine workers were brought much more directly under the control of the representatives of capital and state. In the mines, supervisors were encouraged to eradicate unacceptable activities through the use of sanctions such as fines, suspensions, dismissals and demotions, and to treat their subordinates in the labour force as inanimate factors of production. Meanwhile on the surface, mining camps and key installations were put under the protection of high fencing, while local police forces were provided with armed perimeter posts, floodlights, riot shields and teargas. As an official enquiry into the conditions of mine labour concluded, 'living in a mining compound for a labourer can at best not be far different from living in a barracks'.[42] It was in protest against this new degree of regimentation that the mine workers embarked upon their wave of strikes between 1950 and 1954.

Another significant feature of the strikes of 1950-54 can be discerned in their pattern of participation and mobilization. Of the strikes for which relevant data are available, surface workers took part in all the wage-related stoppages but under 17 per cent of the stoppages related to workplace disputes. In contrast, the underground workers took part in none of the pay strikes, but did participate in over 93 per cent of strikes over disciplinary actions, bonuses, retrenchment, new working methods and supervisory behaviour. Clearly the underground workers, who were most directly affected by the introduction of Scientific Management, had lost none of their longstanding hostility to any strategies designed to bring their productivity more directly under the control of supervisors and management. Moreover, the mine workers received very little help or support from their trade union in their campaign of resistance to the introduction of Scientific Management. Of the 28 workplace-related strikes for which relevant data are available, only one was declared official by the branch and national officers of the MEU.

Other evidence confirms the impression that rank-and-file workers had lost confidence in their union or now perceived it as irrelevant to their struggle against management. After 1948-49, when union membership had reached a peak, it declined slowly, reaching a low of 28.4 per cent of the labour force in 1952-53 before recovering slightly to 31.2 per cent in 1953-54. The alienation of the rank-and-file became particularly explicit at times of conflict with management. In October 1951 a general strike led by underground workers occurred at AGC when a worker with tuberculosis was discharged. Union officials were 'completely overtaken by events and overwhelmed by the magnitude of the strike'.[43] At two further strikes in Obuasi the union was said to be 'overwhelmed by events', and strikers booed the local officials when they suggested a return to work:

> No executive of a trade union cut a more sorry figure at that stage than the local executive. The last minute attempts to regain control received no response whatever from the men, not even the gong-gong appeal from the General President of the MEU.[44]

Similar events were taking place elsewhere. After a spate of four unofficial strikes in the Tarkwa area, the District Labour Officer reported:

> It has been observed with grave concern that in each case there has been an attempt by the NT element to strike without consulting their branch union officers.[45]

This 'yawning gap between the branch union officers and the NT elements' was equally apparent at Bibiani. At this mine over 65 per cent of the workers came from the north, and in 1954 management observed that many of them 'looked to the Northern Territories Association for their help and not to the union'.[46]

The problem of rank-and-file alienation within the MEU was not, of course, a new one for the union leadership, and had reached a peak during the crisis of January 1950 when the northern workers had unambiguously demonstrated their suspicion of the MEU hierarchy. Although that crisis had been resolved without the break-up of the union, events after 1950 combined to perpetuate the tensions which existed within the labour force and between the union leadership and the rank-and-file workers.

The failure of the CPP and TUC to secure the support of the MEU and the mine workers in the general strike of 1950 was considered to be a 'major blunder' by its organizers. With Nkrumah in prison, Komla Gbedemah was left to mastermind the party's campaign. Anticipating a second Positive Action strike, he instigated a campaign to capture the MEU by encouraging a revolt of those elements dissatisfied with Sam and Bissah's timidity during the crisis of January 1950. The campaign culminated in the summer of 1951, when a government official noted 'a considerable split in the established [branch] unions. This has come to a head in the Tarquah and Abosso branch and amounts to a revolt against the leadership of the old established officers'.[47] I.G. Jones was horrified by the prospect of a CPP takeover bid, and told the Chamber of Mines that it would be 'a disaster' if Sam was removed from the leadership.[48] However, he could do nothing to stem the revolt, and at the MEU Annual Conference in July 1951, Sam and Bissah were forced to resign. The leadership of the union was assumed by D.K. Foevie (President), J.K. Arthur (Secretary), C.D. Arthur (Vice President) and A.K. Buachie (Treasurer). Union headquarters were moved from Abosso to Bogosu, where the Togolese Foevie was employed as a track layer at the Marlu mine. In the following months the old branch union officers were also ousted in what one official observer described as 'a series of quite bogus elections'.[49]

This change of leadership had a significant impact on relations between the MEU and the mine workers. The new union leaders were not CPP puppets, or even activists, but the party had supported their takeover bid. Unlike their predecessors, Foevie and his colleagues recognized that the country's future would soon lie with the CPP, and that the union would have to establish a working relationship with it. The rank-and-file, especially the northern workers, did not share this perception, and reacted strongly against the news of Foevie's accession to power. Fears were expressed that a mass withdrawal of MEU members would take place and as a result, Foevie and the new NEC members were forced to play down their political inclinations and intentions. Similarly, the CPP wisely chose to abandon its attempt to forge a close link with the MEU. Nevertheless, rank-and-file suspicions remained, and Foevie had to consolidate his new position in the union. He was a more autocratic and less principled leader than Sam, and quickly used his control of the union's resources to establish a personal network of patronage throughout the union structure. This manoeuvre had profound implications for the democratic mechanisms of the MEU. With Foevie's protection local officials no longer felt obliged to respond to rank-and-file demands by supporting the strikes which workers continued to perceive as an effective mode of resistance. As union officials at the Ariston mine arrogantly remarked, 'they were the truck, and could move without its trailer'.[50]

The most crucial failing of the new leadership was its reluctance to take up the workers' struggle against the introduction of Scientific Management. Like Sam and Bissah, the new leaders perceived the union's main function to be the improvement of wages and conditions, and thought that by assisting management to boost productivity the MEU's position in pay negotiations would be strengthened. Thus in September 1952 the MEU proposed the creation of joint union/management Productivity and Efficiency Committees to examine methods of increasing output. As Foevie argued, if they succeeded, then management would have no excuse for not improving wages. This orientation was assiduously cultivated by the Labour Department's programme of trade union education, which was designed to depoliticize the labour movement, to encourage institutionalized bargaining and to teach union officials that they had 'a vital part to play in educating the Gold Coast workers that it does not pay to be lazy'.[51] The MEU was a principal target of the Department's educational endeavours, and J.E. Quarshie, who succeeded Sam as Branch President at

Abosso, admitted the influence of the programme when he told workers:

> I must make it plain to you that unnecessary strikes, lock-outs and hold ups will do the union more harm than good. I attended the trade union school for ten days at Kumasi and I am now telling you what had been taught to me.[52]

It might not be entirely coincidental that 19 unofficial strikes took place at Abosso in this period, by far the worst record of any mine. Even so, there was a logic to the union's policy. While the Chamber of Mines had no option but to negotiate with the MEU over wages, the Mine Managers made it very clear that they would tolerate no attempt by the union to undermine their authority in the workplace. The union's policy was, therefore, designed to deprive the Mine Managers of one excuse for pursuing their punitive campaign against the MEU and its officers.

Foevie and his colleagues were concerned about the growth of rank-and-file disaffection and its manifestation in the form of unofficial strikes, and used several methods to check this trend. The new General President made a number of tours round the mines, where he attempted to arouse rank-and-file support by vigorous speeches denouncing the Chamber of Mines. Shop stewards were appointed to improve communication between local officials and workers, and in a more sinister move, those officials were encouraged to make surreptitious agreements with management to ensure that unofficial strike leaders would be dismissed. Foevie recognized, however, that there was only one certain means of recapturing rank-and-file support, and that was, as Sam and Bissah had discovered in 1946-47, to win a large wage rise for the workers. As a government official noted in July 1952:

> The new leadership has still to win the confidence of the bulk of the underground labour. The actions of the new union leaders have at all times been governed by the desire to prove themselves 'dynamic' and this could best be done by bringing off some really impressive 'coup'.[53]

The 'coup' of negotiating a large wage rise had several advantages as a means of regaining the workers' allegiance. It would not threaten managerial authority and thereby provoke retaliation from the mining companies. It could be pursued through negotiating procedures recognized by the Chamber and approved by the Government. Above all, in the words of I.G. Jones:

> It had to be remembered that although the NT worker would not lend his support to any political agitation, he would support the union fully in any demand for better conditions.[54]

Between 1954 and 1956 the focus of conflict in the gold mines shifted back from the workplace to the wage negotiating table as the MEU leadership began to pursue its new campaign.

Union Militancy and the Second General Mines Strike, 1954-1956

Between 1952 and 1956 relations between the Chamber of Mines and the Mines Employees' Union deteriorated steadily. This trend culminated on November 20th 1955 when the union's General President, D.K. Foevie, called on the mine workers to withdraw their labour and to support a second general mines strike. The strike was not called off until February 17th 1956, 100 days later, and it remains the longest industrial stoppage in Ghana's history.

Prelude to the general strike

The sequence of events which led ultimately to this strike began in November 1951, when, just four months after becoming leader of the MEU, D.K. Foevie submitted a wage claim to the Chamber of Mines demanding an extra 3/0 per day for all workers. When negotiations about the claim began in April 1952, Foevie raised the claim to a demand for an all-round 50 per cent increase. Discussions soon reached a deadlock, and the following month the MEU dropped its 50 per cent demand and accepted the Chamber's offer of a general 18 per cent rise, with increases of up to 40 per cent for the lowest paid workers. The union's next wage demand was made in October 1953, when the MEU submitted a claim for a 35 per cent increase in basic rates. The Chamber rejected the demand outright at a negotiating meeting in April 1954, and the MEU delegates walked out of the room in protest against the employers' intransigence. After an exchange of acrimonious correspondence the MEU threatened that if the claim was not met, a general strike of mine workers would commence on December 23rd 1954. I.G. Jones reminded the Chamber of the outcome of its obstinacy in 1947, and warned that if negotiations remained deadlocked Nkrumah's transitional Government would appoint an Arbitration Enquiry to avert a strike and to produce a settlement which it found politically and economically acceptable. The Chamber recognized the strength of this argument, negotiations recommenced on December 28th, and the union's threat was withdrawn.

Agreement could still not be reached between the two bodies. The MEU rejected the Chamber's proposal of a new wage schedule that gave a minimum wage of 4/0 and 4/3 to surface and underground workers. As Jones had warned, the Government intervened and announced that a Board of Enquiry into the dispute would start work on January 31st 1955. Foevie refused to present the union's case because the Board's terms of reference did not include related disputes in the manganese and diamond mines, and the enquiry was abandoned. The MEU now attempted to break the deadlock by planning a 24-hour strike for February 18th, but at an all-night meeting on February 15th the NEC decided to postpone the stoppage until a delegation of the Miners' International Federation (MIF) was in the country to inspect the mines. The Chamber responded by withdrawing permission for union officials to accompany the delegation around the mines, and the MEU was forced to cancel its plans for a demonstration stoppage. At the MEU Annual Conference the following month, the union agreed to resume negotiations with the Chamber, and if these failed, to press the Government to appoint another Arbitration Enquiry. Talks started on May 24th and the union accepted 'under protest' the Chamber's December 1954 wage schedule, but three months later Foevie revoked this decision and returned to his demand for a general 35 per cent increase. The Chamber refused to make any further concessions and on November 17th 1955 a strike notice was served for November 20th. The Chamber stood firm, the ultimatum expired, and the '100-day strike' began.

Union, workers, and the negotiating process

To understand the sequence of events which preceded the second general mines strike, it is necessary to look beyond the formal negotiations between the representatives of mining labour and capital, and to examine the dynamics of the MEU's growing militancy in this period. As described earlier in this chapter, having toppled Sam and Bissah from the union leadership in July 1951, and having witnessed the immediate disaffection of the rank-and-file, Foevie needed to achieve 'a really impressive coup' to regain the MEU's grassroots support. Foevie began his campaign ambitiously. After submitting the union's 3/0 wage claim in November 1951, he instructed union officials to prepare for a general strike and arranged mass meetings where 'no effort was spared in whipping the enthusiasm of the mine workers with inflammatory speeches'.[55] The rank-and-file response was not encouraging and the strike plans were suspended. Foevie then renewed his attempt to secure mass support by raising the union's wage claim to a demand for a 50 per cent rise. Once again:

> In spite of attempts to stir up excitement by speeches and placards...the union leaders found ample evidence to show they had not the confidence of the men to the extent where they could confidently risk calling for a General Strike.

In view of this lack of support, Foevie was 'profoundly glad' to accept the Chamber's offer on wages and gratuities the following month.[56]

These events revealed the dilemma confronting the union leaders. They were seeking to regain mass support by securing a large wage increase, but without that support they were unable to make the realistic threats needed to extract large concessions from the Chamber. Nevertheless, the wage increase of May 1952 did aid the union's quest for rank-and-file support. Although it did nothing to stem the rash of unofficial branch strikes over workplace issues, the pay rise restored real earnings to their 1948 level, established the credibility of the new leaders as effective negotiators, and boosted the union's membership from 28.4 per cent (1952-53) to 31.2 per cent (1953-54) of the labour force. When the next round of negotiations began in September 1954, the union leaders had the confidence to adopt a far more militant stance than in 1952, and the positive response of the rank-and-file to this militancy allowed Foevie to issue his first general strike ultimatum in December 1954. Once the ultimatum was suspended after the Labour Department's intervention, branch union officials instructed the rank-and-file to live economically and to avoid sectional and branch strikes in preparation for a protracted confrontation with the Chamber. This advice appears to have been heeded, for the number of strikes dropped dramatically from 18 (12,346 m.d.l.) in 1953-54, to only four (718 m.d.l.) in 1954-55.

Foevie's failure to call a general strike in December 1954, when rank-and-file support had been partially restored, proved to be the first in a series of tactical errors made by the General President. It was, however, an understandable mistake in view of the fragile nature of that support. Foevie's hesitancy in December 1954 was followed two months later by a second error when he decided to boycott the Board of Enquiry. He had expected the Enquiry to be adjourned rather than abandoned and the workers, remembering the benefits granted by the Gorman Award in 1947, were puzzled by Foevie's apparent eagerness to impede the proceedings. Union officials came under fire from angry workers, and the one-day strike planned for February 18th was a face-saving action taken to restore the union's credibility. When this plan was out-manoeuvred by the Chamber's action over the MIF delegation, confidence in Foevie was eroded further and even branch union officials suspected him of 'bungling the affair' for a second time. Recognizing their mistake, Foevie and the NEC were left to hope that the Government would announce another Board of Enquiry and thereby 'bolster their waning popularity'.[57]

By March 1955 the frustration of the rank-and-file was growing. They had given support to the union's wage demands but nothing had been achieved and real earnings had stagnated. Their disillusionment was confirmed by the Government's refusal to establish a second enquiry, and they 'felt that due to their leader's stubbornness they would have to start again and that the union should have sought a mandate for their action'.[58] Branch officers reported difficulty in collecting union subscriptions and membership slumped to 7,400, 26.2 per cent of the labour force. At ABA in Tarkwa the Branch President and Secretary were retrenched, and the union's attempts to mobilize the workers in defence of these officials proved unsuccessful. At Nsuta workers removed the old Executive and elected new officers only to find that they were suspended by the NEC for unconstitiutional behaviour. The suspended President complained that the union was 'becoming a place where lying is an art' and was 'going into bits and pieces'.[59] At Bibiani the earlier north/south split amongst the workers had reappeared and the District Labour Officer reported that 'this, as other branches of the Mines Employees' Union, seems moribund'.[60]

In May 1955 Foevie approached the Labour Department and asked for assistance in ending the stalemate. He and his colleagues were concerned about 'their loss of face with their members, especially the NT element' and were therefore 'genuinely anxious to end the dispute' and prepared to 'behave reasonably' at further negotiations. They were 'so concerned with the ground they are losing among the NT element' that they were prepared to accept a wage rise of 6d per day. The MEU leaders believed that unless they could secure concessions quickly, the union would be left 'with no standing in the industry'.[61]

The union's acceptance of the Chamber's wage offer later that month did not resolve Foevie's predicament. The new pay schedule, which raised minimum wage rates and reduced the length of incremental periods, did not benefit the many experienced workers who had already reached the maximum rate for their category. Workers now suspected that Foevie had been bribed by the Chamber to accept the settlement. On September 6th Foevie met union officials and workers in Obuasi and received a hostile reception from his audience. Recognizing the strength of their feeling, he told the workers that he now realized that they favoured a strike to force a better settlement from the Chamber and asked them to be patient while the union prepared for a stoppage. Two days later Foevie wrote to the Chamber revoking his earlier acceptance of the wage offer.

The NEC's final decision to issue a general strike ultimatum also followed signs of rank-and-file impatience. On September 29th over 5,000 AGC workers went on strike in protest against a new pay system which required all daily-rated labourers to work for 26 days before being paid. The strike, supported by the branch union, lasted 14 days and forced management to abandon the new pay system. The day after the strike ended the NEC met and decided to withdraw their suspension of the strike notice and to inform the Chamber that a general strike would start on an unspecified future date. Between October 4th and 7th the whole labour force at T and A stopped work over the suspension of eight magazine clerks. Workers picketing the mine stoned a car belonging to a government official's wife, broke windows in the mine offices and attempted to overturn company cars. Five days later, after the Labour Department had attempted to dissuade the MEU from calling a strike, Foevie informed the Chamber that the second general mines strike would start on November 20th 1955. The Tarkwa Labour Officer reported:

> It would appear the strike...is likely to receive a great measure of support from the mine workers but only if it does not last too long. It seems to me that the national executive of the union is expecting a Government intervention soon after the strike is called - in order to give the union a moral victory at least.[62]

In fact, the general mines strike was a more protracted and bitter confrontation than the Labour Officer had predicted. Unlike the 1947 strike, the frustration and militancy of the mine workers took a violent form. At Obuasi the houses of blacklegs were stoned and set on fire and there were three 'fairly serious cases of sabotage'. At Bibiani there were 'acts of hooliganism' including two shooting incidents involving blacklegs.[63] At Obuasi African staff members were singled out for attack, and the African Staff Association President's house was dynamited. The Ohene of Huni

Valley, who tried to end the strike in Abosso, had to be escorted from the town by police after being mobbed by angry workers, and in Obuasi members of the police force were attacked when the Police Band began to play in the lorry park at the same time as a mass meeting of workers was due to be held.

Management and Government made strenuous, and frequently devious attempts to end the strike. Leaflets were distributed to workers appealing for a return to work, and posters, local radio and the press were used to impress upon the workers the severity of the industry's financial position. Bulletins were issued which purported to represent the opinions of anti-union workers' organizations. When these strategies failed to undermine the solidarity of the strikers, Ashanti Goldfields sent a Welfare Officer to the Northern Territories, where he gave gifts of £10 to prominent chiefs and asked them to contact the tribal heads in the mining towns, instructing them to call on their people to end the strike. These strike-breaking strategies had, in the words of the Labour Department, 'little apparent result except to irritate the union'.[64] As the strike dragged on strikers were threatened with dismissal and eviction from company housing, and the mines attempted to recruit new workers. These threats also had little effect, for the workers were aware that there was little surplus labour in the mining towns, that new workers could not perform skilled underground work, and that in the close-knit mining towns, few men would risk physical intimidation for the sake of a job in the mines.

The officers of the MEU also came under pressure during the strike. Nkrumah, looking forward to the transition of power to the CPP and now a close acquaintance of General Spears, met Foevie several times in an unsuccessful attempt to end the stoppage. The General President also ignored the advice of the TUC. Since early 1954 the CPP had been engaged in a campaign to centralize organized labour in the colony in order to assert greater control over its activities. Foevie, in loose alliance with the railway, dock and UAC workers' unions, had attempted to obstruct this campaign, and he was therefore not inclined to accept advice from his opponents within the organization.

The Chamber's determination to withstand the MEU's demands and the union's determination to vindicate its decision to call a strike prevented an easy compromise between the two parties. Initially, the MEU rejected a return to work until negotiations or an Arbitration Enquiry had been completed. The Chamber, fearing a repetition of the 1947 situation, would only agree to a fact-finding enquiry, and insisted on a return to work while it made its investigations. Eventually, Foevie was forced to compromise on these issues by a drift back to work at some mines and by the decision of the directors of Tarquah and Abosso, the colony's oldest producing mine, to flood the shafts and dismiss the labour force. By February 17th most branches had agreed to call off the the strike and on March 23rd Foevie agreed that the strike had not been 'suspended' but terminated. The Board of Enquiry sat between January 20th and June 9th 1956. After the publication of the Board's report the Government announced a £200,000 grant to the poorer mines. In August the Chamber of Mines and MEU recommenced negotiations, and the Chamber conceded a 6d per day wage rise to workers on the lowest rates, 1/0 to artisans and improvers, and a 10 per cent rise to all other workers, retrospective to June 1st 1956.

The dynamics of the 1955-56 strike

The dynamics of the first and second general mines strikes were remarkably similar. In 1955, as in 1947, the militancy of the MEU and the willingness of its leaders to engage in a protracted confrontation with mining capital were rooted in the need to overcome the growing alienation of the mass of workers from the union and to combat the disintegrative tendencies inherent to the social structure of the mines labour force.

Although union militancy in 1954-56 stemmed from rank-and-file discontent and action, it would be inaccurate to suggest a simple dichotomy between militant, radical workers and a passive, incrementalist union hierarchy. As this chapter has demonstrated, between 1947 and 1955 MEU officials occupied a very difficult position as broker between the mine workers, the Chamber of Mines, the Government and the CPP, each of which made contradictory demands on the union leadership. The rank-and-file, particularly the underground workers, were reluctant to participate in union affairs or to support the union financially. They would only support the union if it 'delivered the goods', but without the prior assurance of mass support the union lacked the confidence and the bargaining power it needed to win the concessions which would consolidate its credibility. This paradox was reinforced by the demands made by the other principal actors in the situation. The union was under constant pressure from the Chamber and from the Labour Department to restrict its activities to incremental wage bargaining through recognized negotiating procedures, and to avoid any direct challenge to managerial and supervisory authority in the workplace. At a time when mine labour was being subjected to a systematic effort to reinforce workplace discipline, this policy was bound to alienate the rank-and-file. Moreover, as the representative of one of the colony's most powerful interest groups, the MEU was also under pressure to conform to the changing imperatives of the CPP and TUC.

As this chapter has demonstrated, the ultimate response of the MEU to this difficult situation was to disregard the pressures exerted by the Chamber of Mines, the CPP, the TUC and the Colonial Government, and to pursue the aggressive bargaining strategy required to reunite the mines labour force in support of the union. The willingness and ability of the union leaders to pursue this strategy reveals two important features of union/worker relations in the period 1947 to 1956.

Firstly, although the mine workers frequently engaged in collective resistance independently of the MEU, and clearly perceived the union structure to be irrelevant to local-level conflicts with management, they nevertheless recognized the need for institutional resistance by a national organization representing all mine workers in order to negotiate improvements to standard wages and conditions. Moreover, as the pattern of strike activity in the mines in 1954-55 suggests, the workers were prepared to desist from taking independent action once the union demonstrated its willingness to take the initiative against mining capital. Secondly, the sequence of events which culminated in the 1955-56 strike demonstrate that at this time the mechanisms existed whereby rank-and-file workers were able to register their discontent and to force changes in union policy. Unofficial strikes, withdrawal of union membership, non-payment of subscriptions and the creation of alternative organizations were all effective means of keeping the MEU responsive to the workers' demands. The following chapters of the book describe how after 1956 the pressures exerted on the MEU by institutions and individuals whose interests were directly opposed to those of the mine workers became progressively stronger. Chapter 6 examines the impact of those pressures on the democratic mechanisms within the MEU between 1955 and 1966, and analyzes the reaction of the mine workers to the declining responsiveness of their union.

Notes

1. Gold Coast Chamber of Mines (1950) p.21; LA, General Spears, speaking to AGC AGM, 20 May 1948.

2. GNAK, C101, CL to CS, 15 March 1948.

3. Quoted by Buse (1974) p.137.

4. LA, 'AGC Mine Manager's Report', 30 September 1947.

5. AGCO, 15 December 1947.

6. COM, 30 April 1948.

7. GNA, ADM47/1/7, Director of Social Welfare minute, 3 September 1949; GNAS, File 109, 'Bibiani Mine, Inspection Report', 26 June 1948.

8. USA, 848n504/10-1647, US Consul Accra to SS Washington, 24 October 1947.

9. LDT, LT14, 'Handing Over Notes', 6 December 1949.

10. LDA, KD21, 'Speech by J.N. Sam', 5 February 1949.

11. LDT, LT17/1, LOT to RLO, 8 July 1949.

12. GNA, File 118, 'Report by Medical Officer', 22 July 1948.

13. GNAS, A344, DC Cape Coast to Commissioner Western Province, 3 October 1947.

14. SAM, 'Report on Underground Visits', n.d.

15. ARLD 1948-49, p.5.

16. COM, 27 February 1948.

17. PRO, CO96/795/31312, Governor to SS, 3 February 1948.

18. LDT, LT17/1, LOT to RLO, 8 July 1949.

19. COM, 14 April 1950.

20. COM, 31 March 1949.

21. Labour Department File SCR40002/2, Acting COL to CS, 26 January 1950, notes kindly provided by Jon Kraus.

22. GNAS, A357, Acting Senior Labour Officer circular, 11 January 1950.

23. Labour Department File SCR40002/2, loc cit.

24. LDA, 'Trade Unionism in the Colonies', 24 May 1951.

25. COM, 18 January 1950.

26. LDT, LT17/18, Chamber of Mines to LOT, 16 March 1950.

27. GNAS, C89, LOT to RLO, 2 November 1954.

28. Quoted by Buse (1974) p.138.

29. AGCI, 25 May 1952.

30. LDA, KM53, Labour Department minute, 29 October 1953.

31. COM, 14 April 1950.

32. GNAS, C89, LOT to Acting Senior Labour Officer, 22 June 1951.

33. Deputy COL to LOT, 27 December 1951, in ibid.; LDA, 'In the Matter of the Trades Disputes (Arbitration and Inquiry) Ordinance 1941, and in the Matter of a Trade Dispute Between the Gold Coast Mines Employees' Union and Messrs. Bibiani (1927) Ltd. Board of Inquiry Report', ['Bibiani Report'] p.17.

34. COM, 7 December 1950.

35. Fraser and Somerset (1958) passim. All unidentified quotations in this section are taken from this source.

36. Report of the Gold Coast Mines Board of Inquiry. In the Matter of a Trade Dispute Between the Gold Coast Mines Employees' Union and the Gold Coast Chamber of Mines, [Mines Inquiry], p.127.

37. ASG, 'Official Learners' Scheme: Notes on Supervision', n.d.

38. idem.

39. COM, 11 May 1954.

40. LDA, KA93, 'Office Note on H.H. Fraser', September 1954; Interview, R.D. Power.

41. Taylor (1911) p.14.

42. Report of the Mines Labour Enquiry Committee, p.25.

43. GNAS, C86, Senior Labour Officer Kumasi to COL, 31 October 1951.

44. Labour Officer Kumasi to Acting Senior Labour Officer Kumasi, 15 June 1952, in ibid.

45. LDT, LT17, LOT to Acting CL, 10 July 1953.

46. LDA, 'Bibiani Report', p.14.

47. Quoted by Buse (1974) p.182.

48. COM, 14 April 1950.

49. 'Gold Coast Labour', unsigned government report, July 1952, copy kindly provided by Peter Greenhalgh.

50. LDT, LT7/3, LOT to General Secretary MEU, 27 January 1953.

51. LDA, KA93, Labour Department minute, 17 June 1954.

52. The Ashanti Times, 11 July 1952.

53. 'Gold Coast Labour'.

54. COM, 17 February 1950.

55. GNAS, C86, Labour Officer Kumasi to Senior Labour Officer Kumasi, 24 January 1952.

56. 'Gold Coast Labour'.

57. GNAS, C409, LOT to COL, 22 February 1955.

58. LOT to COL, 4 March 1955, in ibid.

124

59. MEU Branch President Nsuta to General Secretary MEU, 12 May 1955, in ibid.

60. LOT to COL, 29 July 1955, in ibid.

61. COM, 17 May 1955.

62. GNAS, C409, LOT to RLO, 15 November 1955.

63. AGCI, 19 December 1955; GNAS, C409, LOT to RLO, 8 November 1955.

64. RLO to COL, 1 December 1955, in ibid.

Chapter 6

UNION ATROPHY AND WORKER REVOLT: THE CPP PERIOD, 1956-1966

As we are aware, in the past trade unionism in
Ghana was different, we fought colonial oppressors.
Today it is our task to re-educate ourselves and
the working peoples that we are no longer fighting
a foreign power, but we are building a new socialist
country according to our own conditions. We must
protect the state's property as our own, we are
working for our state and our government.

M.B. Rockson, National Chairman Ghana Mine
Workers' Union May 1965.

In 1947 and 1955 the Mines Employees' Union had been forced to
organize general strikes for higher pay by the strength of pressure from the rank-and-file workers. Only by adopting an aggressive posture in negotiations with the Chamber of Mines and by ignoring the Chamber's threats and compromise offers had the union
leadership been able to win and retain the support of the militant
mine workers. Between 1956 and 1966 the MEU (renamed the Mine
Workers' Union - MWU - in 1958) came under mounting pressure
to abandon its policy of aggressive wage bargaining, to suppress
rank-and-file demands, and to conform to the imperatives of
mining capital and the post-colonial state. This chapter examines
the origins of those pressures, and demonstrates how they progressively alienated the mine workers from their trade union.

The Mine Workers' Union and the Political Economy of Independence, 1956-1960

After 1956 a number of moderating influences were exerted
on the policy of the MWU. The most immediate of these influences
was the desire of the union leadership to avoid any further protracted confrontations with mining capital. After the 1955-56
strike the Chamber of Mines adopted an extremely aggressive attitude towards the union, threatening to withdraw from all the
negotiating procedures established during the previous decade,
and placing severe restrictions on the freedom of MWU officials to

visit workers in the mines. The Tarkwa Labour Officer reported that the Chamber's policy was 'calculated to force the organization to die' and that 'the union as a national organization is bound to suffer for some time to come, if not for ever'.[1] In view of this punitive attitude, Foevie and the NEC had little choice but to adopt a low profile and hope that the Chamber would continue to recognize the union. In fact, the Chamber did appreciate the value of dealing with a single workers' organization and soon approached the MWU with an offer of reconciliation. The union leadership accepted the offer, and in May 1956 the two bodies began to discuss ways of improving their relationship. The government's fact-finding report into the gold mines, which revealed the precarious finances of the industry, reinforced the union's desire for a rapprochement. It was, according to the Tarkwa DC:

> most educative and critical of each side of the industry towards the other, and the unpleasant results of the last strike have tempered both sides into amiability and it will, I think, take a very long time indeed for relations in the industry to become strained again.[2]

External pressures on the MWU, 1956-58

Foevie's stance at the negotiations held in August 1956 to discuss the union's three year-old wage claim revealed the full range of moderating pressures on MWU policy. Initially, Foevie maintained his demand for a 15 per cent increase backdated to the beginning of the dispute, but in the course of negotiations three factors persuaded him to accept a less favourable settlement. Firstly, the Chamber's threats of further mine closures appeared to be genuine, and Foevie appreciated that if these threats were implemented he would forfeit the confidence of the Chamber, the rank-and-file and the Government. Secondly, Foevie was under pressure from Nkrumah, prompted by General Spears and the LAC, to accept a moderate settlement which would restore the colony's reputation as a safe home for foreign investment capital. Thirdly, Foevie was encouraged to seek a quick settlement, albeit an unfavourable one, by the need to convince the rank-and file that their support for the union during the strike had produced some tangible benefits.

Responding to these pressures, Foevie urged the workers to replace strikes with 'cool deliberations', warned that further stoppages would be suicidal, and asked them to accept a settlement which fell short of the promises he and his fellow officers had made during the 100-day strike.[3] Foevie's appeals were not well received by the workers, who were dismayed by the failure of the three-month stoppage to win major concessions from the Chamber. Understandably, the labour force at T and A was most resentful about the outcome of the stoppage. When the decision to flood the shafts and abandon the mine was announced, 2,000 workers rioted and marched on the mine to demand an explanation for their redundancy. Foevie attempted to placate the workers, but came under heavy criticism for his failure to take threats of closure seriously and his inability to reopen the mine under the control of the MWU, as he had once promised.

The new moderation of the union President was echoed by other senior MEU officials. At Bibiani the Branch Secretary responded to workers' demands for another pay strike by urging them to 'stand firm in support of the union':

> He reminded his audience that the future of the mining industry was at stake, and they must now work harder and endeavour to increase production. The prosperity of the mine must be their concern and would provide greater revenue for the Government who have shown great interest in the improvement of the mine workers' conditions. He then attacked the lazy worker and said that many employees in the past have wasted their time and made a hobby of visiting the latrine during working hours. This practice must stop.[4]

Not surprisingly, the workers were puzzled when they heard such managerial sentiments from the union's officials. They accused Foevie of being bribed by the Chamber, and demanded that he should either threaten another strike or go back to his home in Togo.

Foevie was perturbed by the failure of the general strike to win back rank-and-file support for the union. He had been pushed into the strike by rank-and-file pressure, but now found that the workers did not like the consequences of their own actions. Worried by their opposition to the moderate policy he had been forced to adopt, Foevie attempted to consolidate his personal status in the union hierarchy and to insulate himself and the NEC from the vagaries of rank-and-file opinion by centralizing authority within the union. Regular elections for branch union officers were suspended on the grounds that continuity in office ensured efficient administration. Union finances were centralized to give the NEC greater control over branch executives, and the existing regional councils of branch unions were abolished because they 'appeared in the eyes of certain personages as an aid to help the branches to stand on their own in the regions and to kick against the NEC and Headquarters unconstitutionally'.[5]

Foevie also took steps to restore the union's paid-up membership, which slumped to a mere 2,995 of the 21,000 mine workers in 1956-57. In April 1958 he finally persuaded the Chamber of Mines to deduct union dues from wages, in exchange for an assurance that the union would only recruit daily paid workers. In 1947 William Gorman had rejected the union's demand for a check-off system because 'in the long run it would not be of advantage to the trade union, whose real influence must depend on the intimacy of their contact with their members'.[6] Foevie now admitted that his purpose in requesting the check-off was to insulate the union leadership from rank-and-file pressure. In December 1956 he told the Chamber:

Union officials are not free to take decisions in the best interests of the workers and the industry, because workers can invariably coerce union officials with the threat that they will not pay union dues if their wishes are not acceded to.[7]

The declining responsiveness and militancy of the MWU after the 1955-56 general mines strike was reinforced in March 1957 by the CPP's accession to power. After Independence, Nkrumah and the CPP started to tackle the two perennial problems of the post-colonial state; to consolidate political authority, and to use that authority to promote rapid economic development. Initially conditions appeared favourable for the new Government, but it was not long before the fundamental cleavages in Ghana's political system and the structural weaknesses of its economy began to emerge. Opposition movements flared up in Togoland and Accra, and the parliamentary opposition eagerly supported any manifestations of discontent with the CPP. Doubts were cast over the desirability and possibility of maintaining the liberal-democratic political system inherited from the Colonial Government, and the trade union movement, a well organized interest group with a history of anti-government activity, was now perceived as a threat to CPP hegemony. The trade unions also posed a threat to Nkrumah's economic policy. The cocoa industry was booming, but Nkrumah was determined to pursue an ambitious policy of attaining economic independence by means of externally financed industrialization. In his desire to attract capital investment, particularly for the Volta River Project, Nkrumah was forced to give guarantees that wages would be held down to allow cheap working costs on labour-intensive projects. There was, therefore, a clear convergence of political and economic imperatives pointing to the need for tighter controls over organized labour. The MWU, which represented workers in Ghana's most important industrial sector, and which had always remained independent of the CPP, naturally became a prime target for the party's strategies of institutional labour control.

The strategies employed by the CPP Government to control the MWU between 1957 and 1960 took three principal forms: legislative restrictions on the union's ability to mobilize collective resistance, the integration of the union into the party-controlled TUC, and the integration of D.K. Foevie into the new ruling elite of the post-colonial state.

The Industrial Relations Act of 1958 represented the outcome of a bargaining process, whereby the trade unions accepted new controls over their organization and activities in exchange for a range of provisions designed to consolidate their industrial power, particularly in the private sector. The Act amalgamated numerous small and powerless unions into 24 national unions, compelled employers to bargain with them, and ensured their financial stability through the compulsory check-off system. In exchange for these concessions the unions agreed to conciliation and arbitration procedures which effectively made strikes illegal, and subordination to the TUC through their integration into the organization's 'new structure' devised by Secretary-General John Tettegah. While the Act held some advantages for the smaller unions, it had little to offer the MWU. Strikes, which in 1947 and 1955 had proved necessary to win wage claims and to regain rank-and-file support, were now outlawed. The union was subordinated to an organization whose influence it had long resisted, and it gained nothing from the rationalization of small company unions or the compulsory collective bargaining and compulsory check-off provisions of the Act.

The 1958 Act generated a lively debate within the MWU and between the MWU, TUC and CPP. Initially, Foevie ignored the threats and inducements used by Tettegah to win the union's support for the legislation, and he admitted that the MWU's relationship with the TUC was characterized by 'fear, mistrust, insincerity, disloyalty and lack of confidence in each other'.[8] Foevie insisted that the union should remain independent from external interference and that it should be 'free to criticize the government of the day'.[9] In November 1958, before these issues had been properly settled, the Act became law. Recognizing that further opposition was futile, in January 1959 Foevie issued a statement regretting the 'unfortunate misunderstanding' which had arisen over the union's attitude towards the CPP and TUC:

> The miners and their union are not in any way at any disadvantage as far as the structure is concerned...and will work full-heartedly under the structure and will endeavour to observe all its approved rules.[10]

Foevie's acceptance of the Industrial Relations Act and the TUC's 'new structure' indicated his realistic appreciation of the need to secure a working relationship with the new Government, and his pragmatic desire to avoid any action which might jeopardize his own political ambitions, exclude him from the CPP's patronage network, and restrict his ability to influence party policy from within. What he had not appreciated, however, was the impact that these new restrictions on the union's responsiveness and militancy would have on the pattern of rank-and-file resistance in the mines.

Rank-and-file challenges to the MWU, 1958-60

According to the public statements of the MWU and Chamber of Mines, industrial relations in the gold mines after 1956 were extremely cordial. In March 1958 Colonel Bean, a former army officer who had joined the Chamber's administrative staff in 1944, said that 'never in my memory have relations between workers and management been so good'. Two years later the Chamber still insisted that the gold mining industry was 'a model of good relations'.[11] Strike statistics appear to support such statements, for between 1956 and 1960 the mine workers were responsible for only 6.9 per cent of all man-days lost in strikes throughout the country, a much lower proportion than in any pre-Independence period.

The relative passivity of the mine workers at this time was not surprising given the hardships they had suffered during the 1955-56 general strike, the Chamber's threats of mine closures, and the stability of real incomes between 1956 and 1958. Despite their relative infrequency and small scale, the 20 strikes which took place in the mines between 1956 and 1960 do provide some important indications about the state of union/worker relations in the industry. In many ways, the strikes of 1956-60 were very similar to those which took place in the early 1950's and which were analyzed in the previous chapter. All 20 concerned issues of workplace discipline and authority, all 20 were organized without the support of formal approval of the MWU, and at least 13 of the 20 were led by the traditionally militant underground workers. These stoppages demonstrate, therefore, that despite the MWU's acceptance of legislative restrictions on strikes, the rank-and-file retained a keen awareness of the efficacy of collective resistance and were prepared to defy their union, the Government and the law to defend their interests in this way. More significantly, as the following account of events at Amalgamated Banket Areas and Ariston demonstrates, the mine workers did not only revolt against the incipient atrophy of their union by defying its instructions, but also by attempting to establish autonomous associations which would be more effective than the MWU in leading their struggle against mining capital.

In July 1959, 200 underground workers at ABA stopped work to demand the demotion of a supervisor, a member of the Branch Union Executive who had antagonized workers by suspending an independent benefit society on the grounds that it had 'sinister motives' and was undermining the authority of the union. Management transferred the man to another section but 142 workers there also stopped work. Despite threats from the workers the man returned to his new section, where he was promptly beaten and his life threatened. Foevie was called in to resolve the situation, and he told management that the supervisor should be sent back to work, and the Industrial Relations Act 'let loose' on the workers. The MWU, he said, 'would give no room to subversive elements so exposed, who were agitating to disturb the peaceful and normal operations of the mines against the constitutional provisions of the union'. He would therefore 'recommend the immediate dismissal of these elements'.12

This confrontation took place against a broader background of rank-and-file disaffection in the Tarkwa-Prestea mines. At Ariston a Shop Stewards' Association had been formed in the early days of the union, comprising experienced workers who were empowered to act as a 'watch-dog' over the union and to audit its accounts. In 1957 the Association had become defunct, but in mid-1959 it was re-formed and was pressing branch union officials to present their accounts and to stand for re-election. The Branch Executive resisted these demands, used a new constitutional amendment to suspend elections, and successfully requested the local police to refuse a permit for a mass meeting of workers convened by the shop stewards. The union's uncompromising response to these signs of rank-and-file discontent provoked more serious opposition from the labour force. In Tarkwa a magazine clerk called David Onehene wrote to Foevie protesting about the dismissal of unofficial leaders and accusing him of being 'out to betray the underground elements through whose ability the union has been able to stand'.[13] He stated that without underground support the MWU could not exist, and warned that a Ghana Underground Mineworkers' Union would soon be formed and begin an intensive recruitment campaign.

Perturbed by these attacks on the union, the Tarkwa Labour Officer reported that such events were a 'conspicuous pointer to the way the wind is blowing in the direction of trade union structure' and described the situation as 'remarkable and alarming'. Initially, he had thought that Onehene had 'rushed in with a few fanatics with blind impetuosity to gain notoriety', but it was now clear the proposed underground union was winning support at ABA and at other mines in the area.[14] In response to this challenge, Foevie suspended Onehene from the MWU. In return, Onehene accused Foevie of being 'a liar, black imperialist and liquidator...a leader who is not prepared to listen to those who maintain him as leader'. The MWU he warned, 'should prepare for a challenge'.[15] At Ariston the shop stewards were also improving their organization against the union. In August 1959 the MWU Branch Secretary received letters from 'The Workers Body', reaffirming the demand for publication of union accounts and new union elections. The workers wanted 'honesty, diligency and justice in the union...We are still workers agitating for our rights in demanding active and helpful branch leaders'.[16] The writer of this letter, like his counterpart at ABA, was suspended by the NEC, which then proceeded to warn Mine Managers and District Commissioners of the need to ignore 'illegal' associations of workers. Even these punitive actions failed to stem the growing revolt of the rank-and-file. Early in 1960 The Workers Body reappeared in Prestea to announce that the labour force had passed a vote of no-confidence in the union executives, who had failed to hold elections for six years. In March 1960 a section of underground workers went on strike in protest against the behaviour of a Welfare Officer, and the District Labour Officer reported:

> The fact however remained that this trouble, which ought to have been handled by the union, was entirely in the hands of the workers, who were acting on their own, quite outside of the union.[17]

The workers' willingness to act and organize independently was indicative of the extent to which the MWU's responsiveness had been eroded in the short time since the general strike of 1955-56. Whereas workers had previously ignored the union when it acted too slowly or passively, the rank-and-file now began to perceive the MWU as part of the authority structure which exploited them, and actively to struggle against it. Of course, not all union officials were engaged in a systematic campaign against the rank-and-file, and during this period the MWU and CPP helped to introduce a wide range of benefits for the workers. Such benefits, however, could not prevent conflict from arising between labour and capital, and the workers now found their union very reluctant to take any action on their behalf in the event of a dispute. In 1947 and 1955 the mine workers had demonstrated their alienation from the MWU by withholding and withdrawing their membership, forcing the union leadership into a militant stance. In 1960, under an amendment to the 1958 Industrial Relations Act, the workers were prevented from leaving the union, and the MWU was unwilling to contradict CPP policy by pursuing militant demands. The process of union atrophy and worker revolt which had started in 1956 could not easily be stemmed.

The MWU and the Political Economy of CPP Rule, 1961-1964

1961 witnessed significant changes in the economic and political policies of the CPP Government. By that year, the popular expectations aroused at the time of Independence remained unfulfilled. Cocoa prices fell sharply, and the Government was forced to draw heavily upon the country's foreign exchange reserves and to introduce an austerity budget to restore the economy and sustain the drive for development. In response to the budget and the growing authoritarianism of the CPP, railway and harbour workers went on strike in the first major demonstration of mass discontent since the party took power in 1957. Tensions were also becoming evident at the top levels of the CPP hierarchy. The absence of an effective opposition encouraged factional conflict within the party and stimulated disputes between the CPP and its integral wings such as the TUC and Farmer's Council. Nkrumah purged the party and replaced experienced politicians with weaker figures who were happy to preach the quasi-marxist doctrine of 'Nkrumahism'. The leftward shift in party ideology was reflected in the Government's industrialization strategy, which restricted private enterprise and established many state-controlled corporations, including a State Gold Mining Corporation.

The intensification of state controls

These developments had many implications for the MWU and Ghana's other trade unions. The strike of railway and harbour workers in September 1961 was perceived by the CPP Government as a serious threat to its political authority. To eliminate this threat and discourage further demonstrations of mass discontent, the Government declared a state of emergency, arrested strike leaders and supporters and detained members of the United Party opposition. This uncompromising response was a clear warning to union officials and members that the state would not hesitate to use its coercive powers against them if they dared to engage in such resistance. The deterrent effect of the Government's actions was reinforced by Nkrumah's decision to intensify the existing range of state controls over organized labour by penetrating the unions with reliable party activists. This strategy had no immediate impact on the MWU, since the mine workers were perceived as far less of a political threat than the railwaymen and dockers, who shared a long tradition of political protest and who lived in municipal centres where discontent could be communicated to the wider urban population. Moreover, since Independence D.K. Foevie had proved to be a reliable union leader, prepared to use a combination of initimidation and patronage to control MWU officials and members who wished the union to regain its former militancy.

The nationalization of Ghana's gold mining industry after 90 years of expatriate ownership acted as a further constraint on the ability of the MWU to articulate rank-and-file demands. In 1955-56 four mines had closed, and in the wake of the general mines strike most mining companies gave up the fight to resist rising working costs and adopted a policy of short-term profit making by running down investment and development. When two more mines threatened to close in 1960, Nkrumah rapidly drafted legislation to prevent the closures and made an offer of about $15.4 million for ownership of the mines at Tarkwa, Prestea, Bibiani and Dunkwa. This generous bid was readily accepted and a State Gold Mining Corporation (SGMC) was formed to administer the mines, while Ashanti Goldfields and Konongo remained in private hands.

This major change in the ownership of the gold mines affected union/worker relations in three ways. Firstly, the union's role as the representative of labour was compromised by the fact that any criticism which it now levelled at management was implicitly a criticism of the Government and the CPP. The Government decided that the Chamber of Mines should continue to negotiate standard conditions of service with the MWU, but now that the Chamber was dominated by government representatives, the union's demands had to be tailored to suit the priorities of CPP policy. The union's ambiguous role was reinforced by the appointment of D.K. Foevie (now 'Life General Secretary' and Treasurer of the MWU) to the SGMC Board of Directors. Some union officials correctly perceived that Foevie's new appointment made a mockery of his position in the union, and regarded his new role as a betrayal of his experience as an aggressive negotiator on behalf of the workers. However, most officials were not in a position to question Foevie's activities. They welcomed the end of foreign domination of the mining industry, and believed that Foevie would be able to represent the interests of the union at the highest levels of management.

Secondly, the creation of the SGMC intensified the party's surveillance and control over the MWU and its officers. As Killick has written, relations between the Corporation and Government were characterized by 'a good deal of detailed interference and very little by way of general policy guidance'. Such interference was 'a logical result of the use of state enterprises to reward party activists and to extend the area of political control'.[18] Headed by a veteran CPP opportunist, E.A. Mettle-Nunoo, SGMC management acted as a channel of communication with the Government, providing it with intelligence about the activities of the MWU. Consequently it became even more dangerous and difficult for union officials to support rank-and-file demands which the state deemed unacceptable.

Thirdly, the nationalization of the gold mines gave the MWU greater responsibility for the improvement of productivity and maintenance of industrial discipline. Nkrumah now regarded the trade unions as mobilizers of the country's human resources, and declared in 1962 that their 'former role of struggling against capitalists is obsolete'. They were now to 'inculcate in our working people the love for labour and increased productivity'.[19] This doctrine was faithfully echoed in the speeches of MWU leaders. In April 1963 Foevie announced that the union's new slogans should be 'increased productivity, higher efficiency, more discipline':

> The union now has a new task. They have to teach the workers that they belong to the industry - it is the duty of the union to assist management in improving skills and to make every worker share the responsibility of getting work done, rather than always being critical of management.[20]

In contrast to earlier periods, when the MWU had supported measures designed to increase productivity on the grounds that they enabled higher wages to be paid, the union now expected workers to make greater efforts simply in gratitude for the benevolence of the CPP. To encourage such efforts, in March 1961 the MWU and Chamber of Mines agreed to 'introduce rules that would give effect to Osagyefo the President's national productivity drive'.[21] Under these rules, union officials were required to witness and approve all warnings issued by managers and supervisors to workers guilty of breaches of discipline. While this system theoretically allowed the MWU to protect its members from arbitrary treatment, in reality it merely reinforced rank-and-file suspicions that an alliance had been forged between union, management and government to prevent them from engaging in informal and collective modes of resistance.

The decline of rank-and-file resistance

Despite the new constraints placed upon the MWU's responsiveness to rank-and-file pressure in 1961-64, there is little evidence of the kind of grassroots opposition to the union that there had been in the previous three years. Indeed, the mine workers were uncharacteristically passive in this period, and the Labour Department recorded only two strikes of mine workers between 1961 and 1964.

Why then, did the mine workers not participate more frequently in collective modes of resistance at this time? A number of answers can be suggested. Despite the creation of the SGMC this was a period of great uncertainty in the gold mining industry, and the number of operating mines and consequently the demand for mine workers was declining steadily. At a time of growing unemployment the experienced underground workers who had traditionally led collective resistance in the mines were understandably concerned to retain their jobs. The Government's coercive response to the 1961 strike and the increasingly authoritarian political environment also deterred the rank-and-file from acting independently, while the close scrutiny of branch union officials by party, police and management representatives prevented them from giving covert support to unofficial stoppages. The low level of collective resistance in this period also reflected the tactical awareness of the mine workers. Although the Government's policy of wage restraint and a rising level of inflation were combining to produce a steady decline in real incomes, the rank-and-file appreciated that wage increases were negotiated at national level and could not be won through local unofficial strikes. Finally, strikes were not, of course, the only mode of resistance available to the mine workers. The termination of expatriate ownership of the mines was accompanied by a reduction in the intensity of supervision, and this assisted the mine workers to ignore exhortations from Government, management and union to work harder and more efficiently. Instead of toiling to stakhanovite standards, they displayed an attitude towards their work which was characterized by 'laziness, apathy, carelessness and lack of interest'.[22]

The one major mine strike that did take place in this period is of particular significance as it provides some rare clues to the nature of rank-and-file consciousness between 1961 and 1964. It occurred at Bibiani, a mine with a very poor record of union/worker relations. In the mid-1950's northern workers at the mine had on two occasions threatened to secede from the MWU and to establish an independent union. In January 1961 these tensions reappeared when 200 workers gathered outside the Branch Chairman's home to protest that he had private business dealings with the company and was using the union's money to finance his business. The Chairman, a close associate of D.K. Foevie, was also criticized for failing to issue minutes of Executive Committee meetings and publish union accounts. Bibiani was also the one mine where there is evidence of CPP penetration in this period. In July 1962 even Foevie was prompted to complain to the party about the interference of local CPP officials in the mine and its unsettling effect on the labour force.

The workers' latent discontent with the MWU and CPP was made manifest in the course of a relatively minor dispute with management. In December 1963 the Time Office made a mistake in the calculation of wages, and Bibiani's 1,500 workers organized a six-hour stoppage and demonstration to demand their correct pay. As the workers met to protest against management, their hostility shifted to the CPP and the MWU. At a mass meeting they called for the removal of the branch executives and of party officials working in the mine. They complained about the failure of the union to support their current protest, and demanded the return of money deducted from their wages by the union as a contribution towards the building of new regional CPP headquarters at Sekondi. The workers' attack on the CPP and MWU went beyond verbal denunciations. The MWU National Chairman, A.K. Buachie, and other union officials supported speeches made by management and threatened punitive action against the unofficial strike leaders. The workers interrupted these speeches with heckling, and as Buachie concluded his speech 'chaos and pandemonium' broke out. Stones and bottles were thrown at Buachie and workers smashed the windscreen of his car, shouting that no matter what he said they would strike again. The local Labour Officer concluded that 'the workers would accept nothing short of the removal of the branch union executives'.[23]

Foevie reported that in all his time in the union, workers had never treated its officials in this way. He stated that the workers were 'trying to rob the mine, even though it is their own, state owned', and described the protest as an 'illegal and irresponsible act of hooliganism by anti-party and anti-Government elements and their agents' against 'loyal, honest and sincere party and branch trade union officials'.[24] Foevie insisted that elections would be held at the mine only after he and the NEC were satisfied that the situation there had returned to normal. Only officially approved people at the mine, he said, were authorized to make public statements about labour matters, and in future all unauthorized spokesmen would be asked to explain their actions. Foevie's authoritarian response was not received well by Bibiani's workers. Shortly after issuing these threats he received an anonymous letter threatening another strike and telling him that a bomb made for Kulungugu, where an attack had been made on Nkrumah, had been reserved for him and the branch union executives. Rank-and-file discontent lingered on until early 1964, and when the Regional Commissioner visited the mine in January of that year, the Bibiani workers demonstrated with placards reading 'Remove the Executives'. Despite the relative passivity of the mine workers, their struggle against a trade union which was under growing pressure to act solely as an instrument of labour control had not been entirely abandoned.

Party Penetration and the Destruction of Union Authority, 1964-1966

From mid-1964 onwards the CPP adopted an entirely new approach to the question of labour control in the gold mining industry. Since the early 1940's the colonial and post-colonial state had attempted to control the mine workers by encouraging the MWU to oppose the use of collective resistance and by building up the union's authority over the rank-and-file membership. In contrast, the strategy introduced by the CPP Government in 1964-65 was designed to destroy the union's authority over the labour force and to eliminate the union's role as broker between labour, capital and state.

Given the relatively weak resistance of the mine workers in the preceding four years and the willingness of the MWU leadership to act in accordance with CPP wishes, the Government's desire to tighten its grip over mine labour can only be explained in terms of the party's subjective political imperatives. Since 1960 the party had progressively restricted and penetrated the country's major interest groups, a process that was formalized in September 1964 with the inauguration of a one-party state. Despite the success of this policy in eliminating mass opposition, Nkrumah and his party became increasingly nervous about their security. Attacks were made on Nkrumah's life in August 1962 and January 1964, bomb explosions occurred in Accra, and the judiciary, police, civil service and universities continued to show signs of independence. Political opponents were regrouping in September 1964 with the inauguration of a one-party state. Despite the success of this policy in eliminating mass opposition, Nkrumah and his party became increasingly nervous about their security. Attacks were made on Nkrumah's life in August 1962 and January 1964, bomb explosions occurred in Accra, and the judiciary, police, civil service and universities continued to show signs of independence. Political opponents were regrouping in exile, while within the party factional conflict still flourished. There was growing competition for Ghana's dwindling resources, and an accelerating inflation rate threatened to provoke a recrudescence of mass protest. Stability had not been attained, and it was therefore necessary to intensify restrictions and controls on potential sources of opposition and to extend the party's authority to areas it had not yet penetrated.

The MWU under attack

The first sign of this new strategy came in August 1964 when D.K. Foevie, General Secretary of the MWU, Chairman of the TUC, and a director of the SGMC, was appointed Managing Director of the State Gold Mining Corporation. Foevie resigned from the MWU, while A.K. Buachie became General Secretary, and M.B. Rockson became the union's National Chairman. Early in 1965 Foevie's integration into the ruling elite was completed when the former militant leader of the mine workers was elected President of the Ghana Chamber of Mines. Even in the pragmatic world of Ghanaian politics, the appointment was of unrivalled irony. As a means of consolidating state control over the MWU, Foevie's promotion appeared to be a masterstroke. Since abandoning his opposition to the Industrial Relations Act in 1958 Foevie had proved to be a willing instrument of CPP policy and mouthpiece of party ideology. He had an unrivalled knowledge of the internal politics of the mining industry and a far better grasp of the economics and technology of mining than his predecessor, E.A. Mettle-Nunoo. Foevie had five years experience at the highest levels of the TUC, many of the local and national officers of the MWU were his nominees, while amongst the rank-and-file he retained a network of paid informants and supporters. Who better to destroy the union?

Soon after his appointment as Managing Director of the SGMC, Foevie launched the CPP's assault on the union and its ability to represent rank-and-file interests. In the latter half of 1964 he began to replace MWU officials with CPP officials in negotiating meetings between management and workers, and to encourage the labour force to take their grievances not to their union, but to the party. The impact of these initiatives soon became apparent, and in April 1965 the Commissioner of Labour reported that 'recently party officials have been actively engaged in handling disputes within ABA at Tarkwa. The union's role is gradually fading out'.[25] Assured that his policy was having its desired effect, the following month Foevie formalized the CPP's penetration of the mines by announcing the creation of several new administrative committees within the SGMC, all of which included party representatives. One of these new bodies, the Joint Consultative Committee, was created to investigate the grievances and demands of the labour force, and clearly usurped the functions of the MWU. Later that year, the MWU's role as broker between management and workers was further weakened by the creation of Grievance and Disciplinary Committees in the SGMC mines. These committees were empowered to investigate all complaints made by workers and supervisors, and to administer appropriate corrective action, including the disciplining of workers who breached SGMC regulations. Newly-appointed Grievance and Disciplinary Officers were to act as secretaries to these committees.

The Grievance and Disciplinary Committees had several uses for Foevie and the CPP. By assuming many functions formerly reserved for the MWU they reduced the role and status of union officials and weakened their links with the rank-and-file. They provided the CPP with a legitimate reason for posting party officials to the mines, where they could scrutinize the attitudes and behaviour of management, union and workers. Finally, they provided Foevie with an additional instrument of personal intervention in the administration of the state-owned mines. These aims were clearly illustrated by Foevie's choice of the men appointed to the key post of Grievance and Disciplinary Officer at Tarkwa and Prestea. They were J.V.T. Kwegyir-Paintsil, former General Secretary of the Local Government Workers' Union, and R.E. Dampare, former General Secretary of the Construction and Woodworkers' Union. Both had been dismissed for dishonest practices by TUC Secretary-General, Kwaw Ampah, a personal enemy of D.K. Foevie, and both had been promised new jobs in the state sector by Nkrumah himself. Indeed, when Dampare was provided with his new post at Prestea Goldfields he was introduced to workers as 'the personal representative of Kwame Nkrumah'.[26]

The Labour Department was very wary of the new committees and their secretaries, believing that they could only create trouble in the mines. In February 1966, when Nkrumah and the CPP were eventually ousted from power, the Western Region Labour Officer revealed his concern:

Since no specific injunctions were stipulated in relation to the formation of such committees, it creates embarrassment in a case such as the SGMC where even though adequate and efficient machinery has existed on each mine for many years, Grievance Committees have been superimposed, ostensibly calculated to weaken the activities of the union in the sphere of negotiation - from the local to the national level - 'on all matters connected with employment or non-employment or with the terms of employment or with the conditions of labour of any of the employees'.[27]

Even while the CPP was still in power the Labour Officer remarked that if he were an MWU official he 'would fight tooth and nail against any attempts by management to encroach on the legitimate rights of the union.'28 In fact Rockson did complain that the Grievance and Disciplinary Committees had never been discussed at a Joint Negotiating Committee prior to their introduction, but Foevie simply dismissed this protest and proceeded to humiliate the MWU leadership by dismissing several union officials, banning Rockson's deputy from certain sections of Tarkwa Goldfields, and ordering the SGMC Maintenance Department to stop servicing the union's vehicles. Buachie bravely responded by asking Foevie whether such actions were examples of the socialism he now preached. The subsequent clash between the two men prevented any meaningful communication between the MWU and SGMC, a situation which merely furthered Foevie's purposes.

The revival of rank-and-file resistance

Foevie's campaign to destroy the authority of the union he had once led was to prove decisive in determining the pattern of labour resistance in the gold mines. Between 1964 and 1966, when Foevie was intent on destroying the MWU, the mine workers suffered a rapid decline in real earnings. The inflation rate jumped from just under 10 per cent in 1963 to 24 per cent in 1964, but money wages remained static. The MWU agreed to forego pay rises and to assist with the implementation of new price controls, but these could not prevent the downward slide of the mine workers' real income. In December 1966 Ashanti Goldfields management calculated that a single worker completing his full complement of shifts was living at below subsistence level, while married workers with dependents were now highly vulnerable to malnutrition and its associated diseases.

Of course the mine workers wer enot alone in experiencing such hardships, and the Economic Survey for 1956 revealed that 'it became obvious during the year that there was a strong undercurrent of dissatisfaction with existing wage levels, especially in the face of the rising cost of living'. Significantly, the Survey continued: 'Workers could not effectively press for [higher wages] because of the operation of the Industrial Relations Act'.29 Indeed, the mine workers' ability to resist in any way at all had been severely curtailed. The MWU could no longer articulate their interests, yet they could not withdraw from the union, refuse to pay union dues or attempt to form alternative organizations to represent their demands. Ghana's growing level of unemployment, and the Government's wage policy ensured that pay in other sectors of the economy was no better anyway. Between 1960 and 1963 the mine workers had responded in an uncharacteristically passive manner to these frustrations, but in 1964-65 their mounting discontent was expressed in the form of three major unofficial strikes, all of which attacked both management and the Mine Workers' Union.

The first of these strikes took place at Ashanti Goldfields in November 1964. AGC had enjoyed a spectacular and almost uninterrupted record of profit-making since its creation in 1897, but the CPP Government's desire to safeguard foreign investment in Ghana and its desire to retain the services of the highly-skilled expatriate staff in Obuasi had dissuaded Nkrumah from national-izing the mine. The profitability and private ownership of AGC now represented a serious obstacle to the party's strategy of labour control in the mining industry. The argument that strikes at AGC were 'anti-party' or 'anti-state' was never very con-vincing, and workers at the mine were aware that its great pros-perity would allow AGC management to concede wage rises that the SGMC mines could not affort to pay. Moreover, unlike SGMC management, the managers at AGC had been able to obstruct the CPP's efforts to penetrate the administration of the mine. In August 1963 Foevie had proposed the formation of 'workers com-mittees' at AGC which would include party officials and replace the existing local negotiating committees. This move was con-sidered 'extremely dangerous' by the Consultant Engineer, who warned that it would give the CPP 'substantial control' over labour relations in the mine. When Foevie was told by AGC that the proposal would be 'resisted to the point of law', he quietly dropped the idea.[30]

Even though the state had substantially less control over the mine workers and the MWU at Ashanti Goldfields than it had in the SGMC mines, the expatriate management in Obuasi, under the ultimate influence of General Spears in London, was just as keen to curtail the power of the MWU and to prevent it from mobilizing collective resistance. With this objective in mind, in mid-1964 the Mine Manager promoted the Branch Secretary and Chairman of the union to the managerial and supervisory positions of Personnel Officer and Shift Boss. The two men left the MWU, with the re-sult that 'the voice of the once vocal union became feeble, almost to the point of extinction'.[31] In November 1964 the mine's shaftsmen petitioned the union with a request for extra pay for Sunday work, but according to the Regional Labour Officer, 'nothing happened about the petition, the union officials did nothing about the case'. The shaftsmen then refused to work on Sundays, and when one man was dismissed for absenteeism, all his colleagues went on strike. The District Labour Officer, com-menting on a letter sent to the Mine Manager by the striking shaftsmen, reported:

I suspect the men did not send a copy of their letter to the local union on this occasion because of the weakness shown by the union from the beginning of the dispute.

Only now that the workers had struck independently and against the instructions of the MWU had local union officials 'become con-scious of their ineffectiveness and waning popularity' and moved into 'a state of rediscovery'.[32]

The strike at AGC was quickly followed by a stoppage at Konongo, a small mine which was purchased from its expatriate owners by the Ghanaian Government in 1963 and, like the mines at Tarkwa and Prestea, run at a loss by the SGMC in an attempt to protect jobs and foreign exchange earnings. In July 1964 D.K. Foevie, representing both the MWU and SGMC, had arranged for the other state-run mines to absorb some of Konongo's surplus labour. Under the terms of this agreement any worker who refused to accept a transfer forfeited the right to collect any severance pay. When the Konongo workers heard of this agreement in November 1964 they went on strike for two days to protest about the compulsory transfer clause. Local union officers failed to persuade the men to return and only the intervention of A.K. Buachie finally convinced them to end their stoppage. The General Manager of the mine warned that the men were likely to strike again and that they would not listen to the MWU:

> Because of their desire for a strict observance of the Industrial Relations Act our local union has earned the disapproval of the men to the extent that there is a move afoot to oust them.[33]

The following month, workers at the mine again expressed their dissatisfaction with local union officials and demonstrated with placards reading 'Severance Pay Not Transfer', 'Elections - None for Three Years', and 'Union Accounts to be Rendered'. Workers accused the officials of demanding money in exchange for a guarantee against being transferred, and accused them of being bribed by management. Eventually the union officials were forced to leave the mine under police protection. The following day workers held their own elections for new union officers and demanded that the General Manager recognize them as their spokesmen. Management convened a meeting of union executives, workers and a local Member of Parliament, at which the branch union was accused of 'inaction, arrogance, bribery and corruption'. In return the Branch Chairman, M.B. Rockson (who became National Chairman later that year), accused the workers of 'malice and treachery' and of being 'nation wreckers'.[34] The MP warned that if the unofficial executives met again they would be arrested. This did not happen, for as at AGC the strength of rank-andfile antagonism shocked the union officials out of their complacency and they promised to act more promptly in future. Three months later an Arbitration Enquiry invalidated the compulsory transfer agreement that Foevie had made with management.

Confrontation at Tarkwa

At the beginning of 1965 the mining industry was in considerable turmoil. Two strikes had occurred, both revealing the extent to which the mine workers had lost faith in the MWU. In January discontent spread to Prestea Goldfields, where workers also rejected the incumbent union executives and held independent elections. The national union officers were preoccupied with the clash between Foevie and Buachie, and simultaneously attempting to retain some degree of independence by resisting TUC plans for the centralization of trade union funds. At the height of this turmoil, and at a time when the mine workers' real earnings had slumped to a new low, Foevie attempted to introduce a new bonus scheme at Tarkwa Goldfields, the SGMC mine with the worst loss-making record.

In 1965 Tarkwa Goldfields was losing £69,000 per month. Productivity was falling, and warning notices to the underground workers had failed to persuade them to perform their tasks efficiently. In Foevie's words:

> Some workers had been giving false returns of numbers of holes drilled. When the fathoms reported drilled were related to production the result proved convincingly that the number of holes reported as having been drilled could be false returns.[35]

To prevent this form of bonus-cheating and to boost productivity, Foevie proposed the introduction of a new bonus scheme which would allow a closer check on the relationship between tonnage and the reported number of fathoms drilled, and which would discourage absenteeism by calculating bonuses on a gang rather than individual basis. The underground workers at Tarkwa resented these innovations, complaining that the new bonus scheme made no allowance for mechanical breakdowns and therefore penalized workers for factors beyond their control. Despite the workers' opposition, in March 1965 management, party and union representatives agreed to implement the scheme from the beginning of the next month. Foevie was aware of the strength of rank-and-file opposition to the scheme, and warned that anyone found inciting a strike would be guilty of sabotage and severely punished.

The day after the new bonus scheme was introduced, 500 underground workers walked out of the mine in protest and demanded to discuss the situation with management, using rank-and-file spokesmen rather than union officials as their representatives. The District Labour Officer reported:

> One thing is apparent all along and it is the ineffective action of the local branch union. There is no unity among the union officials who have grouped themselves into two factions, one faithful to the Chairman of the Corporation and the other loyal to the Acting General Secretary of the union.[36]

When negotiations began the workers repeated their complaint that the union had failed to resist or even explain the new bonus before its introduction. I.N. Aikins, the Branch Secretary and Deputy Chairman of the MWU, simply affirmed that the Branch Executive had agreed to the bonus and that strike leaders who opposed it should be dismissed.

Foevie was equally uncompromising. He declared that workers had no right to challenge management, and when the rank-and-file spokesmen said they would rather leave the mines than accept the new bonus he accused them of being 'a menace to the state' and invited them to go ahead with their resignations. If they did so, he said, they would lose their gratuities, receive no pay in lieu of notice, and would be evicted from company housing immediately. Any vacancies left by resignations could be filled by bringing surplus labour from Konongo to the mine. Foevie also used the strike as an excuse to attack his former colleagues in the MWU, making a series of allegations about the inefficiency and corruption of union officials. The MWU representatives left the meeting 'bullied and humiliated' by the SGMC Managing Director. The rank-and-file spokesmen were unmoved by Foevie's threats. They dared not return to their colleagues with the news that they had agreed to the new bonus. To do this, they said, would put their lives in danger and cause workers to believe that they had accepted drinks from the Corporation.

Two days later Foevie convened a mass meeting to resolve the deadlock. Foevie claimed that the present unrest was a plot to discredit him hatched by lazy workers and the unlikely alliance of E.A. Mettle-Nunoo, Kwaw Ampah and A.K. Buachie. A Dagarti student from the Winneba Ideological Institute was introduced to the workers, and he told his fellow northerners in the mine that their strike was 'unpatriotic and colonialist' and urged them to return to work. Foevie then produced his trump card, a 'referendum proforma' which each worker was invited to sign. As a coercive technique of labour control, it was the equal of anything ever devised by that arch-colonialist General Spears. It read:

> I signify hereunder my acceptance/rejection of the new bonus scheme introduced by management in its entirety. In accepting it I undertake to try it for six months without protest or demonstration. I understand in rejecting the scheme I lose my job and all benefits due to me under the Ghana Chamber of Mines Conditions of Service.[37]

Confronted with this threat, the workers agreed to accept the new system on a show of hands.

The acquiescence of the Tarkwa workers soon proved to be merely a tactical gesture. As they had threatened, they now began to resist the new bonus scheme by means of mass resignation. By May 19th 476 underground workers had given their notice to management, forcing Foevie to convene another mass meeting. The workers were equally angry with Foevie for persevering with the new bonus, and with Buachie, who had failed to attend the meeting. One machine driver mounted the platform to complain that in the previous month not a single blastman or machine driver had qualified for a bonus payment, and that of the entire labour force only 90 shovelmen had qualified for extra pay. To reinforce this point, in July the machine drivers arrived for work and went down the mine, but then refused to perform any tasks except those of the unskilled shovelmen. As only shovelmen were earning bonuses, they told their supervisors, there was no reason for them to do their normal jobs. The following day the machine drivers refused to go underground unless the new bonus scheme was withdrawn, and when this request was rejected they returned to their compounds without working. Blastmen and shovelmen joined the stoppage, and when A.K. Buachie arrived to speak to the workers he had to be protected from them by local union officials.

A trial of strength between the Tarkwa workers and D.K. Foevie was now emerging. The SGMC Managing Director wanted to take punitive action against the strikers, but the workers told CPP officials that they had no intention of returning to the mine until a date was fixed for the withdrawal of the new bonus. According to the SGMC Secretary:

> Judging from the attitude of the miners there can be no doubt that they are in no mood whatsoever to accept any sound suggestions of any kind unless their paramount demand seeking the withdrawal of payment of bonuses per month is accepted without condition attached.[38]

The tide was now turning against Foevie. At two important meetings held to discuss the situation at Tarkwa, the Regional TUC Secretary and A.K. Buachie made a spirited defence of the MWU and argued that the current unrest in the mines was the inevitable result of allowing CPP representatives to intervene in the industrial relations of an industry they knew nothing about. All the participants in these meetings stressed the urgent need to end the confrontation, and A.K. Buachie attempted to seek his revenge on Foevie by suggesting that the easiest way to end the dispute was to suspend the new bonus scheme. This proposal was accepted, and Foevie had no choice but to announce his willingness 'to compromise in any decision taken with regard to the new bonus scheme'. There was, he admitted, 'no alternative but to take the easy way out', and the bonus scheme was withdrawn.[39] The Tarkwa workers returned to work in a jubilant mood and the Regional Labour Officer observed that 'peace has returned to ABA Tarkwa, and I have every confidence that will be so for a long time to come'. In fact, the workers were so emboldened by their victory that they continued their go-slow for two weeks, ignoring disciplinary measures by arriving for work at their leisure. When 46 men were locked out for arriving late one morning, they simply 'went proudly home'.[40]

Foevie had suffered a humiliating defeat at the hands of the Tarkwa workers and was determined to seek revenge. In the first two weeks of August 1965 he dismissed the men who, he claimed, had organized the last strike, and dismissed seven other workers. These included a machine driver found inciting workers to organize another strike and a clerk who had the temerity to tell Foevie, 'Do you think we are going to take all that nonsense from you; for us to sit down here and for a Frenchman to come and dictate to us'. Surprisingly, these dismissals did not provoke further protest, and the District Labour Officer wrote that 'Mr. Foevie's action, although drastic, risky and dangerous, has yielded good results'.[41] The MWU, he reported, supported the Managing Director's action and would not assist the dismissed workers in any way.

Although Foevie's intimidatory tactics prevented further outbreaks of collective resistance at Tarkwa, it soon became clear that he had only removed the symptoms rather than the causes of the mine workers' mounting discontent. In January 1966 the

Government announced a reorganization of the Chamber of Mines gratuity scheme, so that only workers who reached the retirement age of 60 or were forced to leave the industry through ill health would be entitled to collect their accumulated benefits. On hearing about this plan, workers at Prestea and Bondaye sections of Prestea Goldfields warned their union representatives that if the decision was not reversed within a month they would stop work until all the gratuities were paid out. The Prestea branch union officers convened a mass meeting and appealed for loyalty to the MWU and the Government. Workers booed and hooted throughout the speeches and mounted the platform to reaffirm their opposition to the plan and to prevent the Grievance and Disciplinary Officer, R.E. Dampare, from speaking in support of the Government's proposal. Workers at the Bondaye section reacted in a similar manner, and at a mass meeting one worker made an eloquent statement of their case:

> Sometimes people think that underground work is like those who work in offices and in the fields where they have natural air. We have no sun or rain underground. Our air is machine air, so we grow older than our age. How can a worker remain in such a place until he is 60 years of age or work until he is weak to die before he is retired and paid his gratuity. We do not want our monies to be paid to anybody when we are dead. We worked for it so we must enjoy the money ourselves. If the Government now feel that the mines are no good as the former managers said before this was bought then they could close it. Whether this letter come from the President, Government or the Cabinet we don't care, we want our old system.[42]

The workers cheered this speech and walked out of the meeting, shouting at MWU officials. The District Labour Officer reported that the workers were unanimous in their opposition, that the MWU could do nothing to placate the workers and that union officials were now very afraid of the rank-and-file.

Following a series of secret meetings between workers at Prestea and Bondaye, the workers adopted the new tactic of a go-slow. At Bondaye tonnage per man dropped from 9.33 in December 1965 to 7.8 in January 1966, and at Prestea overall tonnage dropped from 10,815 in the first half of January to 7,891 in the second half. Sawmill output fell by over 54 per cent in a month, and throughout the Prestea and Bondaye sections headmen reported 'no amount of control from supervisory staff would improve the situation'.[43] When Buachie and Rockson arrived at Prestea on February 18th, and told the workers to end their go-slow and to allow the union to fight their causes for them, the reaction of the rank-and-file was predictable. At Prestea section the workers interrupted the MWU leaders with 'hooting and indecent behaviour', while at Bondaye a mass meeting of 450 workers ended in 'pandemonium'.[44]

This incident provided a fitting end to a decade during which the mine workers had witnessed a steady decline in the willingness of the Government and the Mine Workers' Union to protect their interests and respond to their demands. Six days later the CPP was ousted from power by a group of military and police officers who formed the National Liberation Council Government (NLC). The new military regime remained in power until September 1969, when Dr. K.A. Busia's Progress Party (PP), an organization closely associated with the outgoing military council, won a convincing electoral victory and formed a new civilian government.

The dilemma of the MWU

The strikes at AGC, Konongo and Tarkwa in 1964-65 marked the return of the mine workers' traditional militancy after a four-year period of passivity. In comparison with the general strikes of 1947 and 1955-56 these strikes were short-lived and on a small scale. But, given the unprecedented authoritarianism of the state and mine management in this period, the mine workers' resistance represented a rare challenge to the political economy of CPP rule:

> If such unofficial strikes were tolerated by the union and Government, strikers would continue to make fantastic demands, the result of which may well be disastrous in as much as the security of the state is concerned.45

Government officials who perceived the mine workers' resistance in this way had no doubt that it was a direct result of the new labour control strategy introduced by the state through the person of D.K. Foevie. In the words of the Tarkwa Labour Officer, the 'peaceful coexistence' which had been established in the mines after 1961 was 'severely sabotaged by the maladministrative procedure now in force in the gold mining industry. The Industrial Relations Act has been set aside and blatantly sidestepped by the new Chairman of the SGMC'.46

As this statement suggests, the new strategy of labour control that Foevie was allowed and encouraged to pursue proved within a very short time to be self-contradictory and self-defeating. Foevie's strategy meant that rights and procedures established by law and precedent were ignored, while workers were subjected to increasingly arbitrary treatment. Managerial personnel with no experience or understanding of the industry were appointed to influential positions, and workers with party connections received favourable treatment in matters of pay and promotion. Meanwhile, the mass of workers experienced a steady decline in both their standard of living and their ability to engage in informal and collective modes of resistance. Foevie's policies not only exacerbated rank-and-file grievances, but also destroyed the state/management/union alliance which had effectively eliminated mine worker resistance between 1960 and 1963. In their attempt to destroy the MWU's potential as a source of political opposition, Foevie and the CPP also destroyed the means whereby rank-and-file grievances could be communicated to management for resolution. Understandably, the workers had no confidence in the party-dominated committees introduced to replace the MWU.

Foevie's campaign against his former union exacerbated the longstanding dilemma of the union's officials. Acting as brokers between workers, management and the state, in 1947 and 1955 they had been forced to respond to rank-and-file demands and to ignore the threats and warnings of management and the state. Between 1957 and 1964 they became insulated from rank-and-file pressures, but their authority was maintained by means of their harmonious relationship with management and the state. Now, in 1964-65, they were still expected to act as brokers between the three parties at times of crisis, but had the support and co-operation of none. By 1965 the union was so preoccupied with defending itself from attacks by workers on one hand, and management and the state on the other, that it had neither the willingness nor the ability to pursue normal trade union goals. This trend was epitomized by the MWU Annual Conference of May 1965. The NEC's report to the conference expressed almost no concern for issues such as wages and welfare, and concluded with the recommendation that the rules of the union should 'be rigidly implemented to discourage subversive elements within the union'.[47] By 'subversive elements' the NEC meant both the party representatives who were attempting to destroy the union, and the workers who were attempting to take action independently of it. As Chapter 7 will show, the change of government in February 1966 did little to resolve the dilemma of the MWU, and nothing to check the process of union atrophy which had started in 1956.

Notes

1. GNAS, LWR28/21, LOT to RLO, 10 March 1956.

2. GNAS, F121, 'Handing Over Notes, Tarkwa Labour Office', 12 May 1957.

3. GNAS, LWR28/21, 'Notes on Mass Meeting', 23 August 1956.

4. Labour Officer Dunkwa to LOT, 21 June 1956, in ibid

5. 'MEU NEC's Report, 5th to 7th April 1958', in ibid.

6. Gorman Award, p.16.

7. LDA, K14, 'Minutes of the 18th MJNC', 12 December 1956.

8. GNAS, LWR28/21, loc cit.

9. General Secretary MEU to RLO, 29 April 1958, in ibid.

10. DAT, T18, LOT to RLO, 4 March 1959.

11. The Ashanti Times, 10 March 1958; ARCM 1959-60, p.5.

12. DAT, T18, 'Resolution of the MWU NEC', 19 August 1959.

148

13. D. Onehene to D.K. Foevie, 28 July 1959, in ibid.

14. LOT to RLO, 14 August 1959, in ibid.

15. D. Onehene to General Manager ABA, 26 August 1959, in ibid.

16. 'The Workers' to General Secretary MWU, 18 August 1959, in ibid.

17. GNAS, C109, 'Tarkwa Labour Office Quarterly Report', 31 March 1960.

18. Killick (1978) p.244.

19. Osagyefo in Kumasi, p.17.

20. 'Speech by D.K. Foevie, 20 November 1963', in Ghana Mine Workers' Union (1964); LDA, KL4/8, 'Minutes of the 8th MSNC', 10 April 1963.

21. LDA, KL4/7, 'Minutes of the 4th MSNC', 22 March 1961.

22. SGM, 'Circular to Shop Stewards', 28 September 1964.

23. LDT, LT12, LOT to RLO, 4 December 1963.

24. LDA, KL188/1, D.K. Foevie to Mine Manager Bibiani, 5 December 1963.

25. LDT, LT4, COL circular, 8 April 1965.

26. Report on the Committee of Enquiry Into the Recent Disturbances at Prestea [Prestea Report], p.36.

27. LDT, LT12/8, enc. in RLO to CL, 17 May 1966.

28. ibid.

29. Quoted by Seidman (1968) p.197.

30. ASG, 'Consultant Engineer's Memorandum', 7 August 1963.

31. LDK, LAR16/15/1, RLO to COL, 22 March 1965.

32. RLO to COL, 17 November 1964, in ibid.

33. LDA, KL317, General Manager Konongo to COL, 25 November 1964.

34. Labour Officer Konongo to RLO, 19 January 1965, in ibid.

35. LDT, LT12, 'Notes of a Meeting', 30 July 1965.

36. LOT to RLO, 3 April 1965, in ibid.

37. 'Referendum Proforma', 7 April 1965, in _ibid_.

38. 'Report by T. Ennison', 28 July 1965, in _ibid_.

39. 'Notes of a Meeting', 30 July 1965, in _ibid_.

40. GNAS, LWR28/8, RLO to CL, 5 August 1965.

41. LDT, LT12, LOT to RLO, 11 August 1965.

42. LDA, KD13/10, Industrial Relations Officer Ariston to General Manager Ariston, 24 January 1966.

43. LDT/12/8, 'Senior Labour Inspector's Notes', 7 February 1966.

44. LOT to RLO, 21 February 1966, in _ibid_.

45. LDA, KL331/1, 'Report by Principal Labour Officer', 2 August 1965.

46. LDT, LT12, LOT to RLO, 2 April 1965.

47. GMU, 'Minutes of the 19th Annual Delegates Conference', May 1965.

Chapter 7

UNION ATROPHY AND WORKER REVOLT
UNDER MILITARY AND CIVILIAN REGIMES, 1966-1980

When people are rioting, the first people they get
at are persons in authority.

G.W. Mensah, Counsel for Prestea Goldfields
workers, July 1968.

The period 1966 to 1980 was one of significant changes in Ghana's
political economy, and a time of sharp fluctuations in the pattern
of labour resistance and control in the gold mining industry. Politically, the period witnessed the National Liberation Council's
overthrow of the CPP Government in 1966, a return to civilian
rule under the Progress Party in 1969, and a second coup which
brought to power the National Redemption Council led by Colonel
I.K. Acheampong. Economically, the downward trend of the
country's performance initiated in the latter years of CPP rule
continued unabated, and was manifested in the form of rampant
inflation, serious shortages of essential commodities, and an explosion of illegal economic activities known collectively as kala-
bule. In the mining industry, the mine workers exhibited relatively few signs of discontent for the two years following the 1966
coup and the five years following the 1972 coup. In 1968-71 and
in 1977, however, the mine workers took part in two waves of
strikes and riots of a violence and militancy unprecedented in the
long history of their struggle. This chapter examines that pattern
of resistance.

The Revolt Against Authority, 1968-1971

During the last two years of CPP rule, the mine workers had
shown a growing sense of discontent and a renewed willingness to
express that discontent in the form of collective action against
management, government and union officials. This new militancy
ended abruptly, but temporarily, with the military coup of February 1966. Productivity, which had fallen dramatically in 1964-
66, rose by over 20 per cent in the first year of National Liberation Council Government, and no strikes were recorded in the

mines between February and December 1966. By the end of the year, signs of discontent were beginning to reappear. AGC management reported 'amazing increases' in absenteeism and labour turnover, and concluded that 'perhaps the simplest way for the unhappy, dissatisfied employee to express his feelings is to stay away from work or resign'.[1] Nevertheless, the mine workers still appeared reluctant to protest collectively or overtly, and by the end of 1967 only three minor strikes had taken place.

Between 1968 and 1971 this pattern of resistance changed dramatically. In those three years an explosion of protest took place throughout the gold mining industry. At Ashanti Goldfields there was a week-long general strike in March 1969, culminating in a riot during which two mine workers were shot dead by the police, another died of stab wounds, and 28 other people were injured. In June and July the following year, the mine's 6,500 workers withdrew their labour for almost three weeks, and again scenes of intense conflict took place. Indeed, such was the fear of management that the armed forces were requested to intervene and arrangements were made for the evacuation of the mine's expatriate employees and their families. At Prestea Goldfields major strikes took place in May 1968 and December 1970. The former stoppage escalated into a large-scale riot in which one policeman was killed and several managers, supervisors and union officials received severe beatings at the hands of the workers. Tarkwa Goldfields was the scene of almost continuous unrest between March 1968 and June 1969. As in Obuasi, senior staff at the mine were 'living in perpetual fear' as a result of the workers' actions, which included a series of bloody clashes with armed police and a number of attacks on managers and their property.[2] The smaller mines were not immune from these trends. Strikes and disturbances took place at Konongo in January and March 1969 and September 1971, at Bibiani in January 1971, and at the alluvial Dunkwa Goldfields in June 1969. Altogether, the 19,000 mine workers were responsible for over 200,000 man-days lost during this period, approximately 43 per cent of the country's total.

Why did the pattern of labour resistance in the mines change so dramatically in this period? The relative passivity of the mine workers between 1966 and 1968 was largely a reflection of the high expectations aroused by the NLC coup and the promises made by the new Government. The mine workers had suffered increasing material hardship in the latter phase of Nkrumah's time in power, and they, like workers throughout the country, were elated by the new administration's pledges to check the decline of the national economy, to eliminate corrupt and extravagant government, and to return the country to democratic civilian rule. With the CPP ousted and the new ruling council in power, the mine workers believed that the longstanding decline in the purchasing power of their wages would be reversed and that the MWU would be free once again to represent their interests in an effective manner.

In the first year of military government these expectations were partially fulfilled. Real incomes began to rise for the first time since 1960, and old disputes between the mine workers and the CPP over Social Security payments and gratuity qualifications were settled to the workers' satisfaction. Their hopes of a revival in the trade union movement and the MWU were also confirmed. In an attempt to consolidate popular support and encourage the articulation of pent-up demands, the NLC resisted the temptation to abolish the TUC. Instead, the organization was purged of CPP loyalists and provided with a new Secretary-General, B.A. Bentum, a man with genuine trade union experience and who had a public commitment to an independent and effective labour movement. In August 1966 union elections were held in the MWU, and in a keenly contested election M.B. Rockson was elected National Chairman, while I.N. Aikins from Tarkwa Goldfields replaced the detained General Secretary, A.K. Buachie. The Labour Officer in Tarkwa reported a new air of optimism amongst the mine workers and predicted:

> Now that the Ghanaian mine workers have found a new leader, diametrically opposed to his forerunner in administration and method of approach, it is anticipated that the mine workers will be better off.[3]

The violent strikes and riots which took place throughout the mining industry between 1968 and 1971 were soon to demonstrate that his and the workers' optimism about life under the NLC and the Progress Party were unfounded. In order to explain why the peace established in the mines in 1966-67 was shattered so spectacularly in 1968-71, the following analysis identifies the individuals and organizations who were the targets of the mine workers' hostility in those disturbances, and examines their role in the hierarchy of authority in the gold mining industry of post-coup Ghana. The analysis reconstructs the major characteristics of the mine workers' consciousness, and demonstrates how their apparently chaotic resistance represented a coherent critique of the Ghanaian political economy under the NLC and its civilian successor, the Progress Party.

Targets of attack: senior staff

Between 1968 and 1970 the mine workers' most intense hostility was directed at senior staff and the visible emblems of managerial privilege. At Prestea workers ransacked the Mine Manager's office and the Senior Staff Club. The SGMC Chairman and Secretary were forced to take refuge from the workers in police quarters, while the Mine Secretary and Accountant were caught and severely beaten. At Tarkwa striking workers attacked the Mine Manager's office and a Mercedes car belonging to an SGMC director, and a bus used to transport senior staff to and from the mine was badly damaged. Three senior managers were assaulted and seriously injured, and their bungalows ransacked and looted. The SGMC Managing Director was captured by the workers, dressed in the clothing of an underground labourer, and forced to carry mining tools at the head of a demonstration. In Obuasi AGC workers attacked the Mine Manager's car, forced other managers into hiding and looted the company store.

These attacks and assaults had their origin in the changing power structure of Ghana under the NLC and PP governments. As suggested earlier, in 1966 the NLC needed to consolidate popular support amongst mass interest groups such as the wage labour force and was therefore prepared to make some concessions to them. However, once established in power, both the NLC and PP pursued policies that were inimical to working class interests. In order to broaden their power base, the conservative military and police officers of the NLC entered into an alliance with other reactionary groups which had been excluded from power by the CPP, and which were to form the nucleus of the Progress Party. As a result, the administrative and professional elites, traditional rulers and large businessmen all received a wide range of allowances and concessions designed to boost their income and social status. In contrast, the NLC and PP, encouraged by external capital in the form of the International Monetary Fund and multi-nationals such as Lonrho, had little to offer the working class except rigid wage restraint, mass dismissals and drastic retrenchment.

The elitist policies of the NLC and PP affected both the economic and social status of the mine workers. Between 1966 and 1969 the mine workers' real income fell by 5 per cent, whereas the purchasing power of senior staff salaries rose by at least 15 per cent. Members of management became increasingly indifferent to the needs and grievances of the labour force, and complaints about the deterioration of working and living conditions in the mines were systematically ignored. Such arrogance was typical of the attitudes shared by the beneficiaries of Ghana's new power structure. Senior staff in the mines naturally identified with the new ruling alliance and became provocatively conscious of their privileged status. At Tarkwa, for example, the Mine Manager supported his complaint about the 'apalling state of discipline on the mine' by pointing to the fact that 'workers refuse to doff their hats or stand up, even when the Managing Director passes by'.[4] At Prestea the Chief Security Officer was known to wash his hands whenever an underground worker left his office, while at Konongo the Resident Engineer provoked a strike when he refused to soil his car by conveying a bloodstained injured worker to hospital.

The workers' assaults on senior staff also represented a protest about the failure of the new administrations to rid the management structure of corruption and nepotism. Two prominent targets of the workers' attacks were R.E. Dampare and J.V.T. Kwegyir-Paintsil, the men selected by Foevie and the CPP to undermine the MWU in 1964-65. After the coup both men were demoted and transferred, but they refused to leave their posts and the demotions were eventually revoked. The Labour Department, like the workers, found it 'mysterious the kind of influence Mr. Dampare and Mr. Paintsil wielded on the Board of Directors'.[5] Another target of the Prestea workers was S.K. Acquah, one of Foevie's lackies who remained Accident Prevention and Safety Officer at the mine, even though 'he himself admitted that he has no training at all in the prevention of accidents and safety'.[6]

Labour Department officers had no doubt about the connection between managerial arrogance and corruption and the workers' violent attacks on senior staff members. One officer condemned the 'frigid attitude' of managers who were 'sitting on an ivory tower removed from the practicalities of working conditions'. While workers' grievances were being ignored and bonuses going unpaid, senior staff were 'flying about in Mercedes Benz' and running up huge bills on the SGMC expense account. The Labour Department concluded that 'ostentatiousness beclouds the vision of top management from discerning grievances which, accumulated as time passes, come out in the form of riots'. The workers' violent assaults reflected 'the resentment of those who feel they have been ignored or rejected or even oppressed by outmoded and inflexible bureaucratic systems'.[7]

In their attacks on senior staff therefore, the workers were revolting against the emerging power structure of post-coup Ghana, its unequal distribution of rewards and the elitist ideology of its ruling class. Nowhere was this aspect of the workers' consciousness more clearly expressed than at Ashanti Goldfields, where the longest and most violent strikes took place. The immediate cause of these stoppages was a demand for an ex gratia award or severance payment following a successful takeover bid for the mine by the British multinational, Lonrho. The Government took a 20 per cent holding in the mine but promised Lonrho complete managerial freedom and full assistance in expanding the company's interests in Ghana. The Adansi chiefs who owned AGC's large concession area were given generous financial inducements to accept the takeover bid, while senior staff were assured that the extraordinary privileges they enjoyed would be maintained. The workers' demand for severance payment was based on an accurate perception that while government, chieftaincy and management, the new ruling alliance, had benefited from the change of ownership, they, the producers of the mine's great wealth, had been offered nothing.

Supervisory and disciplinary personnel

A remarkable feature of labour resistance in the mines between 1968 and 1971 was the large number and the violence of the attacks made by workers on managers and senior labourers responsible for supervision, discipline and security. At AGC the Mines Police Office was ransacked and sentry boxes manned by security officers were destroyed. Security vehicles were attacked and rations destined for Mines Police were stolen from a lorry. Senior foremen who tried to persuade workers to end their strikes were heckled and abused by their colleagues. At Prestea the workers' anger focused primarily on R.E. Dampare, who was not only a former apointee of the CPP, but had also been responsible for the maintenance of discipline in the mine. The Prestea workers also chased the Senior Timekeeper into hiding, attacked the security barracks and demanded the dismissal of the Chief Security Officer. The most determined and violent attacks on disciplinary and supervisory personnel took place at Tarkwa, where the Labour Controller, Underground Manager, Medical

Officer, Mine Secretary, Acting Chief Security Officer and the Shift Bosses were all the targets of attacks by angry workers.

It is not surprising that in this period of intense conflict some of the first targets of the workers' hostility should be those individuals most directly and visibly responsible for the control of the labour force. Indeed, the intensity of that control steadily increased during this period, partially as a result of the newly authoritarian managerial attitudes discussed earlier, and partially as a result of the NLC and PP's insistence that the workers' unwillingness to work hard and efficiently should not be allowed to impede the revitalization of a declining industry. At Tarkwa Goldfields, for example, a new form of incentive bonus was introduced in September 1966 which could be withheld at the discretion of the Labour Controller or Senior Timekeeper as a punishment for offences such as unauthorized absence, unpunctuality, indiscipline and refusal to obey instructions. Similarly at AGC, still a highly profitable enterprise, the takeover by Lonrho led to a new campaign to boost productivity by increasing the level of underground supervision, reducing labour complements in work gangs, and by a general reinforcement of security within the mine. Underground workers who were now subjected to anus examinations to prevent them from secreting stolen gold in that part of their anatomy, not surprisingly considered Lonrho to represent the unacceptable face of supervision. Neither were they impressed by the Chief Security Officer's assault on their freedom within the workplace. As the following list demonstrates, like the Taylorist onslaught of the 1950's, this campaign was designed to eliminate every conceivable mode of informal resistance:

Mines Offences Entailing Dismissals of Miners[8]

Mashing or possessing gold quartz
Using helmet for mashing
Helmet bearing evidence of mashing
Possessing mercury
Taking mercury underground
Stealing gold product & concentrate
Loitering on wrong level
Being found idle on wrong level
Chipping rich gold ore
Collecting rich ore in stope/crosscut
Passing by ladder to wrong level
Clocking on and failing to go underground, or escaping
Overstaying underground
Surfacing earlier than closing time
False claim of overtime
General stealing on surface
Deliberate loss of underground lamp
Going underground without authority
Bribing or corrupting security men
Throwing away exhibit when being searched
Threatening and fighting underground
Illegal blasting

By attacking the individuals responsible for the formulation and imposition of such rules, the mine workers were using a crude but effective means of defending their freedom within the workplace and resisting the efforts of management to control their productivity. This aspect of the mine workers' actions was made most explicit at Tarkwa, where the underground workers engaged in a lengthy personal vendetta against the Labour Controller 'for his part in enslaving them'. 'The workers', it was reported, 'want his blood and nothing short will satisfy them'.[9] This quest for freedom within the workplace was not entirely negative, for the Tarkwa workers also proposed that the Labour Controller and Underground Manager should be replaced by former underground workers, and that worker representatives should be appointed to the Labour Control Office, Time Office and Hospital. Predictably, this attempt to secure a small measure of workers' control was rejected by management. Even so, the attacks made on supervisory and disciplinary staff between 1968 and 1970 were to prove a particularly successful form of resistance to the extension of managerial authority in the mines.

The state

The third major target of the mine workers' resistance between 1968 and 1970 was the Ghanaian state and its coercive agencies. At Prestea up to 500 workers armed with sticks, stones and iron rods attacked the Police Station and police barracks. Striking workers assaulted policemen posted at the mine, leaving 12 badly beaten, one seriously injured and one dead. The Inspector of Police believed that the workers were 'determined to kill him' and called for three armed platoons of police reinforcements to restore order and to prevent a threatened bomb attack on the mine.[10] In Tarkwa 2,000 workers armed with bows and arrows, sticks, cudgels and iron rods marched into Tarkwa on two occasions 'like an invading army'.[11] They clashed with armed police in a series of violent confrontations, in the course of which the police used teargas, shot and wounded four workers and arrested a further 60. Workers blocked the Tarkwa to Abosso road and when they were arrested, their colleagues threatened to blast the Tarkwa Court with stolen explosives. During the strike of June 1970 at AGC the Government reported that 'the strike is of grave concern. It is learnt that workers at times deliberately provoked the police in order to lure them into a strife'.[12] This was not entirely surprising, for in March the previous year police had responded to the workers' demonstrations by using teargas and bullets, killing three workers and leaving another nine wounded. In the June 1970 strike the Obuasi mine workers participated in one of Ghana's most dramatic demonstrations of working class power and solidarity. For three days armed workers effectively controlled the town. The police were 'powerless to intervene and themselves afraid', and a management representative went to Kumasi 'to stress seriousness of situation and urge calling in the troops'.[13]

The mine workers' hostility towards the coercive agencies of the Ghanaian state was a direct result of the willingness of both the NLC and PP to use the police, army and judiciary as weapons in their assault upon Ghana's working class. Although the NLC was initially committed to a liberalization of political life, this soon proved to be a very qualified commitment. Strikes were perceived to be a threat to national security (i.e. the security of the ruling class) and stern measures were promised to eliminate them. Even the relatively liberal Labour Department could not dissuade the Government from adopting a punitive attitude towards strikers, and in December 1966 the Department was told to instruct Labour Officers that 'the police should be alerted to arrest the leaders of any group of workers who embark on strikes'.[14] As a result of this instruction, the Labour Officers' former harmonious relationship with the mine workers was destroyed, and they too became the target of verbal and physical assaults.

The police, unlike the Labour Officers, were very willing to play the role of strike breaker. Emboldened by the presence of their senior officers in the NLC, lower ranks of police adopted an aggressive attitude towards the working class and were only too happy to use force against strikers. The official report on the Obuasi disturbances, released by the civilian Progress Party administration in 1970, confirmed that the police had been guilty of 'indiscriminate firing', 'negligent and reckless behaviour' and 'extravagant use of ammunition'.[15] In view of such behaviour, it was not surprising that the official report on the Prestea disturbances should record that 'the sight of police uniforms' had 'an unfortunate effect, on underground labour in particular'.[16]

The Mine Workers' Union

The final target of the mine workers' hostility in the strikes of 1968-71 was the national and local leadership of the Mine Workers' Union. This characteristic of the workers' protest was most evident at Prestea, where the Branch Union Chairman was beaten and the Secretary was forced to seek police protection after being threatened by angry workers. They complained that the branch union was 'completely divorced from the mass of the workers' and said that they had 'genuine reason to believe that the union took instructions from management and failed to fight for their rights'.[17] In the words of the Labour Department, the relationship between the national leadership and the Prestea workers was also 'completely out of gear':

> Mr. Aikins has no support whatsoever from his followers, and scarcely ventures to address the workers during strikes, even though he may pronounce such strikes illegal.[18]

The situation at Tarkwa was very similar. Union officials were 'outspoken in condemning the strike action' but were 'unable to persuade the men to go back to work'. The branch union was 'virtually non-existent' and the Labour Department reported that that 'either the men have no confidence in the leaders or the leaders have lost touch with the men'. Workers complained that the General Secretary was 'nowhere to be seen', and the Labour

Department observed that 'several efforts to get Mr. Aikins to address the workers, even in times of peace, failed to produce results'.[19] Tension between workers and the union was also evident at the smaller mines. When Konongo workers gathered to demand the dismissal of the Resident Engineer, 'member after member condemned the local union executives and indicated the intention of the underground workers to form their own union'. Similarly, the Bibiani workers were 'wont, in times of crisis, to boycott the union', and on one occasion occupied the branch union office in protest against the union's failure to support their demands.[20]

Only at Ashanti Goldfields, now the only privately owned mine, was there any evidence of effective action by the MWU. Following the Lonrho takeover the branch union took up the workers' demand for severance pay, and having been threatened with physical violence if they agreed to a compromise with management, the local officers continued to press for the workers' demand. When management finally announced that the company would pay workers an unspecified 'dash', 'stones, sticks and other missiles were thrown by the workers, and the executives, both local and national, had to flee to safety'. Investigating the strike which followed, the official committee 'found no evidence of any appropriate action by the [national] union officers'.[21] When workers struck again the following year to demand a further payment and the release of the Committee's report, local union officers were again threatened by the workers, and told management that 'they could not do anything but to support the masses stand'.[22]

As Chapter 6 has shown, such examples of rank-and-file hostility towards the MWU were not entirely new, since similar incidents had been occasioned by the atrophy of the union under the CPP's strategies of labour control. But, given that Nkrumah had been ousted in 1966 and that the NLC had come to power with a proven committment to the restoration of a democratized trade union movement, the violence with which the mine workers rejected the MWU in 1968-71 requires further explanation.

Contrary to the mine workers' expectations, after 1966 the MWU was unable to regain the responsiveness and militancy which it had lost during the decade of CPP rule. Indeed, the external and internal constraints on the union's efficacy after the coup were, if anything, greater than they had been in the previous period. Externally, the MWU was severely compromised by the terms of the pact made between the NLC and the TUC. In return for the Government's assistance in reconstructing a decentralized labour movement, Bentum and the national union leaders agreed to 'stabilize' labour relations by urging workers to present their demands peacefully and to desist from unofficial strike action. This agreement soon proved disastrous for the unions. The Government's commitment to free trade unionism was never very strong, and legislative restrictions on official strikes remained in force. Consequently, at a time when government officials and management were pursuing increasingly provocative policies, union leaders were deprived of any real bargaining power. Workers soon discovered that when they presented their demands peacefully, those demands were either rejected or became bogged down in the slow process of formal union/management negotiation. When they tried to bypass or speed up the negotiating process by taking unofficial strike action, they found that their union leaders, attempting to preserve the fragile and unequal _modus vivendi_ established with the Government, joined with management to break strikes and punish rank-and-file activists. The unions' role as broker between the state and the working class became untenable and a wave of wildcat strikes ensued. When Bentum and the TUC finally took up the workers' cause in 1971, Prime Minister Busia promptly disbanded the TUC and introduced emergency legislation to cripple the national unions.

By the time of this national confrontation between organized labour and the state, the mine workers had already demonstrated their total lack of confidence in the MWU, and had violently rejected its leadership at national and local levels. To explain the particular timing and vehemence of the mine workers' revolt against the MWU it is necessary to examine the other constraints which perpetuated the atrophy of the union under the NLC and PP governments.

Surprisingly, in view of his intimate connections with the CPP, D.K. Foevie was not removed from the SGMC after the 1966 coup, but was allowed to retain his position as Managing Director. More significantly, he was allowed to continue his campaign to undermine the union he had once led. Six months after the coup the Western Region Labour Officer admitted:

> Ever since he assumed the reins of Dictatorship, Mr. Foevie seems to have been much more concerned with waging some sort of cold war with the union. Analyses of his speeches indicate imperceptible [sic] attempts to render the union impotent in all its activities.[23]

Foevie started his new campaign against the union by establishing his own loyalty to the new regime. All CPP officials were removed from the SGMC committees which he had established in 1964-65, and at a meeting of management and government representatives Foevie denounced 'the former corrupt regime' and gave a fulsome declaration of his support for the NLC.[24] He then turned on the MWU, accusing the union leadership of installing uncooperative officers on local Executive Committees. The following month, on Foevie's instigation, the MWU General Secretary, A.K. Buachie, was taken into 'protective custody' by the police. The Labour Department had little doubt that Foevie's tactics would perpetuate the atrophy of the union:

> Once again the Managing Director has begun to fan trouble. He controls several strategies with which to outwit the General Secretary of the MWU during negotiations. Mr. Foevie is prone to having as many tentacles in industry as advocated

by the Gestapo Regime of the ousted K[wame] N[krumah].
No one knows the differences in the duties of the Resident
Secretary, Industrial Relations Officer and Grievances Committee, let alone the branch unions. The duties of the former
two in my opinion make no room for any other body to be
charged with the redress of grievances...Plans to rig every
move of the union officials even at the forthcoming new
election of officers, spearheaded by Mr. D.K. Foevie, have
begun.[25]

For a year after the coup, Foevie used these and a variety
of other tactics to intimidate and obstruct MWU officials. He retained a network of clients in the union, and used his powers of
patronage to divide opinion within the NEC and local Executive
Committees. He used his managerial authority to dismiss, transfer
and demote uncooperative union officials, and frequently made
statements that were blatantly untrue in order to embarrass union
officers in the presence of management and government representatives. Significantly, in all these activities, Foevie appears to
have had the tacit support of the NLC, a regime which was publicly committed to the restoration of democratic trade unionism.
Thus in May 1966 the Tarkwa Labour Officer commented:

It is now indisputable that Mr. D.K. Foevie is using the NLC
to silence the union in the same way he used the name of his
former master, the selfish Dictator.

Aikins and Rockson were totally incapable of resisting this onslaught and soon lost the will to fight back. One meeting of a
negotiating committee 'turned out to be a lecture where the Managing Director of the Corporation took the floor for nearly two
and a half hours to intimidate the MWU representatives'. Foevie's
lecture 'dampened the wings of these terrified representatives of
the various branches...with a laden heart this flock of sheep
without a leader bumped into Mr. D.K. Foevie's grip'.[26] Eventually the NLC recognized that Foevie's attacks on the union might
foment rather than prevent labour unrest in the mines, and in
January 1967 he was dismissed and told to leave Tarkwa within 24
hours. By that time the MWU had been silenced for a year under
the new regime, and the mine workers were beginning to suspect
that their union would be no more responsive to their demands
now than it had been under the CPP.

With the dismissal of Foevie a major external constraint on
the efficacy of the MWU had been removed. Nevertheless, serious
internal constraints remained, and it is only by examining these
constraints that the violence of the mine workers' attacks on the
union in the strikes and disturbances of 1968-71 can be explained.

As this chapter has already suggested, within a year of the
NLC coup in February 1966, the mine workers were beginning to
exhibit signs of latent unrest and discontent. Nevertheless, the
rank-and-file resisted the temptation to express that discontent in

independent strike action, and as the Government and the TUC wished, presented their demands through the MWU. It very quickly became clear that the negotiating procedures used by the union invariably took a very long time to achieve very little. Indeed, that was the reason why the NLC was so keen to secure Bentum and the TUC's support for bureaucratic bargaining processes. The frustration which this provoked amongst the mine workers, and their growing efforts to push the MWU into more positive action on their behalf, was perceived as a major threat by incumbent MWU officials. Thus at the end of 1967 M.B. Rockson complained that rank-and-file grievances at Prestea, Tarkwa and AGC were not being 'constitutionally approached through appropriate channels' but were 'influenced by some infiltrators [who] wanted to overthrow the constitutionally elected officers'.[27] These infiltrators were in fact independent associations formed by the workers to articulate their grievances, similar to those which had briefly flourished at Tarkwa and Prestea in 1959-60. At Prestea the Shop Stewards' Association emerged once more, acting as a vigorous rank-and-file pressure group, and was joined by the Machine Drivers' Group which was formed to represent the experienced underground workers. In December 1966 the Group told the branch union officials:

It is the union that settles all mining matters and we have now seen that it is getting to three months and we have not yet heard anything about our case before you and the management...Today we beg to say that we do not want the union to interfere when we go there because we have seen that you have not been able to fulfil your promise.[28]

Similar events were occuring at other mines. At Tarkwa an Underground Workers' Committee was established by rank-and-file workers, and at Konongo underground workers also threatened to establish an independent union. At AGC management still complained that 'the local executives were unable to control the workers' and that 'decisions taken between the union and management could not be implemented by the union'.[29] This statement was soon confirmed, when the Obuasi mine workers passed a vote of no confidence in their branch union and called for new elections to be held.

The growth of rank-and-file opposition to the MWU in 1967 and 1968 worried the incumbent union leaders. If they were ousted they would lose the many privileges they enjoyed as full-time union officials and if rank-and-file discontent took the form of unofficial strike action, they would inevitably be blamed by management and the Government. As the Prestea Branch Secretary was to comment after the disturbances at that mine:

One fact of these unconstitutional strikes is that most of the workers are aware that our particulars have been taken by the Special Branch with our photographs, and are also aware that when there are strikes or trouble, the branch officers would be held responsible.[30]

In order to protect their privileges and to avert the risk of punitive action by the Government, the incumbent leadership of the MWU adopted a number of strategies to stem the incipient rank-and-file revolt. Firstly, the NEC pursued what one rebel official called 'the pernicious policy of democratic centralism'.[31] Constitutional amendments were introduced without discussion or publicity, allowing the national union officers to serve for four rather than two years. The NEC was empowered to suspend branch union elections and to dismiss and appoint branch union officers. When workers attempted to nominate retired workers as candidates for branch elections, thinking that they would be immune from managerial intimidation, the NEC introduced a constitutional amendment requiring all candidates to have worked continuously in the mines for the preceding two years.

Secondly, in the words of the Labour Department, it became 'a widespread practice for trade union officials to foil elections in order to perpetuate themselves in office'. Elections were suspended because the branch union in question was 'not at peace' or because of 'pressure of work' at the union headquarters.[32] When the branch union at the manganese mine in Nsuta rebelled and passed a vote of no confidence in the NEC, the national officers of the MWU quickly suspended the Branch Secretary for 'a diabolical and wicked plan to belittle the dignity of the leadership of the union'.[33]

Thirdly, the NEC and its clients in the branch unions used a variety of tactics to discredit prominent rank-and-file leaders and to disband rebel organizations amongst the workers. Management was naturally eager to 'support the authority of union executives with the workers to prevent the rise of splinter groups and to stop unlawful strikes' and agreed to recognize only the MWU as the workers' representative.[34] The MWU agreed that any worker could be dismissed on the nebulous grounds of 'loss of confidence' and acted in conjunction with management to dismiss potential troublemakers. At AGC and Prestea, branch unions compiled lists of 'subversives' in the labour force and forwarded these to management and union headquarters. At Bibiani the local executives and the Mine Manager joined in a 'concerted effort' to intimidate Kwaku Moshie, a worker who had organized demonstrations against agreements made between management and the branch union without reference to the rank-and-file.[35]

The most vigorous campaign against rank-and-file autonomy was waged by the Prestea branch union. The Secretary, E.G. Williams, urged management to 'take firm and concrete measures against subversionists within the mine'.[36] He asked the police to refuse permits for mass rallies convened by the Shop Stewards' Association and Machine Drivers' Group, regularly requested the Mine Manager to take action against the leaders of these bodies, and invited Rockson to Prestea 'to dissolve the Shop Stewards due to their subversive actions against the union officials'.[37] In an attempt to discredit Augustine Dagarti, his arch-enemy in the Machine Drivers' Group, Williams resorted to even more devious tactics. In July 1969 management, police, MWU headquarters, the

TUC and Labour Department all received a petition, ostensibly written by 24 underground chargehands and senior headmen, complaining that Dagarti was 'assuming undue authority' in the mine, encouraging opposition to supervisory discipline, 'fomenting tribalism amongst the workers' and planning to rig the forthcoming branch union elections. The Regional Labour Officer suspected that the letter was 'a move by the General Secretary behind the corridors', and police investigations confirmed that Williams and Aikins were responsible for the petition.[38]

Fourthly, the NEC attempted to ensure the success of its strategies by means of corruption, nepotism, and maladministration. NEC meetings were held irregularly, at short notice and without agenda or minutes. Auditors' reports which revealed financial mismanagement or embezzlement by branch and national officers were never released, and the NEC provided scholarships, loans and foreign travel to loyal clients in branch union committees. At Prestea, where evidence of financial irregularities was assiduously concealed, union funds were used to bribe the police officers responsible for investigating branch union affairs. In the words of the rebel Branch Secretary at Nsuta, S.K. Cudjoe, the members of the NEC 'showed the happy but guilty satisfaction of Ali Baba and his 40 thieves'.[39]

In view of the union hierarchy's cynical disregard for the interests of the rank-and-file after 1966, it is not surprising that the workers had more confidence in their own ability to extract concessions from management and the state than in the abilities of their nominal representatives in the MWU. While the workers' opposition to the MWU between 1968 and 1970 was indicative of the untenable role of the trade unions in the political economy of postcoup Ghana, it also represented a revolt by the rank-and-file against a wilfully oligarchical leadership which put personal interests before those of the union membership. Nowhere is this interpretation illustrated more clearly than in the following letter sent by the Tarkwa workers to B.A. Bentum and the MWU Branch Secretaries:

> They have chop plenty money in the union building and have no sorrow for the workers. When we go to the union office he doesn't mind us, he has locked the office and drinking with women who are not workers. We are very annoy about this and we want to beat him. One day he will come to Tarkwa mine here. If you don't sack him and anything happen we don't mind. We want you peoples to meet and go to TUC and Government and tell them that we don't want Aikins. When we have come to this union first the headquarters were receiving 35% and we have PLENTY MONEY to buy bus for workers. When the headquarters get 50% we haven't money. WHY? He has chop all money, and when you come to meeting he go to juju man to change your head so when he give you small drink you start to laugh with him and go. We are now telling you that we don't want him again.[40]

As the Chief Labour Officer reported:

> The local union officials and the national union have lost touch with the mine workers...This is prevalent in many trade unions in the country as the result of the check-off system.[41]

In 1968-71 the mine workers could not reject their union by withdrawal of their membership or union dues. They could not prompt the union into more militant action by electing new officers, and their efforts to establish independent associations to articulate their demands were constantly frustrated by the joint action of management and incumbent union officials. In this situation, violent riots, strikes and demonstrations were a rational, and a successful means of expressing grievances and by-passing the inefficacy of the MWU. In the words of S.K. Cudjoe:

> The recent strikes have shown that at long last the rank-and-file have mustered the courage to repudiate the leaders which have been cunningly imposed upon them by means of pseudo-democratic elections. They have demonstrated their lack of respect for, and confidence in the present leadership...It has become evident that the vital industrial medium for workers to readily communicate their problems and grievances to employers, and for the receipt of the employers' decisions and views, is woefully lacking. Thus minor complaints and trivial differences of views are not attended to and develop into industrial upheavals... The emergence of respected but unofficial and unrecognized leadership on most of the mines shows that the workers are yearning for the opportunity to freely elect leaders of their choice at truly democratic elections.[42]

In contrast to the strike waves of 1930-37 and 1950-54, the strike wave of 1968-71 cannot be analyzed by looking at the grievances and demands which provoked the mine workers to take collective action. Indeed, the list of strike issues in the gold mines recorded by the Labour Department in this period reveals a complete absence of any consistent pattern. Moreover, as earlier sections of this chapter have suggested, in the course of their strikes the mine workers' attention shifted very rapidly from specific grievances and demands to a much broader attack on their perceived enemies. This was indicative of an important development in the political consciousness of the mine workers. All forms of labour resistance imply a rejection of certain features of the socio-economic or political status quo. However, the degree to which resistance threatens that status quo and challenges its legitimacy varies enormously. As Chapters 4 and 5 have described, in the 1930's and 1940's Ghana's workers were encouraged to articulate specific grievances because in doing so they acknowledged their subservience to the authority of capital and the state, and restricted their demands to ones which could be accommodated within the prevailing structure of political authority. The mine workers' activities of 1968-71 broke free from this institutionalized model of political participation, and escalated into a serious challenge to the existing configuration of power. Between 1968 and 1971 the mine workers began to perceive that their exploitation and subjugation was perpetuated by a complex network of authority relationships. This network incorporated managers, supervisors, policemen, tribal heads and traditional rulers, politicians, government officials and even their own union representatives. These individuals, and the institutions they represented, had always assumed the right to assert authority and control over the workers. Now, as they attacked their enemies and took control of their compounds, the mine workers were moving beyond a militant expression of grievances and demands, and were proclaiming their right to self-control and autonomy. It would be naive in the extreme to imagine that these incidents were in any sense the beginning of a 'revolutionary' situation. Nevertheless, it is evident that during this critical phase of resistance the mine workers perceived more clearly than ever before the forces which opposed them, and the need to struggle against those forces with every means at their disposal.

Although they rejected the incumbent leadership of the MWU, the mine workers were fully aware of their union's potential role in this struggle, and therefore made strenuous efforts to render it more responsive, democratic and militant. They demanded union elections and went on strike to register their dissatisfaction with entrenched officials. They proposed that Branch Secretaries and Chairmen should be paid directly by the labour force to make them less susceptible to managerial victimization. They created their own independent associations which, like the Prestea Shop Stewards' Association, 'acted as a sort of "pepping up" body to the union'.[43] As the second half of this chapter will describe, when free to do so, they withdrew their membership from the MWU, and at one mine created a completely independent union. Predictably, representatives of management, government and the MWU alleged that such activities were 'backed by some intelligent agent/agencies', and organized 'by men who are not employed in the mine, who are inciting others for their own ends - possibly political'.[44] However, such allegations were never substantiated, and there is no evidence to suggest that these activities represented anything more or less than a declaration by the mine workers of their desire and intention to be represented by an organization which sought to change, rather than maintain, the existing structure of authority within the gold mining industry.

Reform and Revolt: Mine Worker Resistance, 1971-1980

Between 1971 and 1976 the mine workers exhibited none of the militancy which had characterized their actions in the preceding three years. In 1970 the mine workers had been responsible for over 85 per cent of all man-days lost in the country, but in 1971-72 the proportion fell to under two per cent. Between September 1971 and September 1977 there was no major strike in the gold mines, apart from a two-day stoppage at Tarkwa in October 1974, when over 2,000 underground workers participated in an unofficial strike over the calculation of back-pay. As in the previous decade, a period of calm was followed by a period of intense conflict. Between September and December 1977 a series of violent strikes took place at Prestea, Tarkwa, Obuasi and Konongo, in the course of which the mine workers once again demonstrated their antagonism towards management and union officials. The second half of this chapter provides an analysis of this pattern of resistance.

A period of peace, 1970-72

In the 18-month period which separated the Ashanti Goldfields strike of June 1970 and the overthrow of the PP Government in January 1972, the relationship between the mine workers, the MWU and mine management moved into a new, relatively harmonious phase. Despite the bitterness generated by the confrontations of 1968-71, the strike wave had a moderating influence on the parties to the disputes. Management had been both publicly and privately reprimanded by the Government, and was left in no doubt about the need to avoid further provocation of the labour force. Managers who had been guilty of such provocation were weeded out of the SGMC, and a serious attempt was made to rid the mines of incompetent political and personal appointees.

The mine workers were also keen to avoid further confrontations. Their militant resistance in the preceding three years had forced the Government to grant a large number of long-awaited concessions and compelled management to investigate and improve their living and working conditions. The militant underground workers had been rewarded with a doubling of the underground/surface wage differential, and the workers of AGC had forced Lonrho to concede an _ex gratia_ award of three months pay. As a result of their violent attacks on supervisors and disciplinary staff, the mine workers had also very successfully increased their degree of control in the workplace. In January 1969 the Western Region Labour Officer accurately predicted that 'with the recent disturbances in the background, one can be sure that in the direction of enforcing discipline anything that smacks of regimentation will be vehemently opposed'.[45] Management remarked upon the 'reluctance of supervisors to take remedial action against workers', and lamented that 'labour indiscipline, weakness of supervision and hence failure to carry out standard practices...has followed inevitably from the strikes and disturbances of 1968-69'.[46]

Finally, the hard line taken by the Government and management against strikers and rank-and-file activists during the strike wave produced what the Chamber of Mines described as 'a more salutory atmosphere' amongst the workers.[47] However militant, workers had no great desire to become involved in further clashes with armed policemen. Strike leaders received severe sentences in the courts, and even die-hard militants such as Augustine Dagarti at Prestea were now afraid of being held responsible for any further unrest in the mines. Significantly, the

last major stoppage of the strike wave was also the least successful. The AGC strike of June 1970 secured no major concessions,
more than 100 workers were arrested, and the workers' spokesmen
had been forced to issue a humiliating statement of apology for
their actions.

The strike wave of 1968-71 also forced the MWU leadership to
be more responsive to the demands of the rank-and-file. National
and local officials had been criticized by the Prestea and Obuasi
Reports, and the Labour Department was now determined that
pressure should be 'brought to bear on Aikins to put his house in
order'.[48] In September and October 1969 incumbent officials were
instructed to end their delaying tactics and to organize elections.
At these elections underground and northern workers secured a
better representation on local Executive Committees, and at
Prestea E.G. Williams was ousted and replaced by an unemployed
Dagarti. In August 1970 changes were made at national level. The
Finance Officer, General Secretary and Deputy General Secretary
were all dismissed for financial malpractices. Aikins, described by
the Labour Department as a man who had 'miserably failed to meet
the demands of the workers', was replaced by E.G. Williams, who
had been compensated for his rejection at Prestea by a scholar-
ship to Britain and an administrative post in MWU headquarters.[49]
Having borne the brunt of the workers' hostility in the 1968 riot,
Williams was now more aware of the dangers of failing to satisfy
rank-and-file demands. The Government was also putting pressure
on mine management to establish the workers' confidence in their
union. In May 1970 the Minister of Labour produced a cabinet
memorandum on the creation of Joint Consultative Committees in
the mines which would, it was hoped, bring about 'greater common understanding by giving workpeople a chance to know what
is going on and a chance to make a contribution to the running of
the mine'.[50]

By mid-1971 therefore, many of the factors which produced
the strike wave of 1968-71 had been eliminated, and the mine
workers, the MWU and mine management moved into a new, relatively harmonious relationship. This trend was reinforced by
events in the last six months of the Progress Party's administration. After coming to power in October 1969, relations between
the PP Government and the unions steadily deteriorated. The
party's leaders refused to consider wage increases for the poorest
workers, treated TUC and union leaders with contempt, and attempted to weaken the union movement by ousting Bentum and encouraging divisions within powerful unions such as the Railway
Union. The conflict between the Government and organized labour
came to a head in July 1971 when J.H. Mensah's budget announced a wage freeze and a new 'National Development Levy' de-
ductable from workers' wages. Bentum organized the unions in
opposition to the budget, carefully avoiding to support proposals
for a general strike. Despite Bentum's caution, the Government
seized the opportunity to launch a major attack on the unions. In
September 1971 it abolished the TUC, ended the check-off
system, and introduced a range of punitive measures designed to
prevent further opposition by the unions. This confrontation had

a radicalizing effect on the whole labour movement, including the MWU. Although the MWU leadership did not mobilize any strikes against the Government, it did adopt a more militant position than at almost any time since 1956. At an Extraordinary Delegates Conference held in September 1971, Rockson and Williams made a spirited attack on the Progress Party's policies, and the union resolved to join a new trade union centre led by Bentum.

In the aftermath of this confrontation the MWU leadership was given further reason to re-establish contact with the rank-and-file membership. Following the hurried enactment of the Industrial Relations (Amendment) Act on September 10th 1971, the mine workers took advantage of their new right to withhold their union membership. By the end of the year the MWU membership had slumped to under a half of its 1970 level, and the Tarkwa Labour Officer reported that 'the main preoccupation of the MWU is to lure back the members who have opted out'.[51]

The most serious threat to the institutional and personal interests of the MWU leadership came from the 7,500 workers of Ashanti Goldfields. Once the contents of the new Act became known in Obuasi, the idea of an independent union rapidly gained support amongst the AGC labour force. The Branch Union Executive hesitated, but on recognizing the strength of the workers' feelings decided to support the demand for an independent union and separate collective bargaining certificate. Appeals for unity by the national officers of the MWU fell on deaf ears, and the new AGC Employees' Union (AGCEU) issued posters proclaiming 'No More Tarkwa'. Management, Government and the MWU were all opposed to the AGCEU. Lonrho and the Progress Party recognized that the AGC workers would make large wage claims on the basis of the mine's profitability, and that this would encourage the Prestea workers to demand higher wages than workers at the loss-making Tarkwa Goldfields. The MWU leadership was equally concerned by the potential disintegration of the union, and made an unsuccessful attempt to disrupt the new union by dissolving the Branch Executive and replacing it with an appointed interim committee. There was no doubt that the new union had the support of the labour force, and management reported:

> The AGCEU committee are looked upon by the workers as their representatives. The reconciliation with Tarkwa will not be possible until AGEU grievances are satisfactorily settled and the mass of workers agree to that settlement.[52]

Frantic attempts were made to find a compromise solution to the situation, but while negotiations were continuing the Progress Party was ousted by a military coup. The new Government persuaded the Obuasi workers to rejoin the MWU, and the breakaway union was disbanded. In the words of the Principal of the Ghana Labour College, the attempted secession had demonstrated that it was 'naive to ignore the honest feelings of a branch with over 7,000 members'.[53]

Military government and the revival of the MWU, 1972-76

The AGC workers' agreement to reincorporation in the MWU was indicative of the enthusiasm with which Ghana's workers greeted the downfall of Busia and the Progress Party. Recognizing this fact, the new National Redemption Council (NRC) Government, headed by Colonel I.K. Acheampong, quickly introduced a series of measures designed to consolidate the support of organized labour. The NRC re-established the TUC, released its frozen assets and wrote off large debts which the Congress owed to the Accra City Council. Busia's Industrial Relations (Amendment) Act was repealed, and the check-off system restored. Having established a working relationship with the TUC and its new Secretary General, A.M. Issifu, the NRC attempted to ensure the political passivity of workers and unions through a mixture of reward and punishment. To stabilize the cost of living the Government introduced import controls, extended the range of price controls and froze rents. It resumed the CPP's policy of public sector expansion, and took a 55 per cent shareholding in Ashanti Goldfields, a move that was warmly welcomed by the Obuasi mine workers. The new Head of State publicly praised the unions for their opposition to Busia, describing them as 'the Vanguard of the Revolution'.

In return for these concessions the NRC expected the unions to curtail their new militancy. A 2.5 per cent ceiling on wage rises was announced, and the Government called on the unions to observe a 20-year 'industrial truce'. Like the NLC and PP governments, the National Redemption Council retained Nkrumah's restrictive labour legislation, and reinforced it with a Subversion Decree which made incitement to strike an offence punishable by 15 to 30 years imprisonment. Major Asante, the new Commissioner for Labour, placed additional personal pressure on the unions by a policy of direct intervention in trade union affairs, dismissing strikers and dissolving uncooperative union executives.

Despite the many constraints which the NRC imposed upon the trade union movement, the improvement to union/worker relations in the gold mines which had started in 1971 continued unabated. Indeed, the first four years of NRC rule actually witnessed a remarkable revival of the MWU's responsiveness and militancy. This revival was the product of several factors. The strike wave of 1968-71 and the attempted secession of the AGC branch union in 1971 had proved to the MWU leadership the dire consequences of a failure to satisfy rank-and-file expectations. The willingness of the union leadership to articulate the workers' demands was reinforced by the 1972 coup. Although it was vehemently opposed to strikes, the NRC's declarations of support for the trade union movement and its populist economic policy encouraged the MWU to represent the rank-and-file without fear of intimidation. Finally, and most significantly, the incumbent national leadership of E.G. Williams and M.B. Rockson was forced to adopt an aggressive bargaining strategy by the presence of a dynamic new figure on the NEC, R.A. Yeboah.

Although the Obuasi workers had dropped their demand for an independent union, they were still aware of the need for the MWU to be more militant than it had been under the previous three administrations. To this end, in June 1972 they elected R.A. Yeboah as Branch Secretary. Yeboah was a relatively well educated former underground worker who had a total of 12 years experience at five different mines, and who had risen to the senior positions of Shift Boss and Mine Captain. Rockson and Williams regarded Yeboah as a threat to their domination of the union and attempted to obstruct his election. The Obuasi workers were united in their support for Yeboah and accused the NEC of attempting to 'interfere with our unanimous decision to elect competent officers'.[54] Major Asante intervened to break the deadlock, and in July 1972 Yeboah was confirmed as Branch Secretary, despite Rockson and Aikins' allegation that he was an enemy of the Government and should be kept under surveillance.

Yeboah countered the accusations made against him by making flamboyant declarations of support for the NRC, and he then set about fulfilling the expectations of the workers who had elected him. Within six months of his election he was pressing for a five-day week and for worker representation on the AGC Board of Directors. He told the Ashanti Regional Commissioner that he planned 'to expose some of the devilish intentions of this Corporation which has for the past 75 years exploited the mineral wealth of this country with impunity and cheap labour'.[55] Yeboah's aggressive bargaining style rapidly extracted a vast number of concessions from the AGC management, and his dynamic influence was soon felt at meetings of the Standing Negotiating Committee. In November 1973 the MWU called for wage rises of between 30 and 40 per cent, reduced working hours, new housing and better recreational facilities. In June 1974 the union demanded increased overtime payments and a wide range of new benefits and allowances. Observing the negotiations, the Tarkwa Labour Officer reported that the union was 'positively agitated and must be taken very seriously indeed'.[56] A year later the union successfully demanded higher wages and blocked attempts to introduce tighter control over 'malingerers', and in October 1975 Yeboah persuaded the Chamber of Mines to introduce the long-awaited five-day week. The MWU's new dynamism appeared to heal the longstanding breach between the union hierarchy and the rank-and-file. In the four years which followed the NRC coup there was only one major unofficial strike, a two-day stoppage by Tarkwa's underground workers in October 1974.

Renewed revolt: strikes and riots, 1976–77

The passivity of the mine workers between 1972 and 1976, coupled with the improved relationship between the MWU and the rank-and-file, blinded both management and the NRC to mounting discontent in the gold mines. Ghana's economic decline was having a direct impact on the mine workers' living standards. The NRC had been forced to abandon its policy of rigid wage restraint, and allowed the mine workers' wages to rise by almost 200 per cent in four years. At the same time, however, the Government's gross economic mismanagement and world price rises had combined to push up the Consumer Price Index by over 280 per cent in the same period. Moreover, relations between the rank-and-file and the MWU were not quite so cordial as they appeared. In June 1974 the pressure of discontent in the branch unions forced the NEC to request an extraordinary negotiating meeting with the Chamber of Mines, and at Prestea the local union officials claimed that their lives were in danger from angry workers. Even R.A. Yeboah doubted his ability to control the workers in Obuasi. General Secretary Williams reported that the situation was 'now becoming explosive', and that the MWU was under heavy pressure to demand further wage increases.[57] The October 1974 strike at Tarkwa confirmed Williams' fears. The underground workers told the District Labour Officer that they had lost confidence in the union, and only called off their strike after armed soldiers had entered the mine and management had issued threats of mass dismissals.

In 1975 and 1976 the fragile concordat which had been established between the NRC, management and workers came under growing pressures. Inflation was rampant but the NRC, bankrupt of ideas and cash, refused to restore the real value of the workers' incomes. In February 1976 the incumbent leadership of the MWU faced its first challenge since the resignation of D K. Foevie in 1964. At the first Quadrennial Delegates Conference, R.A. Yeboah challenged E.G. Williams for the position of General Secretary. The NEC's Constitutional Committee ruled that Yeboah was not eligible to stand as a candidate but Yeboah had mobilized opinion within the union against Williams. Fearing a defeat the incumbent General Secretary stood down, allowing Yeboah to fill the post.

The combination of growing rank-and-file discontent, an increasingly authoritarian government, and a militant MWU General Secretary soon proved to be explosive. In January 1975 the NRC had taken control of the African Manganese Company at Nsuta. Remembering the award granted to the AGC workers at the time of the Lonrho takeover, the Nsuta workers demanded a goodwill award of three months' wages. The branch union of the MWU failed to appreciate the strength of rank-and-file opinion on the issue, and an unofficial eight-day strike ensued. In September 1976 the workers raised the issue again, now supported by the new General Secretary. Yeboah reiterated the demand for three months' wages at a meeting with the Board of Directors on October 29th 1976. While negotiations were in progress, workers besieged the bungalow where the meeting was being held, smashing windows, throwing stones and damaging the company's vehicles. The Board, unable to leave the building, now agreed to the workers' demand. The following day the NRC, now renamed the Supreme Military Council (SMC), repudiated the settlement and sent riot troops to Nsuta to forestall any further protest. The 1,340 strikers at the mine were dismissed and told to reapply for employment and to sign guarantees of good behaviour. The six members of the Branch Executive were not re-engaged, and three strike leaders were jailed for between six months and a year.

This incident at Nsuta, the first example of violent mine worker protest since 1970, was symptomatic of the impending political crisis confronting the SMC. Inflation, corruption, food shortages and black marketeering had all reached unprecedented levels throughout the country. In 1972 there had been only 13 strikes and 4,991 man-days lost. In 1976 the figure jumped to 50 strikes and 31,790 man-days lost. In the major municipal areas educated and professional elements were coordinating a campaign of protest against the Government's incompetence and authoritarianism, and threatening to give direction and coherence to the frustration and anger of the masses. In response to this crisis, Acheampong and the SMC attempted to buy off and suppress working class protest simultaneously. Minimum wages were doubled, and when this strategy failed to curtail the workers' disaffection, the Government resorted to less subtle measures. Striking workers were dismissed and forced to reapply for work under stringent conditions, uncooperative union officials were summarily removed from office, rank-and-file leaders were subjected to harsh corporal punishment, and Special Branch agents infiltrated unofficial workers' associations.

The SMC's strategy of labour control was manifestly self-contradictory. By printing money to increase wages, the Government merely boosted the rate of inflation and exacerbated the country's other pressing economic ailments. By suppressing popular protest and political participation so ruthlessly, the SMC simply provoked further opposition, both from the workers and the educated and professional class.

These contradictions were amply illustrated by events in the gold mines in 1977. As a result of Yeboah's support for the Nsuta workers' demands and his aggressive wage bargaining campaign, the MWU General Secretary was now perceived as a major threat to the Government's attempts to eliminate political opposition and to regain control of the economy. The Labour Department and M.B. Rockson, National Chairman of the MWU, were also keen to see the radical Yeboah removed from the union. Consequently, a plan to oust the General Secretary was set in motion. Following his election as General Secretary, Yeboah attempted to ensure that his own nominee was elected as Branch Secretary at Obuasi. This nominee was defeated in a rigged election, and in March 1977 the new Branch Secretary announced that owing to irregularities in the branch union accounts, an investigation would be held into Yeboah's handling of union finances between 1972 and 1976.

While this investigation was in progress discontent was growing amongst the mine workers. Despite a wage rise from 2.50 to 4.00 cedis in April 1977, the workers demanded higher wages to counter the rapidly rising cost of living. Trusting in Yeboah's abilities as a negotiator they did not take independent action, but expressed their dissatisfaction through other modes of resistance. Many resigned or stayed away from work, preferring to earn their money by farming. Others simply did less work, and a consultant's report completed in May 1977 at Tarkwa Goldfields stated that 'the very poor level of productivity in all areas of the mine was apparent'.[58] The workers' discontent came to a head in September 1977, when the Chamber of Mines refused to implement new government wage guidelines, which would have raised the minimum wage in the mines to 5.42 cedis. Tension was mounting, and Yeboah doubted his ability to control the workers.

At precisely this time when discontent was at its peak, the Government, aided by management, Rockson and the Labour Department, made its move against Yeboah. On September 16th 1977 the Obuasi branch union released its audit report, and alleged that Yeboah and four other branch executives had embezzled a total of 22,000 cedis between 1972 and 1976. The five men were indicted, and Yeboah had no choice but to leave the union. An Emergency Delegates Conference was held, at which Yeboah's position as General Secretary was filled by the conservative Jonathan Mamah, a draughtsman from northern Ghana.

The removal of Yeboah from the NEC acted as a catalyst to the discontent of the rank-and-file. They had no faith in Rockson and Mamah, and now that the union lacked effective leadership they had no reason to use it as a means of articulating their demands. As a result, the last three months of 1977 witnessed a series of major unofficial strikes at Tarkwa, Prestea and Obuasi. At Tarkwa underground workers struck on December 8th to demand an end of year production bonus. They rejected managerial claims that production targets had not been met, and chased clerical and surface workers from the mine. They emphatically told the Mine Manager, 'No bonus, no work'. The strike ended unsuccessfully two days later, when the strikers were dismissed and instructed to reapply for employment. At Prestea three strikes took place in November and December 1977. In the first, three-day strike, workers demanded the payment of overtime and wage arrears, and the dismissal of the Labour Controller, Stores Manager and Underground Manager. The Underground Manager was asked to stay away from the mine and the strike ended, but when he returned the workers struck again. During this second stoppage MWU officials were abused and assaulted, and the SGMC Managing Director was first besieged and then kidnapped. On the instructions of the Regional Commissioner the Underground Manager was permanently removed from the mine, and an enquiry into the workers' grievances was initiated. On December 22nd, when seven leaders of the strike were dismissed, the workers downed tools again. Following the example set by the Tarkwa management, the strikers were dismissed so that 'undesirables and troublemakers' could be permanently excluded from the mine.

The Ashanti Goldfields workers provided the most serious opposition to management and Government in the last quarter of 1977. 1,032 underground workers struck between 15th and 17th September when 25 workers were suspended for gold stealing. The strikers successfully demanded the transfer of the Underground Manager and Shift Bosses who had discovered the thefts, and management decided to take no further action against the 25 men. A second strike took place ten days later, when 55 hospital workers successfully demanded the introduction of new wage rates. Inspired by these successes, on October 3rd all 7,900 workers at the mine went on strike to demand the implementation of the Government's wage guidelines. After a three-day stoppage the SMC agreed to introduce new minimum wages of 6.27 cedis for surface workers and 6.92 cedis for underground workers. Throughout November and December rumours of further strike action were rife in Obuasi. Among the demands which the workers intended to make were the removal of all military personnel from the mine, the reinstatement of R.A. Yeboah, pay for the three-day strike period the previous month, the dismissal of the mine's Medical Officer, and the removal of the branch union executives. The Regional Labour Officer observed:

> Members of the union planning a strike for the second time without knowledge of the local union executives would indicate a loss of confidence in the executives or a poor relationship between the workers and their leaders.[59]

The executives recognized their lack of rank-and-file support and now moved to consolidate their position. The Branch Secretary told the Mine Manager:

> The union is prepared to take any joint action with the management over this issue, even if it requires appealing to the Government for any action in this regard.[60]

The mine's and the Government's intelligence agencies were now operating at full strength, attempting to infiltrate the workers' ranks and to ascertain the likelihood of further strike action. On October 12th a high-powered sub-committee of the SMC produced contingency plans for future strikes and ordered troops to Obuasi. Three days later eight rank-and-file leaders were summoned by the Government and required to give an undertaking that there would be no more unrest at the mine. They were told that they were under constant surveillance and would be held responsible for any strikes which took place. These measures had their intended effect, and although rumours of another strike were rife, 1977 ended without further trouble at the mine.

Informal and collective resistance, 1978-80

The coercive tactics employed by the SMC and Ashanti Goldfields at the end of 1977 achieved their objective of curtailing the mine workers' collective resistance. What those tactics could not do, of course, was to prevent the mine workers from expressing their discontent in other ways. The following extracts from a meeting between the branch union and management at Ashanti Goldfields in March 1978 illustrate some of the many ways in which the mine workers were able to continue their struggle against the post-colonial state and international mining capital:

> The General Mines Manager stated that the total [production] achievement for the month was actually 27% below the point where a bonus can be earned and 37% behind earning a full bonus. The cumulative rating of 66.3% was way behind the

target set, and present signs indicated a worsening of the situation...it appeared so far that the poor performance seemed to have no effect on the labour... A recent study report had revealed that the underground night shift in certain working places produced nothing for the whole shift... This could not be attributed to lack of supervision because the ratio of Shiftbosses to the number of working places was better and higher than at many other mines... Management was at present concerned about the increasing rate of absenteeism. Sickness which used to average 5% had now increased... Also fewer people were turning up for work on Friday night, Saturday morning and afternoon when called to do so... The General Mines Manager said there has been an alarming increase in the apparent theft of miners boots on the mine... The Chief Engineer pointed out that light bulbs issued free of charge with AGC embossed on them had been purchased by a messenger sent to the village to buy bulbs for the Company. The number of bulbs being used was out of all proportion to actual requirements.[61]

Beneath the calm surface of industrial relations in the gold mines, therefore, the daily struggle of the mine workers against their exploitation and subordination continued. Moreover, beneath that surface the threat of violent outbursts of collective resistance was ever present. In October 1979, for example, the entire labour force of Ashanti Goldfields withdrew their labour when management withdrew certain grants and allowances from workers suffering with tuberculosis. Although the allowances were immediately restored by management, the workers continued their strike for no less than two weeks, and demonstrated their anger by smashing car windscreens, breaking down doors and windows in the Mine Hospital, and destroying seven company Land Rovers.

The period of military government between 1972 and 1979, when Ghana was once again returned to civilian rule, revealed in very clear terms the dilemma confronting capital and state in their efforts to control the mine workers. Since the early 1940's two broad strategies had been used to achieve that objective. The first was to allow the MWU a reasonable degree of autonomy, hoping that the union would articulate rank-and-file grievances, but would do so in a predictable and peaceful manner to negotiate incremental benefits. Between 1972 and 1975 the NRC, like the Colonial Government, had discovered that given such autonomy, the MWU was liable to be responsive to rank-and-file militancy and to become the mobilizer and organizer of collective resistance. The second strategy was to place severe restrictions on the independence of the MWU, hoping that the union could be transformed into an instrument of labour control and that the rank-and-file could be coerced into passivity. In 1976-77 the NRC, like its post-colonial predecessors, discovered that given such restrictions the mine workers would simply by-pass their union, mobilizing collective resistance independently as they had done during the long period of struggle before the formation of the MWU. In both cases, the neat formulae of labour control devised by capital and state were fatally flawed by their failure

to recognize the strength of the mine workers' militancy and solidarity. More than 100 years of struggle in the gold mines have
demonstrated that it is a militancy and solidarity which cannot be
legislated out of existence, eliminated by the incorporation of the
MWU and its leaders into the machinery of state, or suppressed
by the use of crude coercive tactics. The origins of that militancy
and solidarity, and its broader significance within the political
economy of Ghana, are the subject of the next and final chapter.

Notes

1. ASG, 'Memorandum on Wage Demand', December 1966.

2. LDT, LT12, LOT to RLO, 28 June 1969.

3. LDT, LT13/8, LOT to RLO, 18 July 1966.

4. LDT, LT12/8, 'Minutes of a Meeting', 12 January 1967.

5. Prestea Report, p.166.

6. ibid., p.26.

7. LDA, KL331/5, RLO to CL, 3 July 1968.

8. Undated memorandum, supplied by AGC Chief Security
    Officer.

9. LDT, LT12, LOT to RLO, 11 January 1968.

10. Prestea Report, p.26.

11. Interview with an eye-witness in Tarkwa.

12. LDA, KL331/2/2, Cabinet Secretary to Permanent Secretary
    Ministry of Labour, 25 July 1970.

13. ASG, 'Diary of Events - Stoppage of Work, 3rd April to 7th
    July 1970', p.7.

14. LDA, KL331/2/2, CL circular, 28 December 1966.

15. Report of the Commission of Enquiry into Obuasi
    Disturbances [Obuasi Report], pp.39-40.

16. Prestea Report, p.177.

17. ibid., p.191.

18. LDT, LT12, LOT to RLO, 13 May 1968.

19. LDA, KL331/5, RLO to CL, 14 October 1968; LDT, LT12,
    LOT to RLO, 4 July 1968.

20. LDK, LAR16/15, 'Office Notes', 12 March 1969; LDT, LT12, RLO to CL, 28 April 1969.

21. Obuasi Report, pp.18 and 33.

22. LDK, LAR16/15, Labour Officer Obuasi to RLO, 29 May 1970.

23. LDT, LT12/8, RLO to CL, 31 August 1966.

24. 'Minutes of a Meeting', 18 March 1966, in ibid.

25. LOT to RLO, 19 April 1966, in ibid.

26. LOT to RLO, 9 May 1966, in ibid.

27. GMU, 'Brief Report of the National Organizer', n.d., p.3.

28. Prestea Report, p.86.

29. LDC, L03/12, Liaison Officer AGC to General Secretary MWU, 8 September 1967.

30. Prestea Report, p.140.

31. LDT, LT13/8, S.K. Cudjoe to General Secretary MWU, 20 August 1969.

32. LDA, KL331/3/1, Acting Deputy CL to Deputy CL, 25 August 1969.

33. LDT, LT13/8, 'Minutes of an Emergency Meeting of the MWU NEC', 23 May 1969.

34. COM, 12 November 1970.

35. LDT, LT13/8, General Secretary SGMC to Mine Manager Prestea, 9 May 1967.

36. Prestea Report, p.139.

37. GMU, loc cit.

38. LDT, LTC5; LDA, KL331/3/1, passim.

39. LDT, LT13/8, S.K. Cudjoe to General Secretary MWU, 20 August 1969.

40. J.F. Koomson 'for all ABA workers' to TUC Secretary-General, n.d., in ibid.

41. LDA, KL331/5, CL to Permanent Secretary Ministry of Labour, 11 July 1968.

42. LDT, LT13/8, loc cit.

43. *Prestea Report*, p.198.

44. *ibid*., pp.57 and 61.

45. LDA, KL188/2, RLO to CL, 20 January 1969.

46. SGM, 'Technical Operations Report', n.d.

47. COM, 12 August 1969.

48. LDT, LT13/8, RLO to Acting CL, 4 July 1969.

49. LOT to RLO, 18 August 1969, in *ibid*.

50. SGM, 1/22, 'Notes on the Formation of a Joint Consultative Committee', n.d.

51. LDT, LT5/1, 'Quarterly Report', 31 December 1971.

52. ASG, Untitled memorandum, 3 January 1972.

53. LDA, KD13/11, J.F. Nortey to CL, 10 February 1972.

54. LDO, LO3/12, 'Resolution Confirming the Election of Officers', 27 January 1972.

55. LDA, KL188/3, R.A. Yeboah to Ashanti Regional Commissioner, 16 November 1972.

56. LDA, KD13/2, LOT to RLO, 2 July 1974.

57. LDT, LT13/8, General Secretary MWU to Commissioner of Lands, 3 July 1974.

58. SGM, 'Report on Survey of Productivity', May 1977.

59. LDA, KL331/2/3, Ashanti RLO to CL, 17 October 1977.

60. MWU Branch Secretary and Chairman Obuasi to General Manager AGC, 7 October 1977, in *ibid*.

Chapter 8

THE LIMITS OF MILITANCY: MINE WORKER
RESISTANCE AND POLITICAL CHANGE IN GHANA

> Because of certain betrayals and widespread cor-
> ruption, some people look upon political action as
> something to be avoided. But politics are not bad,
> just because there are some bad politicians.

Ghana Mine Workers' Union, Members Pocket Guide.

From the beginning of capitalist gold mining in the 1870's to the
present day, Ghana's mine workers have been engaged in a determined struggle to resist their exploitation and subordination. Obstructing and defying the relentless efforts of capital and state to
control their activities, the mine workers have persistently as-
serted their autonomy, displaying a degree of militancy and solidarity rare amongst African workers. This concluding chapter
identifies the roots of the mine workers' tradition of militant resistance, examines the way in which this struggle has shaped their
consciousness, and assesses the impact of the mine workers' resistance on Ghana's political and socio-economic structure.

The Roots of Mine Worker Militancy

The mine workers' characteristic militancy, their propensity
to engage in sustained conflict with capital and state, has its
roots in the peculiar conditions of life and work in the gold
mining industry. Work in the mines is gruelling, monotonous and
exceedingly dangerous, particularly for the underground workers.
Such inherently unattractive features of mine work have been exacerbated by the persistent reluctance of mining capital and the
state to commit expenditure to the improvement of working and
living conditions. Supervision in the mines has always been intense and authoritarian, and despite the successful resistance of
the labour force to the imposition of workplace discipline,
management has been able to retain extensive powers of control
over rebellious workers. The financial rewards offered to workers
in the mining industry have never been great, and although the
mine workers have successfully obstructed managerial and official

attempts to impose a rigid wage freeze, incomes and prospects of promotion in the mines are not appreciably better than those offered to workers in far less onerous forms of labour.

The militancy provoked by such unattractive conditions of service has been reinforced by the sharply contrasting lifestyle traditionally enjoyed by management. Workers have had to live in dilapidated company compounds or in overcrowded and over-priced private accommodation, inconveniently situated in the hot and humid valleys of the mining areas. Senior staff have been provided with commodious, well appointed bungalows, built on the relatively cool hilltops, overlooking the immaculately kept golf courses maintained for their enjoyment. The mining companies have always been reluctant to provide transport for their labour force, leaving workers to walk as much as five miles to and from the mine every day, whereas managers have been given chauffeur driven cars and coaches to convey them the short distance to their place of work. The mine workers have never been able to buy foodstuffs at officially controlled prices, and have been at the mercy of market traders and caterers. In contrast, managers enjoy expertly cooked meals in subsidized restaurants and have a guaranteed supply of cheap and otherwise unobtainable commodities from company stores. After a day (or night) of arduous toil, the workers can only afford to relax by drinking pito or akpeteshie in their compound. Senior staff spend their leisure time in sumptuous, well equipped clubhouses, now amongst the very few places in Ghana where one can be sure of finding a supply of cold beer.

The impact of such contrasts (which could be listed ad nauseam) on the mine workers' consciousness has been confirmed by the provocative attitudes and behaviour of management. Inheriting the acute elitism of their expatriate predecessors, Ghanaian managers (especially those in administrative posts) make no secret of their contempt for the 'rats' who work underground, constantly remind workers of their inferior status, and do not attempt to hide their antagonism to the workers' demands for better working and living conditions. In short, there are few places in Ghana (or indeed, anywhere else) where the inequalities of capitalist society are quite so brazenly displayed. The failure of institutionalized bargaining procedures to reduce such inequalities, and the apparent collaboration of the MWU leadership with this highly privileged managerial elite, has simply fuelled the mine workers' militancy and reinforced their long-established belief in the efficacy of independent collective resistance.

The mine workers' willingness to participate in collective modes of resistance has been encouraged by their strong bargaining position. Much of the machinery in a mine must be operated continuously to prevent shafts from flooding and to allow the excavation of gold-bearing rock. The ease with which production can be disrupted, the unique cost structure of the gold mining industry, and the marginal status of most Ghanaian mines have made the strike an extremely effective weapon, and prevented mine management from using a favourite strategy of the Ghanaian employer, the lock-out. At national level the mine workers have also enjoyed considerable leverage. Economically, the mining industry has provided around 10 per cent of the country's much needed foreign exchange earnings in the post-colonial period, and the performance of a company such as Lonrho can have a decisive impact on the willingness of foreign capital to invest in Ghana. Politically, although the mining towns of Tarkwa, Prestea and Obuasi are relatively isolated from the country's major municipal areas, the threat of civil disorder amongst the large concentrations of workers in the mines inevitably poses a threat to the political authority of a ruling regime, especially one which is committed to the elimination of mass political participation.

Understandably, the mine workers with the greatest bargaining power, the underground workers, have also been the most militant. In the words of the SGMC Managing Director:

> The underground workers, especially the machine drivers and the blastmen, hold a very special and peculiar position in the production process in the mines... Almost all strike actions are taken by them owing to their being fully aware of the important production work on which they are engaged.[1]

The peculiar militancy of the underground workers is an important and long-established characteristic of the mine workers' political culture. Chapter 4 described how in the 1930's the underground labour force, led by a core of skilled and relatively stabilized workers, mobilized a series of strikes which forced the colonial administration to abandon its purely coercive strategy of labour control and to introduce the new strategy of institutionalization. After the creation of the Mines Employees' Union in 1944 these same workers continued to exercise a decisive influence on the pattern of resistance and control in the mining industry. It was their unremitting demand that the MEU should 'deliver the goods' that pushed the union leadership into general strikes in 1947 and 1955. It was their insistence that the union should 'keep out of politics' that prevented the participation of the MEU in the 1950 Positive Action strike, and their concerted opposition to the introduction of Scientific Management that was responsible for the unofficial strike wave of the mid-1950's. After Independence, the underground workers, still led by the machine drivers and other skilled categories, spearheaded the workers' revolt against the atrophy of the MWU, defying the union's renunciation of collective resistance, threatening to secede from the union, and leading the wave of violent protest that shook the mines in 1968-71.

The Sources of Mine Worker Solidarity

The mine workers' traditional militancy has been accompanied and reinforced by their distinctive solidarity. This ability to transform latent discontent into active, collective resistance which transcends horizontal and vertical cleavages in the labour force, again derives from the unique conditions of life and work in the mining towns. Prestea, Tarkwa and Obuasi are classic examples of occupational communities, self-contained social and geographical entities where the majority of the population is engaged by the same employer in similar kinds of work. In such communities workers of different ethnic origin, levels of skill, status and experience are thrown together, not only in the workplace, but also in the intimate atmosphere of a densely populated compound or suburb. During the day, the heterogenous elements of the labour force work together in small, mixed teams, facing the same dangers, sharing bonuses and subject to the same supervisory pressures. After work they spend their free time together, discussing grievances, formulating their demands, and sharing their aspirations.

In such an environment it has not been difficult for the 'adamant radicals' of the labour force, the skilled and experienced underground workers, to mobilize their colleagues.[2] Plans for strikes or demonstrations devised by these unofficial leaders (or as they prefer to be called, 'spokesmen') can be rapidly communicated to other workers.[3] Less experienced members of the labour force, especially newly-arrived migrants suffering a particularly harsh and intensive form of proletarianization, respond naturally to such dynamic leadership, while potential blacklegs amongst the more established and surface workers can readily be eliminated by the threat of intimidation or use of violence.

The mine workers' consciousness of common interest has been strengthened by the steady process of labour stabilization in the mining industry since the 1930's, when the Gold Coast first experienced a labour surplus. At Ashanti Goldfields, for example, annual labour turnover is now as low as 11 per cent, and as Konings discovered in 1975, nearly 40 per cent of all unskilled and semi-skilled workers at the mine have been employed by the Corporation for more than three years. Thus the mine workers are becoming increasingly proletarianized, a self-reproducing sector of the Ghanaian working class, separated from their rural origins and fully committed to wage-earning employment. In Konings' words, 'farming has played little or no part in the miners' lives. They are to a large extent (and some even completely)...freed from the land'.[4]

Of course, the solidarity of the mine workers is not, and never has been, total. As earlier chapters have described, the overlapping regional and occupational split between underground/ northern and surface/southern workers was the source of some division in the labour force in the late 1940's and early 1950's. In the critical period of mass resistance between 1968 and 1971, the mine workers' unofficial leaders mobilized mass opposition to the southern-dominated MWU by appealing to such allegiances. However, these loyalties are not necessarily detrimental to the workers' militancy or solidarity. Ethnicity or regional origin has never been an issue of overt conflict between the workers, and when Dagarti or Frafra mine workers go on strike, attack managers or threaten to dynamite a court house, they do so as mine workers, not as Frafras or Dagartis. Their interests as workers transcend ethnic or regional allegiances, a feature of the mine workers' political consciousness evidenced by the persistent failure of capital and the state to use tribal heads and Paramount Chiefs as strike breakers.

To conclude this brief examination of the mine workers' militancy and solidarity, it is important to recognize that such attributes are historically self-reinforcing. As Jeffries suggests in his study of the Sekondi railwaymen, consciousness is shaped by the experience of struggle.[5] Therefore, political action is informed not only by contemporary circumstances, but also by past experiences and the mythology of those experiences. In the gold mining industry this observation is evinced by the strong element of continuity in the pattern of collective mine worker resistance. As previous chapters have demonstrated, this pattern, originating in a period when trade unions were outlawed, persisted through a brief period during which the mine workers' union proved responsive to rank-and-file pressures, and re-emerged more vigorously once the union had been rendered insensitive to the grievances and demands of its members. Through their experience of conflict, their victories and their defeats, the mine workers have developed a keen appreciation of the efficacy of collective resistance, and a strong awareness of the need for such resistance to transcend the many potential divisions of interest within the labour force.

Mine Worker Consciousness and its Limitations

To what extent can the mine workers' resistance be regarded as a force for progressive change within the Ghanaian political economy? The history of Ghana in colonial and post-colonial periods is a testament to the susceptibility of the Ghanaian state to the threat of popular unrest and protest, and of the failure of successive regimes to eliminate mass political participation. The 1938 cocoa hold-up, the 1948 riots and the 1950 Positive Action strike all acted as significant catalysts to colonial policy in the Gold Coast. The 1961 Sekondi strike represented a watershed in CPP policy, and in 1971 the confrontation between the trade union movement and the Progress Party was directly related to the NRC coup of January 1972. Six years later, in June 1978, General Acheampong was deposed by his colleagues in the Supreme Military Council in a desperate attempt to stem the rising tide of popular protest, and the failure of this cosmetic operation to defuse mass political consciousness prompted the junior officers of the Armed Forces Revolutionary Council to seize power a year later.

Given the sensitivity of the colonial and post-colonial state to urban and rural mass protest, it might be imagined that the mine workers, with their tradition of militant resistance and their high degree of bargaining power, constitute an important force for change within the Ghanaian political economy. Unfortunately, the historical evidence presented in this study precludes such a conclusion, for the mine workers' militancy and solidarity has hitherto operated within three clearly defined and closely related boundaries, which have served to reduce the direct impact of mine worker resistance on Ghana's political and socio-economic structure.

Firstly, the mine workers' militancy and solidarity has always been defined in <u>occupational</u> rather than <u>class</u> terms. While they have a strong appreciation of their common interests as mine workers, and a keen awareness of their tradition of militant resistance to exploitation, they have never identified their suffering and struggles with those of other members of the working class, and have consistently rejected the opportunity (most notably in 1950, 1961 and 1971) to act in unison with other workers.

Secondly, the mine workers have traditionally displayed very little interest in participating in the national political arena. As Chapter 1 explained, while the resistance of wage labourers to the control of their productivity and wages cannot be dismissed as apolitical in either motivation or effect, and has an indirect impact on the national political economy, overtly political participation has a more profound, and usually a more immediate impact on the status of wage labour vis-à-vis capital and the state. The mine workers have never, even at the height of their militancy and solidarity in 1968-71, consciously used their resistance as a means of effecting progressive change within the prevailing national power structure.

Thirdly, and concomitantly, in spite of their militancy the mine workers have never espoused any radical political ideology, or, like the railwaymen, developed a 'radical political sub-culture' in which 'the aims and propellants of protest extend beyond narrow occupational grievances to a desire to effect radical alterations in the prevailing political and socio-economic order'.[6] The mine workers remained impervious to the socialist anti-colonialism of I.T.A Wallace-Johnson, did not adopt the radical nationalism or quasi-socialism of the CPP, and were relatively unmoved by the democratic populism of Bentum's TUC. As Konings discovered in his survey of Ashanti Goldfields workers in 1975, the mine workers have a keen sense of deprivation relative to the dominant classes of their country and 'strongly resent the present social inequality in Ghanaian society', but such feelings 'have not given rise to the emergence of a revolutionary but to a reformist consciousness':

> Miners do not want to seize political power; they do not even possess a vision of alternative socio-political order unless some vague notions of a more democratic and more prosperous society. Quite a few workers and union leaders told me that workers in Ghana do not bother much what kind of government Ghana has, socialist or capitalist or anything else, as long as the politicians are honest, prepared to listen to workers' grievances and demands and 'to deliver the goods'.[7]

To summarize, throughout their long history of militant resistance, the mine workers have displayed very little interest in acting in alliance with other workers. They do not have clearly defined political ideals, and remain highly sceptical of the value of participation in the national political arena. Their support for politicians and governments, like their support for trade union officials, is conditional and instrumental. It seems unlikely, therefore, that the mine workers will assume the role so effectively played by the railwaymen, 'radical populists' who share a coherent ideal of an open and responsive political system, who are committed to participation as an effective independent force in national politics, and who project themselves as the spokesmen of the masses, particularly the labouring poor.

Ironically, these distinctive features of the mine workers' political consciousness derive from the very conditions of life and work which have also shaped their militancy and solidarity. The isolation and insularity of the mining communities, the intensity of their struggle against managers, supervisors and union officials, and the domination of the mine workers' political culture by northern underground workers suspicious of 'southern' politics and politicians, have all enabled the mine workers to defend their interests with a significant degree of success, but have simultaneously limited the impact of their resistance on Ghana's broader political and socio-economic structure.

The Mine Workers, Trade Unionism, and Political Change

Superficially, it appears that the mine workers' trade union could have transformed the mine workers' militancy and solidarity into an extremely powerful force for progressive political and social change, coordinating action with other workers and unions, using the mine workers' bargaining power as an effective weapon in national politics, and imparting to the workers a broader awareness of the need to struggle for changes in the prevailing distribution of authority and resources. The inability of the MWU to play this mobilizing role lies predominantly not in the opportunism or cowardice of a few union leaders, nor in the inherent tendency of trade unions to become bureaucratized institutions incorporated into the structure of state power. Rather, it stems from the highly (and perhaps unrealistically) conditional nature of the mine workers' support for their union.

As previous chapters have described, the mine workers expect their union leaders to 'deliver the goods', and will not lend their support to the union unless it appears able to do so. When such expectations are not realized, they rapidly revert to alternative modes of resistance, initially learnt in the long period of struggle before the creation of the MEU in 1944. In the colonial era the union leadership was able to attract popular support by adopting an aggressive bargaining policy, but in the post-colonial period the paradoxical nature of this union/worker relationship became evident. Confronted by new, more determined strategies of labour control, the union leaders found it more and more difficult to 'deliver the goods' by means of institutionalized bargaining procedures. As a result, the union lost its popular support, and without the assurance of that support the leadership was further inhibited in any attempt to extract concessions from capital and the state. The process of union atrophy and worker revolt now became self-perpetuating and self-reinforcing. Finding themselves opposed by the workers on one hand and management and government on the other, the leadership succumbed to the latter, and attempted to bolster its position against attacks from the rank-and-file. Reacting to the union's declining responsiveness, the workers turned to alternative modes of resistance, and increasingly directed their attacks not only at their employers and the Government, but also against their nominal representatives in the MWU. Threatened by this trend, the union leadership moved more vigorously against the rank-and-file, which provoked an equally vigorous, and now violent reaction from the workers. Thus the contradictions in the relationship between the mine workers and their union, which existed from the very beginning of the union's history, were not fully worked out until the late 1960's.

Again, the contrast between the mine workers' perception of their union and that of the railwaymen is illuminating. As Jeffries has described, the railwaymen have a distinctively 'participant' attitude not only towards national politics, but also towards union membership. Leadership in the Railway Union has always been highly valued, and the union contains a 'superabundance of men experienced in union officialdom and determined to retain or accede to the limited number of posts available'.[8] Such competition, or 'leadership factionalism', has frequently proved divisive, but has simultaneously forced incumbent officers and their competitors to remain responsive to their rank-and-file constituents. In contrast, there is little evidence of leadership factionalism within the MWU. The mine workers, especially the militant underground workers, expect the union to 'deliver the goods' and to respond to their demands, but they have relatively little interest in competing for office. Branch union committees have therefore been dominated by skilled and clerical surface workers (or as the underground workers somewhat derisively label them, 'the politicians'), while the NEC has been tightly controlled by a small caucus of long-serving officers, most notably D.K. Foevie (1951-64) and M.B. Rockson (1964 onwards). The marked absence of factional conflict within the MWU has made it particularly susceptible to the state's strategies of labour control, and allowed the union leadership to adopt the unresponsive attitude towards rank-and-file consciousness described in the preceding two chapters.

Of course, in the absence of the dynamic relationship between union leaders and union members which was responsible for mobilizing the first and second general mines strikes, the mine workers have been able to defend their interests with a significant degree of success. The ability of supervisory staff to impose workplace discipline has been curtailed, managerial and official efforts to impose a rigid wage freeze have been thwarted, and other benefits have been extracted from recalcitrant governments and mining companies. Indirectly, the mine workers have contributed towards the removal of unpopular and authoritarian regimes, and have forced successive governments to take some account of working class interests in the formulation of policy. Nevertheless, the political limitations of the modes of resistance employed by the mine workers in achieving these ends are only too apparent. Informal modes of resistance such as reduced productivity, bonus cheating and theft have increased the workers' degree of freedom in the workplace, supplemented their declining real incomes, and provided some psychological redress against capital and the state, but these forms of action operate within the prevailing organization of production, structure of political authority and distribution of economic resources. Unofficial strikes, riots and demonstrations have proved a remarkably successful means of securing short-term demands, but such modes of resistance have rarely (if ever) united workers at different mines, let alone workers in different sectors of the economy. The mine workers' efforts to establish autonomous associations have provided a clear indication of their desire to be represented by a responsive and militant institution, but such associations have had few financial or organizational resources, and have proved relatively easy to suppress. Moreover, they tend to undermine the mine workers' solidarity by reinforcing latent divisions within the labour force, representing the interests of those workers (for example, machine drivers, blastmen, and the Ashanti Goldfields workers) who enjoy the greatest bargaining power.

To conclude, the MWU, despite its record of accommodation with capital and the state in the post-colonial period, cannot be dismissed as irrelevant to the mine workers' struggle against their exploitation, or indeed to the broader struggle for progressive change within the Ghanaian political economy. Trade unions have the potential to represent unified occupational and class interests, and the ability to aggregate the bargaining power of all groups of workers, irrespective of their individual strengths and weaknesses. They can mobilize and coordinate resistance, not only in the workplace, but also in the national political arena. In the unstable states of post-colonial Africa they represent one of the few means whereby authoritarian and elitist regimes can be held in check, or even removed. As the speedy removal and subsequent incarceration of R.A. Yeboah in 1977-78 indicates, such regimes will not tolerate popular and dynamic trade unions easily, perceiving them as a serious threat to their desparate efforts to consolidate political authority. Nevertheless, Ghana's mine workers have demonstrated in the past their willingness and ability to rally in defence of colleagues subjected to such crude forms of intimidation. When they are able to perceive union officials as colleagues, rather than as part of the hierarchy of authority which perpetuates their exploitation and subordination, then the mine workers' historically rooted militancy and solidarity might become a more influential force for progressive political change.

188

Notes

. Prestea Report, p.135.

2. LDA, KL331/3/4, LOT to RLO, 22 October 1974.

3. Prestea Report, p.23.

4. Konings (1978) p.40.

5. Jeffries (1978) p.192.

6. ibid., p.3.

7. Konings (1978) pp.71-2.

8. Jeffries (1978) p.142.

BIBLIOGRAPHY OF SOURCES CITED*

ARCHIVES

AGCI   Incoming Correspondence (Obuasi Office to London Office) of the Ashanti Goldfields Corporation, Guildhall Library, London (1897-1940) and AGC, Obuasi (1941 onwards)

AGCO   Outgoing Correspondence (London Office to Obuasi Office) of the Ashanti Goldfields Corporation, Guildhall Library, London (1897-1940) and AGC, Obuasi (1941 onwards)

ASG   Records of the Ashanti Goldfields Corporation, Obuasi

BMA   Basel Mission Archive, translated typescript, Centre of West African Studies, University of Birmingham

COM   Minutes of the Meetings of the Gold Coast/Ghana Chamber of Mines, Ghana Chamber of Mines, Accra

CP   Edwin Cade Papers, Centre of West African Studies, University of Birmingham

CHP   Joseph Chamberlain Papers, University of Birmingham Library

DAT   Records of the District Administration Office, Tarkwa

GMU   Records of the Ghana Mine Workers' Union, Tarkwa

GNA   Ghana National Archives, Accra

GNAK   Ghana National Archives, Kumasi

* For a full bibliography of the sources used in the preparation of this book, see Crisp (1980) pp.538-580.

GNAS	Ghana National Archives, Sekondi
GNAT	Ghana National Archives, Tamale
LA	Lonrho (Technical) Ltd. Archive, London
LDA	Labour Department (Accra) Archive
LDK	Labour Department (Kumasi) Archive
LDO	Labour Department (Obuasi) Archive
LDT	Labour Department (Tarkwa) Archive
MP	F.W. Migeod Papers, Royal Commonwealth Society, London
PRO	Public Record Office, Kew
RHO	Rhodes House, Oxford
SAM	Private Papers of J.N. Sam, Abenase
SGM	Records of the State Gold Mining Corporation, Tarkwa
USA	United States National Archive, Washington

OFFICIAL PUBLICATIONS

Government of Great Britain

Further Correspondence Regarding Affairs of the Gold Coast. Colonial Office, African No. 249, 1883.

Further Correspondence Regarding Affairs of the Gold Coast. Parliamentary Paper C3687, 1883.

Further Correspondence Relating to Medical and Sanitary Matters in Tropical Africa. Colonial Office, African No. 966, 1911.

Government of Gold Coast/Ghana

Annual Reports on Ashanti

Annual Reports on the Gold Coast

Annual Reports on the Labour Department

Annual Reports on the Medical Department

Annual Reports on the Mines Department

Annual Reports on the Transport Department

Annual Reports on the Western Province

Gold Coast Legislative Council Debates

Enquiry Into the Wounding of Eight Africans at Prestea on 15th September 1930. Sessional Paper No. 19 of 1930-31.

In the Matter of the Trades Disputes (Arbitration and Inquiry) Ordinance 1941, and in the Matter of a Trade Dispute Between the Gold Coast Mines Employees' Union and the Gold Coast Chamber of Mines; Award of Arbitrator, 1947.

Report of the Mines Labour Enquiry Committee, 1953.

Report of the Gold Coast Mines Board of Inquiry, In the Matter of a Trade Dispute Between the Gold Coast Mines Employees' Union and the Gold Coast Chamber of Mines, 1956.

Osagyefo in Kumasi, 1962.

Report of the Committee of Enquiry Into the Recent Disturbances at Prestea, 1968.

Report of the Commission of Enquiry Into Obuasi Disturbances, 1970.

PERIODICAL PUBLICATIONS

Annual Reports of the Gold Coast/Ghana Chamber of Mines

The Ashanti Times (Obuasi)

The Financial Times

The Mining Journal

West Africa

SECONDARY SOURCES

BENING, R. (1975) Colonial Development Policy in Northern Ghana, 1898-1950. Bulletin of the Ghana Geographical Association, vol.17, pp.65-79.

BERG, E. (1960) The Recruitment of a Labour Force in Sub-Saharan Africa. University of Harvard PhD thesis.

BLAY, J. (1950) The Gold Coast Mines Employees' Union, Ilfracombe, A.H. Stockwell.

BURTON, R. and Cameron, V. (1883) To the Gold Coast for Gold (Volume 2), London, Chatto and Windus.

BUSE, J. (1974) Gewerkschaften in Ghana, Bad Godesburg, S. Neue Gesellschaft.

CARDAN, P. (n.d.) Redefining Revolution, Solidarity Pamphlet, no.44.

CARDINALL, A. (1931) The Gold Coast, 1931, Accra, Government Printer.

COHEN, R. (1976) Hidden Forms of Labour Protest in Africa. University of Birmingham Faculty of Commerce and Social Science, Discussion Paper C30.

CRISP, J. (1980) Labour Resistance and Labour Control in the Ghanaian Gold Mining Industry, 1870-1980. University of Birmingham PhD thesis.

DICKINSON, J. (1939) Notes for the Guidance of Europeans in the Gold Coast, Accra, Government Printer.

DUPONT, H. (1901) Les Gisements Aurifères de la Côte d'Or d'Afrique, Paris, Dupont et Banquiers.

EATON-TURNER, G. (1947) A Short History of Ashanti Goldfields Corporation, London, AGC.

FOSTER, D. (1912) Labor and Superintendence on the Gold Coast, Mining and Scientific Press, February 1912, pp.202-203.

FRASER, H. and Somerset, O. (1958) Scientific Management Principles Applied to West African Mining, Transactions of the Institution of Mining and Metallurgy, vol.67 no.7, pp.285-348.

GHANA MINE WORKERS' UNION (1964) Written Addresses and Messages Delivered at the Third Miners' Day Celebration on 20th November 1963 at Tarkwa, Ghana, Accra, Government Printer.

GILES, Lieutenant-Colonel (1905) Sanitation and Anti-Malarial Measures in Sekondi, the Goldfields and Kumasi, Liverpool School of Tropical Medicine, Memoir no.15.

GOLD COAST CHAMBER OF MINES (1950) Gold From the Gold Coast, London, Millard.

GOODY, J. (1956) The Social Organization of the Lo-Wiili, London, HMSO.

GREENSTREET, D. (1966) The Transport Department: The First Two Decades (1901-20), Economic Bulletin of Ghana, vol.10 no.3, pp.33-44.

GUGGISBERG, F. (1922) The Gold Coast: A Review of the Events of 1921-2 and the Prospects of 1922-3, Accra, Government Printer.

GUTKIND, P. (1974) The Emergent African Proletariat, Montreal, Centre for Developing Area Studies, Occasional Paper no.8.

HYMAN, R. (1975) Industrial Relations: A Marxist Introduction, London, Macmillan.

JEFFRIES, R. (1978) Class, Power and Ideology in Ghana: The Railwaymen of Sekondi, London, Cambridge University Press.

JONES, I. (1949) A Trade Unionist in the Colonial Service, Corona, August 1949, pp.21-23.

KILLICK, T. (1978) Development Economics in Action. A Study of Economic Policies in Ghana, London, Heinneman.

KONINGS, P. (1978) The Political Potential of Ghanaian Mine Workers: A Case Study of AGC Workers at Obuasi, Typescript, Leiden, Afrika-Studiecentrum.

MARX, K. (1901) Capital (Volume 1), London, Swan Sonnen-schein.

McCARTHY, E. (1909) Early Days on the Gold Coast, The Mining Magazine, vol.1 no.4, pp.291-293.

_____ (1918) Incidents in the Life of a Mining Engineer, London, George Routledge.

MEEK, C., Macmillan, W. and Hussey, E. (1940) Europe and West Africa: Some Problems and Adjustments, London, Oxford University Press.

MURRAY, A. and Crocket, J. (1941) An Interim Report on the Prevalence of Silicosis and Tuberculosis Among Mine Workers in the Gold Coast, Accra, Government Printer.

PRAH, K. (1976) Essays on African Society and History, Accra, Ghana Universities Press.

ROSENBLUM, P. (1972) Gold Mining in Ghana, 1874-1900, University of Columbia PhD thesis.

SEIDMAN, A. (1968) Ghana's Development Experience, 1951-1965, University of Wisconsin PhD thesis.

SKERTCHLEY, J. (1878) A Visit to the Goldfields of Wassaw, West Africa, Journal of the Royal Geographical Society, no.48, pp.274-283.

SONGSORE, J. (1975) Wa Town as a Growth Centre, 1897-1973, University of Ghana PhD thesis.

TAYLOR, F. (1947) Fundamentals of Scientific Management, Reprinted in Scientific Management, New York, Harper and Brothers.

THOMAS, R. (1973) Forced Labour in British West Africa: The Case of the Northern Territories of the Gold Coast, 1906-1927, Journal of African History, vol.14 no.1, pp.79-103.

WALKER, L. (1971) The Gold Mining Industry in Ghana, University of Edinburgh PhD thesis.

WRAITH, R. (1967) Guggisberg, London, Oxford University Press.

INTERVIEWS

Interviews with the mine workers of Tarkwa, Prestea and Obuasi, and with the informants listed below, were conducted in 1977 and 1978. Direct quotations from this source have not been used in the text due to the sensitive nature of the subjects discussed.

J. Ahinful-Quansah, Publicity and Information Officer, Ghana TUC.

I. Aikins, former General Secretary, MWU.

G. Amadu, Chief Security Officer, Tarkwa Goldfields.

G. Amoako-Atta, Labour Officer, Tarkwa.

S. Azu, Deputy Chief Labour Officer.

K. Baah, District Chief Executive, Tarkwa.

B. Bartlett, Director of Technical Services, SGMC.

L. Bean, former Managing Director, Gold Coast/Ghana Chamber of Mines.

H. Benyah, Chief Inspector of Mines.

R. Blay, Chairman, Committee of Enquiry Into Prestea Disturbances.

W. Box, General Mine Manager, AGC.

J. Cave, Director of Technical Services, AGC.

E. Crentsil, former Labour Officer, Tarkwa.

C. Dagarti, Branch Union Executive, MWU, Prestea.

A. Darkoh, Chief Personnel Officer, AGC.

E. Ephson, Regional Labour Officer, Western Region.

S. Forson, Medical Officer, Tarkwa Goldfields.

Major G. Habib, Chief Security Officer, AGC.

M. Kofi, Principal, School of Mines, Tarkwa.

V. Kondoh, former Labour Officer, Tarkwa.

C. Kuta-Dankwa, Legal Advisor, SGMC.

J. Kwegyir-Paintsil, Chief Personnel Officer, Prestea Goldfields.

J. Mamah, General Secretary, MWU.

A. Muhammed, Deputy Secretary-General, Organization of African Trade Union Unity.

P. Nuamah, Labour Officer, Obuasi.

G. Osei, Labour Officer, Ashanti Region.

J. Phillips, former Commissioner of Labour, and Labour Officer, Tarkwa.

R. Power, Managing Director, AGC.

A. Prah, Secretary, Ghana Chamber of Mines, and former Principal Secretary, Ministry of Lands and Mineral Resources.

A. Quagraine, Industrial Relations Officer, Ghana TUC.

M. Rockson, National Chairman, MWU.

J. Sam, co-founder and former General President, MEU.

G. Scott, General Mine Manager, Prestea Goldfields.

E. Williams, former General Secretary, MWU.

Colonel G. Yarboi, Deputy General Manager, AGC.

INDEX

www.ingramcontent.com/pod-product-compliance
Ingram Content Group UK Ltd.
Pitfield, Milton Keynes, MK11 3LW, UK
UKHW031249020325
455689UK00008B/154